The Volunteers' Guide to Fundraising

Raise Money for Your School, Team, Library or Community Group

Ilona Bray

FIRST EDITION   MAY 2011

Editor   JANET PORTMAN

Cover Design   JALEH DOANE

Production   SUSAN PUTNEY

Proofreading   ROBERT WELLS

Index   SONGBIRD INDEXING

Printing   DELTA PRINTING SOLUTIONS, INC.

Bray, Ilona M., 1962-
The volunteers' guide to fundraising : raise money for your school, team, library or
community group / by Ilona Bray. — 1st ed.
       p. cm.
 Summary: "A comprehensive guide to raising money written for volunteers and staff
who aren't necessarily professional fundraisers. Containing insights and stories from
a team of nonprofit experts, this book covers both the practical and the fun, creative
aspects of fundraising."—Provided by publisher.
 ISBN-13: 978-1-4133-1332-1 (pbk.)
 ISBN-10: 1-4133-1332-9 (pbk.)
 ISBN-13: 978-1-4133-1508-0 (epub e-book)
 1. Fund raising—United States. 2. Fund raising—Law and legislation—United States.
I. Title.
 HG177.5.U6B734 2011
 658.15'224—dc22
                          2010052787

Please note

We believe accurate, plain-English legal information should help you solve many of your own
legal problems. But this text is not a substitute for personalized advice from a knowledgeable
lawyer. If you want the help of a trained professional—and we'll always point out situations in
which we think that's a good idea—consult an attorney licensed to practice in your state.

NOLO Products & Services

⇨ Books & Software

Get in-depth information. Nolo publishes hundreds of great books and software programs for consumers and business owners. Order a copy—or download an ebook version instantly—at Nolo.com.

⇨ Legal Encyclopedia

Free at Nolo.com. Here are more than 1,400 free articles and answers to common questions about everyday legal issues including wills, bankruptcy, small business formation, divorce, patents, employment and much more.

⇨ Plain-English Legal Dictionary

Free at Nolo.com. Stumped by jargon? Look it up in America's most up-to-date source for definitions of legal terms.

⇨ Online Legal Documents

Create documents at your computer. Go to Nolo.com to make a will or living trust, form an LLC or corporation or obtain a trademark or provisional patent. For simpler matters, download one of our hundreds of high-quality legal forms, including bills of sale, promissory notes, nondisclosure agreements and many more.

⇨ Lawyer Directory

Find an attorney at Nolo.com. Nolo's consumer-friendly lawyer directory provides in-depth profiles of lawyers all over America. From fees and experience to legal philosophy, education and special expertise, you'll find all the information you need to pick the right lawyer. Every lawyer listed has pledged to work diligently and respectfully with clients.

⇨ Free Legal Updates

Keep up to date. Check for free updates at Nolo.com. Under "Products," find this book and click "Legal Updates." You can also sign up for our free e-newsletters at Nolo.com/newsletters.

Acknowledgments

The word "acknowledgment" doesn't begin to convey what I owe the many people who contributed their advice, experience, and knowledge to this book. Although much has been written about how to fundraise for nonprofits, it's usually meant for the larger, more established groups. Researching the universe of volunteer-led fundraising required picking up the phone and finding out what's actually happening on the ground (or the playground). Luckily for me, the person at the other end often turned out to be a delight, and a source of not only wisdom but inspiration.

The chapter advisers took a particularly active role in this book, by not only lending their expertise, but reviewing individual chapters to help make sure they were complete and helpful to the intended audience:

- **Hydeh Ghaffari,** CPA, MBA, Senior Partner of Ghaffari Zaragoza LLP, in Oakland, California.

- **Sandra Pfau Englund,** attorney and founder of Pfau Englund Nonprofit Law, PC, in Alexandria, Virginia; and founder of Parent Booster USA.

- **Jan Masaoka,** writer and editor of *Blue Avocado*, based in San Francisco.

- **Gail Drulis,** Executive Director of the Albany YMCA in Albany, California; Board Member of the Albany Education Foundation; and member (and former board member) of the Albany Rotary Club.

- **Edie Boatman,** Director of Fund Development for SHARP Literacy in Milwaukee, Wisconsin, and board member of the German Immersion Foundation and several other nonprofit organizations.

- **Melissa Irish,** provider of philanthropic counsel to Nonprofits in the Bay Area of California.

- **Grace Boone,** Events and Communications Manager at Girls Incorporated of Alameda County, in California.

- **Peter Pearson,** President of The Friends of the St. Paul Public Library, a library foundation in Minnesota.

- **George Hofbauer,** Principal, St. Joseph School (kindergarten through 8th grade) in Seattle, Washington, and board member of the Fulcrum Foundation.

- **Cherie King,** Volunteer cochair of the 2010 Candler Park Fall Fest in Atlanta, Georgia; chairperson of the Mary Lin Education Foundation; and board member at Clifton Sanctuary Ministries.

- **C.J. Hirschfield,** Executive Director of Children's Fairyland in Oakland, California.

- **Philip Skabeikis,** founder and annual chairperson of the Richmond Hill House and Garden Tour, by the Richmond Hill Chapter of the Friends of the Queens Library in New York City.

- **Gary Stewart,** Director in the Office of Government and Community Relations at Cornell University, in Ithaca, New York; and longtime supporter and past board member for Hospicare & Palliative Care Services, also in Ithaca.

- **Sylvia D. Hall-Ellis, PhD,** Associate Professor, Library and Information Science Program, Morgridge College of Education, University of Denver, Colorado.

A number of other people generously contributed advice, help, and sample materials. I'll list them below—with apologies that I can't include complete professional affiliations for everyone, but have tried to highlight their roles as relevant to this book.

They include the staff of the Foundation Center in San Francisco, particularly C. Davis Fischer, Training Coordinator, and Jean Johnson, Senior Librarian; Jerry Aldaroty, Director of Sales and Hospitality at Golden Gate Fields in Albany, California; Jose Aponte, Library Director, San Diego County Library; Bob Baldock, Events Coordinator at KPFA radio in Berkeley, California; Craig Buthod, Director of the Louisville Free Public Library and *Library Journal*'s 2010 Librarian of the Year; Nini Curry, Marketing Director at Fentons Creamery in Oakland, California; Hilary Cooper, parent-volunteer and cochair of Spring

Fling 2011 (a Piedmont, California, Tri-School Fundraiser); Michael Crowe, board member of the Oakland Heritage Alliance; Marcia Eaton, President of the Band Boosters group at College Park High School in Pleasant Hill, California; Ken Edelstein, Editor and Publisher of *Green Building Chronicle*; Debbie Essex, volunteer and former PTA president in Albany, California; Jan Etre, organizer of annual KPFA Crafts Fair in San Francisco; Christy Fell, coordinator of Tulsa's Living with Art in the Garden Tour, in Oklahoma; Rhona Frazin, President of the Chicago Public Library Foundation; Sydney Goldstein, founder and Executive Director of City Arts & Lectures in San Francisco; Sue Hall, coordinator and lead consultant with Library Strategies in St. Paul, Minnesota; Lisa Handley, Community Responsibility Manager for the law firm Orrick, Herrington, & Sutcliffe LLP, in San Francisco; Fran Hildebrand, Development Director of the Community Music Center, San Francisco; Paul Irwin, attorney, Arlington, Texas; Helaine Isaacs, Event Director of the Parkinson's Unity Walk, held in New York City; Gretchen Lightfoot, Director of Development at Harmony Project, Los Angeles; Kim Litland, Director of the Brookfield Public Library, in Illinois; Matt Lovett, past PTA President at Pleasant Hill Elementary School, in California; Robin Lydick, former concert production assistant at Swallow Hill Music Association in Denver, Colorado, and former Concert Director at the Colorado European Festival; Mike Mansel, CIC, based in Pleasant Hill, California; Mike Maxwell, nonprofit professional in California; David McRee, Certified Public Accountant in Saint Petersburg, Florida, and author of *Form 990: Penalty Relief Manual*; Saoirse McClory, Director of Community Support at Hospicare in Ithaca, New York; Margo Palmer, PTA volunteer in Tacoma, Washington; Mary Randolph, parent-volunteer in Berkeley, California; Laura Reichgut, volunteer with the South Mountain PTA in New Jersey; Alix Robinson Tew, Development Director at Camp Happy Days in Charleston, South Carolina; Nancy Schwartz, of Nancy Schwartz & Company in New York City, providing marketing planning and implementation services; Cindy Shelby, former PTA president in the Bay Area of California; Emily Shem-Tov, cochair of Silicon Valley Puzzle Fest; Vivian Shnaidman, volunteer in Princeton, New Jersey; Fran Smyth, Manager of Arts Services, Arts & Business

Council of New York; Luan Stauss, owner of the Laurel Bookstore in Oakland, California; Gene Takagi, attorney in San Francisco; Jackie Thompson, parent-volunteer in the Bay Area of California; Amanda Vender, former board member of DAMAYAN Migrant Workers Association; Simon Wang, volunteer with the student-run Suitcase Clinic at the University of California, Berkeley; Kaleo Waxman, parent-volunteer with the Belmont Oaks Academy in California; and Kyung Yu, volunteer with children's hockey teams in Paoli, Pennsylvania.

At Nolo, special thanks go to Marcia Stewart for helping conceive of and bring about this project, Stan Jacobsen for research help well above and beyond the call of duty, my ever-supportive editor Janet Portman (who also took on the task of creating the forms on the CD-ROM), Rich Stim for advice on contract and music law matters, as well as Kathleen Michon, Mary Randolph, Jackie Thompson, and our creative and accommodating Production team.

Table of Contents

CD-ROM Table of Contents

Bonus Chapter

Forms

Your Fundraising Companion

Raising money for a community group like a school, club, or sports team; or for a church, synagogue, or other religious organization, has always been a challenge. Lately that's even more the case, with unemployment high and government funding for various institutions dwindling. If not for the work of many dedicated volunteers—and sometimes even staff, such as schoolteachers and librarians who take on extra responsibilities—many of these groups wouldn't last another year.

And that, apparently, is where you come in. If you've volunteered to help fundraise for a nonprofit group, you deserve some serious kudos even before you set to work. Many people run from anything with the word "fundraising" in it. The assumption that fundraising is going to be awful is actually odd, because people involved in volunteer fundraising often report loving what they do, typically because it:

- expands their social network and sense of community
- helps them maintain or build new skills during a period out of the job market
- involves creating fun activities for many to enjoy, and
- leads to tangible results, and a sense of personal satisfaction, at having brought about positive change for one's family and community.

In fact, you'll hear many stories from fundraising volunteers in this book, who will share both their best tips and their worst moments, for your inspiration and careful consideration. And that's just the beginning of what this book offers you, by way of a crash course in how to fundraise effectively using the minimum amount of time, effort, and resources. We've brought together a team of experts, including directors and board members of nonprofit organizations, PTA parents, accountants, lawyers, librarians, a school principal, a Friends of the Library group director, and more. They'll address not only the various methods for fundraising that are appropriate to volunteer-led efforts or small groups, but how to fundraise without running afoul of the law or getting into financial trouble.

We'll answer questions from the broad-brush to the nitty-gritty, like:

- Where do you start when it comes to fundraising for your nonprofit group and getting other volunteers involved?
- Do you have to worry about violating any laws, like health codes at bake sales, or tax laws if you sell things at a profit?
- What's better, a live, silent, or online auction?
- How many portapotties do you need for a walkathon or festival?
- Is there an alternative to selling gift wrap?

Helpful Forms, Done Your Way

This book also supplies you with a number of forms, which will help you achieve everything from collecting walkathon and phone pledges to selecting artists to put up booths at your festival. Each form appears as a filled out sample in the book and as a file on the CD-ROM. (A few forms, for legal reasons, should be individually drafted by a lawyer for your group—but we have supplied examples of those.)

Most of the forms are designed for use on a computer. They have fillable fields, which you select with your cursor; then you type the needed information. They look like this: _____*[date]*_____. After you've typed the text, the underline, brackets, and instructions will go away, leaving only the original surrounding text and what you've added.

You may prefer to fill out some forms by hand, rather than on the computer. It's easy to convert a fillable field to a blank line—just print the form as is. The gray shading and the bracketed instructions will disappear, and you'll have a blank line on which to write the information.

As a bonus, the CD-ROM at the back of this book contains material on whether and how to approach foundations for grant funding. It also features three audio podcasts, including "Interview With Author Ilona Bray," "Bringing Creativity to Your Fundraising Efforts," and "The Down

Economy's Impact on Grassroots Fundraising." (You can also hear these at www.nolo.com/podcasts/podcasts.html.)

With the help of this book, you'll soon be fundraising like a pro—and maybe even better than the pros, in some situations. That's because, as a volunteer or someone whose job wasn't meant to include fundraising, you've got a passion for the cause and a knowledge of your group's work that can't help but inspire the people whom you approach for financial support. ●

The Basics: What Your Group Can and Can't Do When Raising Money

Meet Your Adviser

Hydeh Ghaffari, CPA, MBA, Senior Partner of Ghaffari Zaragoza LLP

What she does: "I've been handling financial management for nonprofits for over 25 years, along with teaching at the University of San Francisco as adjunct faculty, giving financial management workshops at CompassPoint for Nonprofits in San Francisco and at the AICPA National Not-for-Profit annual conference, and presenting other workshops. I've also served—and continue to serve—on several nonprofit boards."

Earliest memory of taking part in a charitable activity: "That was actually at my first job in the United States, as an accountant with a large, established nonprofit. In fact, it was my first exposure to the nonprofit sector. My most vivid memory is from soon after I started working there, when the receptionist delivered the deposits that I needed to record that day and said, 'Look what we got!' It was a check for $1 million, from a donor's bequest. That didn't happen every day."

Likes best about her work: "The challenge of trying to sort out the various financial issues facing nonprofits. Most groups—even when they're trying to do things right—have some area of their financial activities they've got issues with, whether it's to do with accounting, unrelated business income, or governance—or the lack thereof. I can help them get back on track, and back to the work they do best."

Top tip for people new to nonprofit fundraising: "Even if your organization is tax exempt, it's only exempt from income taxes. You still have to comply with the rules and obligations concerning all other types of taxes, such as sales tax, payroll tax, property tax, use tax, unrelated business income tax, and any others applicable in your state. Also, you may face tax-compliance issues around the various types of fundraising, including specific types of information which, by law, you have to give to donors, whether they're coming to a dinner or getting their car washed."

Having signed up to help out with a group's fundraising efforts, you're probably eager to dive in and make things happen. But before you do, take a moment to figure out the lay of the land. Understanding a few basics, like the legal ramifications of how your group is organized (incorporated or not), and your obligations vis-à-vis the IRS, will avoid many questions (and perhaps some problems) later on.

You may already be asking sensible questions like:

- Are the tax authorities keeping an eye on our group—for example, if we hold a bake sale or bring in other money, might we have to pay tax on it?

- If I and others donate money to our group, or rack up expenses due to volunteering, will these be tax deductible?

- Does "nonprofit" mean we're not allowed to make a profit?

- Could our own money or assets be on the line if the group gets sued?

- Are some types of fundraising illegal?

- How should we handle money that comes in?

First, let's start with some reassurance. Things will probably turn out fine. Both federal and state laws are mostly set up to protect volunteers and charitable groups, in order to encourage your work without overexposing you to lawsuits and tax hassles. And law enforcement authorities are not going to be spending a lot of time looking over your shoulders.

But there are limits on what you can do, and potential trouble spots to avoid. It would be a shame if, merely for lack of knowledge, your group got embroiled in a lawsuit or lost its tax-exempt status.

What Type of Group Are You With? Incorporated, or Not?

Many of the questions noted just above have answers that depend on how your organization is structured. Whether or not your group has incorporated under your state's nonprofit incorporation laws and (after a separate process) received IRS recognition of tax-exempt status can make all the difference. If you don't know, ask your group's leaders. The processes of incorporation and applying for tax exemption are sufficiently worky that, if your group has done either or both within recent history, its leaders will not have forgotten.

We'll explain the consequences of each group type in later parts of this chapter. For now, the table below outlines the four major ways your group may be organized.

Your Nonprofit's Legal Structure			
Group Type	**What This Means**	**Is This Legal?**	**Why Your Group Would Choose This—Or Not**
Incorporated nonprofit with tax-exempt status	The group has both success-fully applied to its state to become a non-profit corpora-tion and also applied to the IRS for federal recognition of its tax-exempt status.	Yes. In fact, most of the major nonprofits you can think of choose to both incorporate and apply for tax-exempt status. (Examples include the national Parent Teach-ers Association (PTA), many Friends of the Library associations, the Red Cross, the Sierra Club, the Rotary Club, and so on.)	It's the obvious choice for those who want to establish an official presence or be ready for future growth. Incorporation allows a group to shield its directors and staff from personal liability. Tax exemption allows it to avoid paying taxes on certain types of income, and (under Section 501(c)(3) of the Tax Code) assure donors that their donations will be tax deductible.
Incorporated nonprofit, without tax-exempt status	The group is a nonprofit that has filed for in-corporation, but hasn't applied for or received formal fed-eral (or state) recognition of tax-exempt status.	Yes, so long as the group is willing to live with the possibility of its income being treated like that of any ordinary business at tax time. Some groups really should be reporting and po-tentially paying taxes on their income, but don't bother.	A group may choose to go without tax exemption, perhaps because it doesn't need to (churches and groups whose annual gross receipts don't normally exceed $5,000, for example, are considered automati-cally exempt). Some groups think of themselves as hav-ing a charitable mission, but in practical terms, wouldn't qualify for tax exemption, perhaps because they're engaging in substantial business activities.

Your Nonprofit's Legal Structure, continued			
Group Type	**What This Means**	**Is This Legal?**	**Why Your Group Would Choose This—Or Not**
Unincorporated nonprofit, with tax-exempt status	The group has not applied to incorporate, but is an association that has gained IRS and possibly state recognition of its tax-exempt status.	Yes. Incorporation is not a prerequisite to applying for tax-exempt status, though it can make it easier to get.	Some groups figure they'd rather avoid the hassles of incorporation—at least for the moment—and face little risk of liability anyway, but would like the benefits of tax exemption.
Unincorporated nonprofit, without tax-exempt status	The group is an association that operates without either corporate or recognized tax-exempt status.	Yes, although some groups really should be making themselves known to the IRS by reporting and potentially paying taxes on their income, but don't bother.	This avoids all the hassles of dealing with applications and fees, and is a common choice by very small groups such as a local native plant society or a cheerleading squad, whose donors may be more focused on the personal benefits the group offers rather than tax deductions.

Will the Tax Authorities Take Bites Out of Your Group's Income?

Any time money changes hands, you can count on the federal and possibly state tax authorities wanting to know about it—or at least wanting you to assure them that some of that money isn't owed in taxes. With any luck, however, your group won't owe a thing.

The first deciding factor is whether your group has either been recognized as tax exempt or automatically qualifies for this status, most likely under Section 501(c)(3) of the federal Tax Code. We'll look at some of the advantages to 501(c)(3) status in this section, as well as whether and when it makes sense for very small groups to put off applying to the IRS for determination of their tax exemption.

What Does It Mean to Be Tax-Exempt?

A nonprofit is a business, but a special type with aims that involve the public good rather than individual profit. In recognition of that fact, certain nonprofits qualify for exemption from paying federal and state income taxes. Under the most commonly used federal tax exemption, Section 501(c)(3) of the Tax Code, the nonprofit is allowed to:

- avoid paying federal taxes on its income, so long as that income is related to its charitable purposes
- offer its donors the added incentive that their donations will be tax deductible
- allow its volunteers to deduct certain expenses associated with their work, and
- in states that follow the federal exemption (as most do, either auto-matically or after the nonprofit files an application), avoid paying state income, property, and sales tax as well.

The 501(c)(3) exemption can be used by nonprofits engaged in one or more of the following purposes (but not engaged in political campaigning):

- charitable
- religious
- educational
- scientific
- literary
- fostering national or international amateur sports competitions, and
- preventing cruelty to children or animals.

Nevertheless, Section 501(c)(3) is not the only exemption out there. For example, many groups whose main purpose is social, recreational, or business-related are not eligible for 501(c)(3) status. But they might instead apply to be a 501(c)(5), which is meant for labor, agricultural, and horticultural organizations; a 501(c)(7), for social and fraternal clubs;

or a 501(c)(4), for civic leagues, social welfare organizations, and local associations of employees.

The 501(c)(3) organizations enjoy a particular advantage over other 501(c) groups. While the non-(c)(3) groups won't have to pay taxes on income, their supporters won't be able to claim tax deductions for donations. Such groups can still legally raise money from others, but can't offer this added incentive toward giving.

Federal Tax Deductions Available to Your Volunteers

The tax deductions available to volunteers at a 501(c)(3) nonprofit may not add up to big dollars, because volunteers can't deduct the value of the actual hours they put in. Even a highly skilled volunteer, such as a graphic designer or lawyer, can't deduct the value of time spent helping out your group.

But volunteers for tax-exempt organizations can get some dollar return for other expenses they incur, including:

- **Car and transportation expenses.** Volunteers can deduct the cost of using their cars or other transportation as they go back and forth from their homes to your worksite, or to meetings or other sites (such as a special event, or to deliver food to a homebound senior). For driving, volunteers will need to choose between deducting actual gas and oil used, or taking a mileage deduction at the rate of 14 cents per mile (2011 tax figures— note that the allowed deduction is always shockingly lower than that allowed for business-related mileage deductions). Given the high cost of gasoline today, most volunteers are better off keeping track of actual driving expenses. Volunteers can also deduct parking fees and tolls; and those taking public transportation can deduct those costs.

- **Travel expenses.** Volunteers can deduct travel expenses such as airfare and other transport, accommodations, and meals when working for your organization away from home. This might include trips to attend a convention or board meeting, taking schoolkids or scouts on a camping trip, or monitoring environmental destruction. However, the deduction won't be available if the volunteer gains significant personal pleasure, recreation, or vacation from the travel. (Don't ask how the IRS expects to monitor how much fun your volunteers are having!) The volunteer must also really be working—tagging along on an outing while performing nominal duties, or even no duties for significant parts of the trip, won't cut it.

- **Other out-of-pocket expenses.** Board members, for example, might deduct unreimbursed phone, postage, and copying charges associated with preparing for meetings. Volunteers at an animal rescue facility can deduct the treats that they're asked to provide in order to help train animals. Sunday school teachers can deduct classroom supplies.

- **Uniforms.** If you ask volunteers to purchase a uniform and wear it while performing services—for example, an apron identifying them as an event helper—they can deduct both the purchase price and any upkeep costs. However, the uniform must not be suitable for everyday use (providing a T-shirt with a logo or asking ushers to wear black, for instance, won't be enough).

Volunteers should keep reliable written records or other receipts in order to back up their deduction claims in case of an IRS audit.

How Does a Group Become Tax Exempt?

An organization that wishes to be treated as exempt under Section 501(c)(3) of the Tax Code must give notice of this fact to the IRS, and receive IRS approval. This is done by filing Form 1023, along with supporting documents and financial data, within 27 months of the group's formation. If your group needs information on the details of this process, see *How to Form a Nonprofit Corporation* (national edition), by Anthony Mancuso (Nolo); or *How to Form a Nonprofit Corporation in California*, by Anthony Mancuso (Nolo).

A few groups are considered automatically exempt, and don't need to formally apply for tax-exempt status unless they want to, including churches, synagogues, temples, mosques, and their auxiliaries and associations, as well as very small groups that meet the 501(c)(3) criteria and whose annual gross receipts (total income from all sources) are not normally more than $5,000. (See our discussion under, "Is It Worth Keeping Your Gross Receipts Low Enough to Qualify for Automatic Exemption?" below.) Note this exception doesn't mean that every group of people with gross receipts normally below $5,000 is automatically considered a 501(c)(3). David McRee, a Certified Public Accountant who works with nonprofit organizations in Saint Petersburg, Florida (and the author of *Form 990: Penalty Relief Manual*) reminds us that, "Such groups still have to meet the organizational and operational requirements as set forth under Section 501(c)(3) of the Tax Code. A good example of an organization that failed to meet these requirements is the Ann Arbor Dog Training Club. It wanted to qualify as 'educational.' But 'education,' according to the federal tax laws, relates to people, not animals. A court ruled that although the dog owners did receive some training, the primary training was for the dogs, so the organization didn't meet the organizational and operational requirement. (*Ann Arbor Dog Training Club, Inc. v. Commissioner*, 74 T.C. 207 (1980).)"

Some groups operate under a group exemption through their subordinate affiliation with a "central" or parent organization. For example, groups that join Parent Booster USA, a nonprofit formed by adviser Sandra Pfau Englund (whom you'll meet in Chapter 2), receive immediate federal tax-exempt status via their membership, without having to separately apply in their own name. Churches and local Boy Scouts groups also make use of these group exemptions.

As an alternative, you might ask an established nonprofit organization—one with a similar mission—to become your "fiscal sponsor." This allows you to basically ride on the other group's 501(c)(3) coattails (typically for a fee of at least $100 a month), while it handles any money you receive and assumes legal and financial liability for your activities. You can offer donors the right to claim tax deductions, and rely on the sponsoring organization to report and fulfill other requirements to the IRS and your grantmakers, plus help out with payroll, insurance, and other "back office" services (potentially saving you from hiring accounting and other administrative staff). But your group is not considered a 501(c)(3) in its own right, and your sponsor has primary control over any donations made to you—and indeed, over your whole group, if it chooses to wield that power. If you haven't chosen a well-managed, trustworthy organization, you could find yourself chafing under the control, or having to double-check where your money has gone. Therefore, this is typically a temporary measure used by groups working their way toward a 501(c)(3) application. For more information and lists of currently active fiscal sponsors, see www.fiscalsponsordirectory.org.

Also, adviser Hydeh Ghaffari warns, "You'll need to understand the responsibility the fiscal sponsor is taking on for you. Be very clear as to who is responsible for what in terms of handling cash and disbursements, and put the whole arrangement into writing. As an example of what can go wrong, I know of a small environmental organization that started out fiscally sponsored by a larger organization, which promised to include the smaller group's income within its tax returns. But then the smaller group raised so much money that it kicked the sponsor's total income over $2 million. Because the nonprofit groups were located in California, they were subject to the California Nonprofit Integrity Act, requiring nonprofits with income of $2 million and over to obtain an audit of their financial statements. The fiscal sponsor didn't want to deal with the audit, saying it wasn't what it agreed to, and told the smaller to file its own tax return after all. By that time they were already late."

Reasons to Obtain IRS Recognition of Tax Exemption

A number of groups decide to avoid the hassle of applying for tax exemption, and operate without formal recognition of such status—even beyond the groups that are considered automatically exempt because, for example, they're religious organizations or their gross receipts fall under $5,000 a year. Nevertheless, your group will be in a much better position to raise money if it has already obtained such recognition.

As explained by CPA David McRee, "Two major downsides to a small organization choosing not to seek official recognition are that it makes it much harder to solicit corporate donations, and almost impossible to solicit donations from private foundations. Both of those types of donors will almost always demand to see an organization's 501(c)(3) determination letter before writing a check. The corporation does so because it wants assurance of deductibility. The private foundation does so because it wants to avoid exercising expenditure responsibility under Sec 4945(d)(4) of the Internal Revenue Code—in other words, the foundation doesn't want to become legally responsible for monitoring how you actually spend the funds, which it won't have to do if your group is a recognized 501(c)(3)."

Also, if and when you try to broaden your donor base, you'll find it increasingly important to tell prospective donors with confidence that gifts to your organization are tax-deductible. They can still try deducting their contributions to you without this recognition, but if they're audited, and the IRS auditor isn't convinced that your group meets the 501(c)(3) criteria, both the donor and your group could be in for trouble.

Besides, as explained below, going without IRS recognition of your tax-exempt status doesn't excuse you from annual IRS filing requirements— that's a separate issue for every nonreligious group. In fact, if you earn any appreciable amount of income, David McRee notes, "The IRS is likely to view your activities as some sort of business endeavor—and expect you to pay tax accordingly."

Is It Worth Keeping Your Gross Receipts Low Enough for Automatic Exemption?

The short answer is, "No." Maintaining a normal level of gross receipts below $5,000 puts an absurdly low ceiling on your activities, especially after you understand what gross receipts really means.

The IRS defines "gross receipts" as "the total amounts the organization received from all sources during its annual accounting period, without subtracting any costs or expenses." In other words, the definition of gross receipts has nothing to do with where the money came from, much less whether the money is taxable. Regardless of whether you're bringing in individual donations, grant funding, sales proceeds from garage sales or pancake breakfasts, or room rentals in your building, it all counts as gross receipts. (For details, see the IRS regulations contained in the Code of Federal Regulations, available in many libraries or at www.nolo.com; the specific cite is 26 C.F.R. § 1.6033-2(g)(4).)

Take special note of the part of the definition that says that costs and expenses are not omitted from gross receipts. Let's say your group earned $5,500 from holiday wreath sales last year, but paid $5,000 to the wreath maker, so that your profit was only $500. The gross receipts from that venture alone are still $5,500.

And the consequence? As described above, if you're a small group that was planning to avoid having to file for tax exemption by staying small, that may soon be over. However, it's not as simple as saying that once you hit $5,000, the game is up. The point at which your group is considered to have hit the $5,000 mark depends not only on exactly how much was earned, but how that compares to your group's earnings over the previous one or two years. It's all about what's "normal" for your group. (See 26 C.F.R. § 1.508-1a.3.i.) Your "normal" is still below $5,000 if:

- during the first taxable year, your organization brings in gross receipts of $7,500 or less;

- during its first two taxable years, your organization brings in gross receipts totaling $12,000 or less, and

- if your group has been in existence for at least three taxable years, its aggregate gross receipts from the preceding two tax years, plus the current year, add up to $15,000 or less.

So, your group could, for example, bring in $7,000 in its first year and still not need to file for tax exemption; another $4,500 in its second year and still not need to file (because the aggregate hasn't exceeded the $12,000 limit); and another $3,000 in its third year, and remain just at the allowable three-year total of $15,000.

As soon as your group realizes that it has exceeded any of the limits described above, the IRS gives you 90 days within which to submit a Form 1023, requesting official determination that you're tax exempt. So if your fundraising has even a chance at regularly bringing in $5,000 or more, it really would make sense to apply for tax exemption now, rather than fret over the numbers.

Responsibilities That Come With Tax-Exempt Status

Tax exemption comes with some responsibilities, too. The most important ones include:

- filing an annual informational tax return, and

• paying tax if your group brings in certain types of income, especially from activities unrelated to its charitable purposes.

Filing an Annual Informational Tax Return

Your group *must* file an annual tax form with the IRS, even if you're automatically exempt and the IRS has never otherwise heard of your existence. Groups whose gross receipts are normally less than $25,000 a year need only file a simple electronic form called a 990-N. The 990-N is what's known as an "information return." Its purpose, explains adviser Hydeh Ghaffari, is "simply to let the IRS know you're still in existence and announce that your gross receipts are less than $25,000. The Form 990-N doesn't even collect any financial information; though if your group earns income on which tax is owed (such as through unrelated business activities), you'd have to use a separate form to report on that, called a 990-T."

The only exception to the annual filing requirements is for churches and religious organizations—they need not file any version of the 990. (See the IRS's *Tax Guide for Churches and Religious Organizations*, available at www.irs.gov.)

CAUTION

Had trouble filing the online Form 990-N? At the time this book went to print, filing Form 990-N was difficult for groups that hadn't already received IRS recognition of tax exemption, due to the way the IRS computer system is set up. You could deal with this by calling the IRS 45 days before submitting Form 990-N, giving the IRS time to set up a computer file for your organization. It's possible this problem will have been solved by the time you read this (or the solution changed), so check with other nonprofits or your tax pro.

Groups whose receipts are normally higher than $25,000 a year must file either a full Form 990 or a midsized Form 990-EZ. These tell the world about the group's activities (demonstrating that it still meets the qualifications for tax-exemption), and about matters like the group's executive salaries and program expenditures.

When 501(c)(3)s Need to Pay Taxes

Although the IRS tends to lump all types of income together when deciding whether your group qualifies for an automatic exemption and which tax form it needs to file, it allows for more fine distinctions when determining what types of income your group, assuming it's a 501(c)(3), will actually owe tax on. Some of your group's largest sources of income may be from grants (from foundations or corporations) or individual donations. These won't be taxed, because both are assumed to be related to your group's charitable purposes. The same goes for the following types of income:

- fees for your group's services (for example, the fees you charge to attend your summer day camp)
- income from business activities that are mostly run by volunteers (for example, when your volunteers cultivate and sell native plants)
- income from sales of donated merchandise (as with a garage sale, auction, or thrift shop)
- income from a business that isn't carried out on a regular, continuous schedule (think Girl Scout cookies), and
- income from business activities that operate mainly for the convenience of your group's members, students, patients, officers, or employees (as with an on-site hospital pharmacy or coffee shop).

But if a tax-exempt nonprofit starts regularly operating a business that's not substantially related to its nonprofit purposes, and earns more than $1,000 a year at it, its income may become what the IRS calls "unrelated business income" (UBI) and subject to tax at federal corporate rates. That doesn't necessarily mean you've done anything wrong, as long as the business activities remain a minor part of what your nonprofit does. It does, however, mean that you'll have the hassle of computing (and paying) the tax you owe.

The fundraising strategies described in this book are unlikely to draw you into the realm of UBI. But it's something to keep in the back of your mind. What if, for example, someone in your group suggests, "Let's buy a coffee cart and hire someone to operate it on the sidewalk outside our building for passersby, and use the profits for our programs?" Not a bad idea—but the resulting income would in all likelihood be considered UBI, so you'd have to remember to figure federal and probably state income tax obligations into your estimates of profits. (And who wants to worry about computing and paying state sales tax, which might also apply?) Then there's the worst-case scenario: If the coffee-cart project got so big that it took over the purpose of your nonprofit, perhaps with carts on various street corners throughout your city, your group could actually lose its tax-exempt status.

State Tax Obligations That Apply to Nonprofits

If your group has received federal recognition of tax exemption, your state's government is likely to honor that as well (though you may need to apply for confirmation of your exemption). But this isn't always the way it works— some states simply exempt all nonprofits, while others require them to submit a separate application for state tax-exempt status. You'll need to check with your state's tax-regulating authorities to find out the details.

Does "Nonprofit" Mean You're Not Allowed to Make a Profit?

A nonprofit is expected to work for the public good, motivated by a mission other than making money for individual shareholders or business owners, as is the case with for-profit enterprises. But obviously, you need to make enough money to carry out your good deeds. And you don't have to give everything away for free, work within a bare-bones budget, or never set money aside for the future. Nothing could be further from the truth.

For starters, if you're providing goods and services to the public, you're allowed to ask people to pay for them. This is true whether you're dealing directly with clients, perhaps low-income people, or with others. Of course, when dealing with clients, it won't serve your mission to try and make a financial killing off of them—but setting at least nominal fees can both help your group's finances and remind clients that you're providing something of value.

In the case of selling goods and services to the public, what you charge is limited only by what you need to do to protect your tax-exempt status—for example, if you haven't yet formally applied for tax-exempt status and are trying to keep your gross receipts to a level that's normally below $5,000 a year, then you obviously wouldn't want to start selling expensive goods. And venturing too far into the territory of unrelated business income could threaten your tax-exempt status. But these are outside limits, and don't stop many nonprofits from, for example, selling baked goods, greeting cards, tickets for tours, and much more, sometimes at higher-than-market prices.

Then there's the matter of setting some funds aside for the future, or for a rainy day. In an unhappy coincidence, on the very day I'm writing this, the Humane Society just one block from my office is trying to recover from a devastating midnight fire. Yes, property insurance will cover rebuilding, but it won't cover other costs like continued medical care for the animals that they're placing in temporary foster homes and the fundraising costs to ask the public to help. It's not easy to set aside money when very little comes in to begin with, but if you choose a small percentage and stick with it, it will start adding up. Aim for a six-month surplus.

What Protects You From Personal Liability If Your Group Gets Sued?

There's a reason we asked you to find out whether your group has become a nonprofit corporation, as opposed to remaining an unincorporated association. Incorporation is an important step in protecting people associated with a group from personal liability for lawsuits.

Your Group Has Incorporated: How Does That Help You?

If your group has become a nonprofit corporation, this means that it has arranged with a state office to become a separate legal entity—in fact, has become legally equivalent to a separate person. It will have filed articles of incorporation, paid a fee, adopted bylaws, appointed a board of directors, and so forth. The incorporation process is similar to that undertaken by for-profit businesses, except that nonprofit corporations don't have shareholders or issue dividends.

Once formed, the corporation can sign contracts, enter into debts, and pay taxes in its corporate name. Its separate existence also acts as a shield, protecting its board, staff, and members from personal liability for mistakes made during the course of their duties as directors, employees, and members. That means that if someone sues your group—perhaps a cookie company to which it owes money, a local personality claiming slander for a portrayal in your group's newsletter, or a visitor injured at your holiday bazaar—the person suing will have to name your group as the defendant (and not individual members or volunteers) and claim any damages from the group's funds (not from any individual's personal assets). If your nonprofit corporation has insurance—which it should—any claims, settlements, and verdicts can be satisfied with insurance proceeds.

Exceptions do exist, however, for cases in which a group's board, staff, or other member behaved badly enough to be found personally liable. The most likely examples are when someone within your group personally and directly injures someone, or deliberately misuses nonprofit funds. In addition, if a group representative personally guarantees a bank loan made for the corporation's benefit but then defaults, the bank can demand payment from the individual (which, of course, was the point of asking for the personal guarantee).

In short, if your group is an incorporated nonprofit, you can feel pretty comfortable that, unless you do something seriously out of line, you'll be protected from personal liability. But don't panic if your group hasn't incorporated—there are other ways in which you may be protected, as discussed next.

Your Group Is Still an Unincorporated Association: Is That a Problem?

Many small groups, such as garden, bridge, or ethnic clubs, do just fine without incorporating. An unincorporated association can still be called a "nonprofit." And it can carry on its regular activities without feeling that it has to have "official" status. These groups aren't operating in a shady, underground manner; we all have a constitutional right to gather. Also, many states' laws govern unincorporated associations in the same way as they do incorporated nonprofits.

But what about the personal liability issue? Without the shield of a separate entity, members of an unincorporated association can, unfortunately, be sued for damages based on their activities with that group. Thinking about liability is probably the last thing you want to do when planning a rose garden tour or a playground carnival, but you never know when someone will get angry enough to sue over an unpleasant encounter with thorns or the dunk tank. Still, the chances that you'll actually face a claim may be slim, if one or more of the following are true:

- **You're a volunteer, protected by federal law.** The federal Volunteer Protection Act (VPA), passed in 1997, says that unpaid volunteers for groups that operate for public benefit and primarily charitable, civic, educational, religious, welfare, or health purposes, enjoy limited immunity from liability. So long as you, personally, were acting within the scope of your volunteer responsibilities, with any necessary licenses, certification, or authorization, and didn't do something intentional, criminal, reckless, or grossly negligent, and weren't driving a vehicle, boat, or aircraft, you're protected from liability.

- **Your group doesn't engage in high-risk activities.** If, for example, you're working with a music club or an organization dedicated to raising funds to restore a local fountain, it's unlikely (though not impossible) that you'll face the expensive suits arising from personal injuries.

- **Your group has taken out insurance.** Many groups' general liability policies cover staff and board members against lawsuits. Adding coverage for regular volunteers is also possible, and possibly worth looking into for your group. In the meantime, if you'll be holding events or conducting activities where people might get hurt, consider asking a lawyer whether drawing up a waiver (in which the participant gives up the right to sue you if your carelessness causes injury) would be legally effective in your state, and if so, to draft one for your group. Then ask participants to sign the waivers when they sign up or show up for your events.

- **Your state's laws protect members of groups like yours.** A number of states have passed legislation protecting members of unincorporated associations from personal liability. In fact, several of these states have adopted what's known as the "Uniform Unincorporated Nonprofit Association Act," or "UUNAA," giving unincorporated nonprofits the status of a separate entity when it comes to liability. People working for this entity can't, under most circumstances, be held liable for its actions.

Your group should also implement commonsense strategies to protect against the most likely risks. Sit down with your organization's leaders (or fiscal sponsor) and discuss what these are—whether injuries, debts, or something else—and how to deal with them. For example, if you'll have a lot of volunteers working directly with children, it's wise (and in some states, legally required) to carefully screen the volunteers (including a background check for criminal infractions). We'll explain how to do this in Chapter 2.

Deciding Whether to Remain Unincorporated

Incorporating has its benefits, as you can see. But if your group is small enough—and plans to stay small or even disband in a few years—and your activities don't present substantial risks, don't feel pushed. Perhaps dealing with the administrative requirements and paying the fees aren't worth it.

If your group has growth plans in its future, however, formalizing your organization might make sense—in fact, it might aid in your growth plans. Grantmaking foundations typically restrict their giving to nonprofit groups that have both incorporated and filed for recognition of 501(c)(3) status.

Incorporating will also help you succeed if you plan to file an application for 501(c)(3) tax-exempt status. As attorney Paul Irwin, who advises nonprofit groups in Arlington, Texas, notes: "The IRS's expectations very nearly require your group to become a corporation. Before granting 501(c)(3) status, the IRS wants to see a board of directors in place, and no individual ownership of the group's assets. So if you have to create a board anyway, and you need to create an entity to own the assets, your most logical move is to incorporate. Do so early in your group's existence, unless you plan to stay very small. It's sort of like politics: The best time to run is when you have no record, so there's nothing to attack you on."

Formalizing your status as a separate organization will also help you when it comes to fundraising. Oftentimes, prospective donors to public institutions (such as public schools and libraries) worry that their money will get sucked right into some distant government budget, perhaps never to be seen by your school or library again. By incorporating and gaining formal status as a 501(c)(3) in your own right, you can reassure people that their donations will go to straight to your organization.

If you think it would be a good idea for your group to incorporate, it's never too late to do so. If, however, your group received tax-exempt status (discussed above) before incorporating, you'll have to reapply for it under your new, corporate name.

Why Organizational Structure Matters		
Group type	Liability	Tax Obligations
Incorporated nonprofit with tax-exempt status	Staff, directors, and members protected from personal liability	File an annual return. No tax on income related to charitable purposes; but tax owed on unrelated business income (UBI). If exempt under Section 501(c)(3), donors can take tax deductions for gifts.
Incorporated nonprofit, without recognition of tax-exempt status	Staff, directors, and members protected from personal liability	File an annual return. Pay tax on all forms of income (unless qualified for automatic tax exemption, in which case your group will be treated like a tax-exempt organization, described above).
Unincorporated nonprofit, with tax-exempt status	Staff, directors, and members must rely on insurance and other risk-prevention laws or measures	File an annual return. No tax owed on income related to charitable purposes; but tax owed on unrelated business income (UBI). If exempt under Section 501(c)(3), donors can take tax deductions for gifts.
Unincorporated nonprofit, without tax-exempt status	Staff, directors, and members must rely on insurance and other risk-prevention laws or measures.	File an annual return. Pay tax on all forms of income (unless qualified for automatic tax exemption, in which case your group will be treated like a tax-exempt organization, described above).

Now that you know some of the ramifications of incorporating (or remaining an unincorporated association), take a look at "Why Organizational Structure Matters," above. This table summarizes the personal liability and tax consequences of the four ways to structure your organization, introduced earlier.

Are Some Types of Fundraising Illegal?

Federal law does not restrict how you fundraise. State and local laws are another matter, however. The main things to check into are:

- laws and regulations concerning particular activities, such as raffles, bingo games, and bake sales, and

- registration or licensing requirements.

State and Local Regulation of Particular Fundraising Activities

In some localities, you'll need separate permission before carrying out certain activities. Or, you may have to follow local regulations or heed restrictions on specific types of fundraising. Commonly regulated activities include door-to-door solicitations, selling baked goods or other foods, raffles, and bingo games.

For example, you may need to get a permit in order to hold a garage sale or bake sale. A liquor permit may also be required if you plan to serve or sell beer or wine at your group's event. And holding a raffle may be entirely illegal (as in Alabama and Hawaii, where raffles apparently resemble gambling too closely for governmental comfort), or you may need to apply for advance permission to hold raffles (as in New York and Indiana).

Exactly which government office you'll need to check with depends on where you live. It may be the state attorney general, the local police, or a finance, tax, licensing, or commerce department. The chapters that follow address each type of fundraising, with information on the most common restrictions and requirements.

Nonprofit Registration Requirements

Every single one of your group's fundraising activities may actually be illegal if you haven't yet registered your group and its fundraising intentions with state, city, or county authorities—and kept up your registration with annual renewals. There's no nationwide law requiring this, but state and local registration laws are on the increase. And they're being enforced more than ever, by authorities hungry for new sources of revenue.

If the notion of registering surprises you, that's understandable. Although such laws have been on the books for some time, they were regularly ignored by the IRS. Most nonprofits didn't need to worry about registering until 2007, when the IRS added a question to Form 990, inquiring whether the group had complied with state registration requirements.

Failing to register, at least in your own state or locality, may subject your group to fines or prohibitions on fundraising until after you've registered. Worse yet, the liability may extend to individual board members. The scandal resulting from noncompliance won't help your group's reputation, either.

To avoid trouble, start by checking with your local government offices regulating businesses. At least make sure you've met the registration requirements for the area where your office is located and where you solicit your donations.

But your inquiry isn't over yet: If your group is or will be reaching out to potential donors in more than one state, whether in person, at events, via print or advertising, or by a website or some other means, you might have to comply with those states' registration requirements as well. In fact, if you have a website with a "Donate Now" button, or a means of accepting online contributions, that alone can trigger some states' registration requirements. At last count, 39 states plus the District of Columbia required out-of-state groups that solicit funds there to register—and to do so before making the solicitations, not after receiving any actual gifts. (California is an exception; it gives you 30 days from the time you receive your first contribution to register.)

States That Don't Require Nonprofits to Register

Good news if you're based in, or will be soliciting donations in one of the following 11 states: They don't require nonprofits to register.

- Delaware
- Idaho
- Indiana
- Iowa
- Montana
- Nebraska
- Nevada
- South Dakota
- Texas (requires only "public safety" charities to register)
- Vermont
- Wyoming

All of the registration states and the District of Columbia grant exemptions to certain types of groups, however. There's a good possibility you fit into one of these exemptions. For example, all states except Arizona exempt churches and religious organizations from registering. Some states exempt nonprofit libraries, educational organizations, groups that solicit funds only from their members (such as fraternal, social, or alumni organizations), groups raising money to help a particular person (for example, a medical fund), or groups whose annual receipts of individual, nongrant donations—from all states, not just the one in question—are below a certain amount. That amount currently ranges from $1,500 to $50,000, with $25,000 the most typical figure. In a few states, having only a small number of donors will also qualify your group for exemption.

The trouble is, not all states grant all the exemptions just described, or even the same set of exemptions. For example, some require even tiny groups to register, regardless of how low their revenues or how few their donors. Some states count grant funding as revenue. Therefore, you'll need to look further into the matter if there's any chance your group, or anyone working on its behalf, will be making requests for charitable contributions from donors of other states—including via your website.

If you determine that you're exempt for the moment, great—but don't stop your inquiry there. For one thing, 12 states won't grant you the exemption automatically. You'll need to apply for it, and in some cases pay a fee.

Also realize that you could lose your exemption in the future, possibly quite unintentionally. For example, if your revenues go up, your group is given a few moments on national television to pitch your cause, or you team up with a corporate sponsor that will be selling products nationwide featuring your logo and information on how to contribute, you may need to start registering in a number of states.

RESOURCE
Looking for more information on the complex topic of state registrations? You'll find information to help you deal with registration, including discussions of when the requirements are triggered by Internet and email fundraising, in *Nonprofit Fundraising Registration: The 50-State Guide*, by Stephen Fishman (Nolo).

How Should You Handle and Safeguard Money?

Now let's jump ahead to that happy moment when you've held an event or sale, or asked for donations, and successfully raised money for your group. This book isn't about nonprofit accounting, and assumes that your group will have a treasurer, accountant, or finance committee focused on learning about and dealing with the details of such issues. However, everyone in your group who's involved with raising money should be aware of how important it is to:

- open a separate bank account for your group
- put any incoming money into a secure and separate place right away, until you can get it to the bank
- create a paper trail and a system for double-checking where the money came from and went to
- take precautions against mistakes and theft
- use money for its intended purposes, and
- thank the donors, for the sake of politeness and IRS rules.

A Bank Account Is Crucial

If your group has no separate bank account, where will you put money that comes in? Unless you put your faith in mattresses and freezers, it's most likely to go into one of your group leader's bank accounts. In that case, however, the person would need to report the money to the IRS as income.

A better option is to open up a bank account for your group. This is a fairly simple process. You'll need a federal Employer Identification Number (EIN) first, but can easily get one online, at www.irs.gov (search for "EIN").

Where to Stash the Cash on Its Way to the Bank

Money has an unfortunate way of disappearing, even in an environment where you think everyone is friendly and trustworthy. So your number one goal, whether you're accepting donations in person, by mail, or at an event, is to get the money into a safe place, for example by instituting the following measures.

- Designate a person or persons at your organization to handle finance matters, including collecting money and making deposits to the bank account.

- Develop a clear timeline and system for transferring cash and checks to that person.

- Minimize the number of people handling money. For example, at events involving games and food, use a central cash box that sells tickets for both (thus avoiding multiple cash boxes at different booths). One of your finance people should regularly stop at this main cash box to remove extra money (beyond what's needed for making change) and put it in a safer place.

- At ongoing fundraisers (such as a week-long membership drive), use an on-site safe or locked drawer where money can be kept temporarily until your finance person is ready for a bank run. For example, school fundraisers might use the desk in the principal's office.

TIP

Consider setting up credit card or PayPal accounts. Credit cards are convenient for the donors, avoid the transfer of real money, and don't bounce like checks. For many small groups, however, the effort it takes to set up a credit card account isn't worth the effort. The next best thing is to use a service like PayPal, allowing donors to transfer money online; see www.paypal.com.

Create a Paper Trail

Whether you're answering to an individual donor ("Did you get my check?") or to an IRS auditor ("Where are the receipts for this?"), being able to say where money came from—or went to—is critical. Your grant funders, as well as your state government's oversight branch, may also take a keen interest in your group's finances, and require it to submit an annual financial report.

The best practice is to keep a record of every cent that passes in or out of your organization's hands (as well as of all correspondence with donors, a topic we'll discuss in Chapter 6). Let's say you're an event-planning volunteer with a parent-teacher organization, and a parent hands you a $50 cash donation. It may seem like the most natural thing in the world to turn around and spend that money on balloons for the event, but that's not a good idea. Instead, you'll need to give the donor a receipt on the spot (even if it's only handwritten on a blank sheet of paper), transfer the money to your group's finance person, and either request petty cash to pay for the balloons or use your own funds and request reimbursement later—having, of course, saved the receipt for the balloons. That way, the donor will be reassured that the money was recorded and the organization will be able to keep accurate records of who has donated and how much, along with how much was spent for event costs.

That said, it's true that there's no actual law saying you have to give a receipt to everyone who gives your group money—in fact, IRS rules for 501(c)(3)s require giving receipts only for gifts of $250 or more. Nevertheless, providing receipts for smaller gifts is a good idea. Relatively new IRS rules demand that donors claiming tax deductions keep receipts for all donations, regardless of amount. A bank record will work for checks or credit card donations. But if a donor makes a cash donation, claims it as a tax deduction, and is later challenged on the legitimacy of the deduction, the donor won't have a record unless you've supplied it. It's simplest—and better for donor relations—to send a receipt regardless of the amount donated.

Written receipts also avoid suspicion and disputes, along the lines of, "Why are you asking me for my dues when I already gave $50 to Joe last week?" We'll show how to draft thank-you letters that incorporate receipts for donations in the next section.

Make sure that everyone who might accept or handle money for your organization knows these basic principles. For someone who'll be regularly receiving money, pick up an actual receipt book from an office supply store.

Take Precautions Against Internal Mistakes and Theft

A good cautionary measure is to give not one, but two people the ultimate power and responsibility for handling your group's money. Both should be responsible for checking the other one's work. Drawing checks from your group bank account should require both signatures. No matter how trustworthy they each are, mistakes happen, and everyone will appreciate catching these early and internally.

As Margo Palmer, a mom in Tacoma, Washington, who's been active in PTA fundraising explains, "We learned early on that if cash is left unguarded, it's soon gone. There's nothing worse than having to be suspicious of others, wondering who had access—and you certainly don't want that suspicion to land on you. To avoid such situations, we always had two people count out the cash every night after events like the annual book fair. Usually the PTA treasurer would take care of the bank deposits, but she wasn't necessarily available for cash-counting. So the school librarian and I would go through the till after the fair, leaving behind enough change for the next day. I'd watch her lock the till into the closet, and I'd take the profits, put them in a bag, and deliver it to the PTA treasurer, sometimes at her home."

A policy stating that anyone from within your group's leaders or members can examine your group's finance books at any time is also helpful, and serves to project a positive image to the public.

Using Money for the Purposes That Donors Intended

For the most part, your group will solicit funds for its general purposes, as you do, for example, when inviting people to "Buy brownies to help the school marching band!" There's nothing wrong with using those donations for any valid project or purpose—you haven't earmarked the expenditure. But be careful that you don't accept money that's designated for a specific, limited reason, then use it for something else. For example, it's a mistake to say, "Buy brownies to help the school marching band travel to England!" but end up using the excess earnings on new uniforms or to raise the director's salary. Such actions would violate the donor's wishes, which might not only upset the donor (or soon-to-be ex-donor), but supply potential grounds on which to sue your group.

Attorney Paul Irwin, of Arlington, Texas, notes, "This is an issue I see a lot among people new to fundraising. Let's say, for example, that a Boy Scout troop goes out and raises money for a charity like Ronald McDonald House. It brings in $10,000. But then the troop uses $5,000 of this for a camping trip, to celebrate. Using a little bit of this money would have been okay, perhaps for a celebratory dinner—but if you spend significant amounts that donors meant for another purpose, that's a no-go. In most cases, you're supposed to go back to the donor and say, 'Would you like the money back, or prefer that we transfer it to our unrestricted funds?' Many donors will agree to the switch. Yet a lot of charities, being afraid of refusal, don't bother to do the right thing and ask."

Thanking Donors—While Providing Receipts for Donations

Thanking donors early and often is one of the most important tasks for anyone involved in raising money—and one that often gets overlooked. It doesn't matter that your group is full of committed supporters who see a direct benefit from the money they put in. Even if it's their own kids who get to participate in school sports, or their own mosque that gets a remodel, everyone likes the recognition of being thanked, the affirmation that their contribution made a difference, and of course the proof of any tax deductions they're due. On the flip side, people who don't receive acknowledgment get disgruntled, and start thinking your group isn't very well managed.

So, having made a point of carefully recording every donation that comes in, be sure to follow up by sending out a thank-you letter soon after. A postcard or an email may be acceptable, depending on the culture of your supporters (and both are okay by the IRS, whose requirements we'll discuss next). But real mail adds a note of thoughtfulness. In fact, we know of instances where donors so appreciated the personal touch that they sent thank-you letters in response to the thank-you letters!

If your organization is a 501(c)(3), so that its donors are eligible for tax exemptions, your thank-you letters need to meet IRS requirements and otherwise help donors claim the deductions they're due. A good thank-you letter (or postcard or email), and one that will more than satisfy the IRS, should state the following (also see the sample below):

- The basics, including your organization's name and the donor's name. If the donor is a business, include both the name of your contact there, his or her title, and the business's name and address.

- A reminder of why the gift is important, and what it will help your organization to achieve. This is not required, but is good for donor relations. For example, you might say something like, "Your support will help us ensure that the team travels to the regional championships this year."

- The dollar amount donated.

- In the case of a noncash gift, such as a painting or a jar of handmade jam to be sold at your silent auction, a description. Be sure to adequately identify the gift, so there's no question as to what your organization received. Your organization is not obligated to estimate how much the item is worth. That's the donor's job, if he or she decides to claim the gift as a tax deduction. (However, for auction items, you will eventually have to estimate the item's fair market value for the bidders' sake, as discussed below.)

- Whether the donor received anything of value in return for the gift other than a token or low-cost item (such as a tote bag or stickers; for more information on this, see "Token or 'Low-Cost' Items," below). If so, you must state the amount of their contribution that's tax deductible after subtracting the fair market value of what they received. For example, if a donor bid $90 at an auction for a fruit basket that retails for $50, the tax-deductible portion of the contribution is $40. If the retail value isn't obvious, your good faith estimate of its worth is enough—no need to hire a professional appraiser. For ticket purchases to a gala dinner, for example, you'd need to factor in things like how much dinners at local restaurants cost, and make a reasonable estimate of its value to the donor. Unfortunately, notes adviser Hydeh Ghaffari, "A number of nonprofits have no choice but to put a value on the dinner and music that's higher than or equal to the ticket price!" If the donor didn't receive a return gift, state in your letter that nothing of value was given in exchange for the contribution.

CAUTION

Don't confuse fair market value with the cost to your organization. Adviser Hydeh Ghaffari explains, "I see many organizations assume that because, for example, a painting was donated to them, they don't need to estimate its value for purposes of advising the donor who buys it at auction. That's not the case—you need to tell the donor the fair market value of the item, regardless of whether you got it for less. If you don't give donors these estimates of fair market value, it could catch up with your group someday—most likely because one of your donors gets audited, and then shows the IRS the letter from your group as support for the claimed tax deduction."

- The fact that, if your organization is a 501(c)(3), the gift may be tax deductible. Our sample adds the language "to the extent allowed by law." That sidesteps the possibility that you'll be seen as giving out tax advice, impliedly leaving the final judgment to the donors' tax advisers or personal research. You need to give donors enough factual information with which to analyze their tax situation (such as the fair market value of goods bid on, as described above), but you shouldn't go further and actually provide tax advice.

CAUTION

Never over-promise when it comes to tax deductions. A lot of nonprofits loosely throw around the phrase "tax deductible!" not realizing how many exceptions exist. For example, money spent buying raffle tickets isn't tax deductible; neither are in-kind gifts of services or uses of property for a limited time period (for example, when donors offer haircuts, swim lessons, or weekends at their time-share for your next auction). Again, it's the donor's job to figure out the details.

Token, or "Low-Cost" Items

When thanking donors, there's no need to mention or subtract the value of either:

- token items like a tote bag, coffee cup, or stickers, so long as they bear your organization's name or logo; nor
- items that are low-cost in comparison to the overall donation.

According to the IRS, "token" goods or services must cost your organization no more than $9.70. To take advantage of this exception, the contribution received must have been at least $48.50. (And again, the items must have your organization's name or logo on them.)

There's also an exception for "low-cost" items, either with a fair market value of up to $97, or worth up to 2% of the donor's payment, whichever is less. When you run the numbers, you'll find that you'll almost always end up bound by the 2% limit.

(The above token and low-cost limits apply to calendar year 2011; these are regularly adjusted.)

Does everyone deserve a thank-you, even for a few dollars? Yes. If a few dollars was all someone could give, then it was a significant gift for them. And for purposes of cultivating ongoing relationships with your group's supporters, sending out thanks is a good investment of your time. For gifts at the high end of your donor range, you'll want to do more than merely send a letter, but also call the person, invite him or her to lunch or a tour of your facility or activities, and otherwise make such donors feel like an important part of your work.

Now, a word on the tone of your thank you letters. Notice how the letter below keeps the focus on the cause, rather than your group. The message is "Thank you for joining in the effort to achieve X," not just "Thank you for giving us your gift." The former reminds the donor that you're all working together in service of a greater goal; the latter sets up a gulf between the group and the donor. You'll have a better chance of keeping donors if you make them feel like part of the group's efforts, rather than like outsiders.

You'll find a blank thank-you letter on the CD-ROM at the back of this book.

Sample Donor Thank-You Letter

Eggmont High School
Shakespeare Players

October 2, 20xx
Candace Thimblewine
3233 Grape Arbor Lane
Eggmont, NC 12345

Dear Mrs. Thimblewine:

Thank you for your lovely gift of $60 to the Eggmont High School Shakespeare Players. Your support will help make sure that the group is able to travel to Scotland this year for the Edinburgh Festival.

No goods or services were provided in exchange for this donation. Eggmont High School Shakespeare Players is a 501(c)(3) organization. Your contribution is tax deductible to the extent allowed by law. We advise you to keep this acknowledgment of your donation for your tax records.

Again, thank you for your generosity. We look forward to continuing with our mutual efforts to bring quality theater instruction and performance opportunities to the public schools. For more information on upcoming events and activities, see our Facebook page or contact me at mayar@email.com.

Very truly yours,

Maya Rodriguez

Maya Rodriguez
Parent, Chair of Committee to Support the Eggmont High School
Shakespeare Players

Share Financial Information With Members

Your group has to compile financial reports and statistics for the IRS, and there's no reason not to make this information available to individual members and donors. You'll enhance your credibility—and convey that your group is committed to good planning, wise spending, and rigorous oversight practices—by letting people know where to find this information. Beyond the dry numbers, it's also helpful, and very effective for fundraising, to break down expenses on a "per unit" basis, such as "every $10 allows us to buy art supplies for one child."

Your group's website, if you have one, is an excellent place to post this sort of information. Make it easy to find. Include financial information in any newsletter or email updates you regularly send to supporters, as well. For example, if you're discussing a particular program, you might discuss the challenges of raising funds when "bus rentals for our educational tours cost $5,000 alone." Specific dollar figures catch people's eyes and make them better understand why you're tackling an ambitious financial goal.

As for the hard-copy records, do your best to find a permanent location in which to store them. Moving boxes and files from one garage to the next is a recipe for loss and confusion. ●

Getting Volunteers Eager and Ready

Meet Your Adviser

Sandra Pfau Englund, attorney and founder of Pfau Englund Nonprofit Law, PC, which provides legal services to nonprofit organizations; and founder of Parent Booster USA, which provides tools, tips, and immediate tax-exempt status to school support groups (parent-teacher organizations and sports, music, and other booster clubs).

What she does: "I talk to people daily about how to start new nonprofit groups, and how organizations like school booster clubs can operate legally from the start."

Earliest memory of taking part in a charitable activity: "Putting change into the church offering plate is probably my first memory of helping raise money. My Mom and Dad gave me the change, so I wasn't really putting much thought into it then. But I think that I do what I do now because my parents volunteered a lot. While I was in law school, it all clicked: I realized that I could combine my interest in volunteer-based organizations with the legal profession."

Likes best about her work: "Working with people who really care about what they're doing. Many of them, I identify with—like a parent with kids who's trying to raise money for their baseball team, lacrosse team, or something else. In other cases, I may not have a burning passion for the particular cause, but the person who calls me does, and I can believe in that. It's satisfying to feel, at the end of the day, that I've made someone's life easier. People already have enough to deal with just getting the groceries and making dinner! So if I can take some of the load off, perhaps by helping them get their group's tax-exempt status or answering a question about a Form 990, I'm happy."

Top tip for people new to nonprofit fundraising: "I have two tips: (1) Make sure you are allowed by law to hold certain events, like raffles and auctions; and (2) Make sure you are insured to cover accidents and losses related to the event."

W e're assuming in this chapter that you're in a leadership position that involves organizing volunteers, even if you yourself are also a volunteer. (If you're simply one of many volunteers, can you skip this material? Yes, but you might gain some ideas here worth passing along!)

Volunteerism is alive and well in the United States, where people collectively put in around eight billion unpaid hours every year. Even some established organizations rely heavily on volunteer support, or have more volunteers than paid staff. And of course, it's traditional for a nonprofit's board of directors to volunteer its services. (This chapter won't focus on board members, but will include tips regarding their role.)

Fundraising is an area where volunteers can be incredibly useful, performing tasks like reaching out individually to donors, coordinating and helping with events, offering up unique skills (a magic show at your carnival?), or providing behind-the-scenes support.

Volunteers can also reduce your need to fundraise, by providing services you might otherwise have to pay for, such as photography, graphic or Web design, sound tech services, food preparation, and even helping at a library's circulation desk. The principles described in this chapter will help in your efforts to make good use of this type of volunteer, as well.

Now, it's just a matter of finding the right volunteers—and keeping them.

TIP

Who's your point person? Managing volunteers can be a full-time job. You might want to ask someone to be a point person, who will focus on creating a functional program and be the one to approach with questions.

> ### What Do Nonprofit Board Members Do?
>
> Nonprofit board members are a special breed of volunteer. Legally, they are the top-level decision makers, responsible for determining the group's mission and goals and providing financial oversight and assistance on strategic, managerial, and other matters, including fundraising. Most board members serve terms of one to three years, with one or more renewals (as set out in your group's bylaws).
>
> Due to the perennial issue of some board members showing very little interest in fundraising, however, some nonprofits pare the board down to ten or fewer members, but ask these members to farm out work—including some fundraising—to committees. The committees may be composed of non-board volunteers who will work on, say, a donor campaign or a special event.

Recruiting Volunteers

If there's a silver lining to the recent economic downturn, it's that some unemployed people have time to spare, and some people who can't afford to make gifts to charity have decided to volunteer, instead. But plenty of working people volunteer, too. In fact, recent reports show working mothers as the most active volunteers. Key parts of the volunteer recruitment process include:

- getting your message out among your existing circle and beyond, and
- making use of volunteer-matching organizations

TIP

Aim to sign up at least double the number of volunteers you think you'll need. No-shows are inevitable, both at initial meetings and in later follow through. Adds Margo Palmer, an experienced PTA mom, "You can expect that 20% of the people will do 80% of the work."

Get the Word Out

Some people may not know that your group needs help, or what kind of help they can meaningfully offer. So your first task is to put the facts in front of them, whether in your newsletter, website or Facebook page, signs posted at your facility, or elsewhere. After years chairing a book fair for her daughter's school in Tacoma, Margo Palmer found that, "The PTA at my daughter's middle school did something that I thought was brilliant: In the beginning of each school year, they'd add a volunteer form to the packet that goes home asking parents to join the PTA and providing other information. It asked, 'Which of these volunteering categories would you be interested in?' and offered many choices. That gave me a list of people to contact right away for help with the book fair."

Assemble materials that will excite potential volunteers' interest, such as descriptions of your group's fundraising activities and upcoming events, press coverage and photos of accomplishments, and a list of committees (highlighting those in need of members). These can be distributed at meetings or events, added to your group's website (if any), or emailed around.

Explain the exciting projects and volunteer positions available for participation, how much time people can expect to put in, and the vital goals they'll be helping your group to reach. Explain what's in it for them. For example, Fran Smyth, Manager of Arts Services, Arts & Business Council of New York, says, "I work with a placement counselor who reminds unemployed people that, when they finally get their first job interview, and the interviewer leans across the table and says, 'What have you been doing with your time?' that's not the time to say, 'Duh, nothing.' Far better to explain your world-improving volunteer achievements."

Personally Contact Potential Volunteers

Think about how you can go beyond passive messaging to proactively reach volunteers. You can ask current group members for suggestions, or simply talk to friends. Professional associations, local graduate schools, chambers of commerce, alumni associations, service clubs (such as Rotary, Lions, or

Kiwanis) and other such groups are good sources of prospective volunteers. Some will allow a representative of your organization to make a pitch at one of their meetings or events.

Don't forget to distribute your recruiting materials and announcements to your group's existing volunteers. Some may be ready to step up to a higher level of service, or have friends who'd like to get involved.

Get Help From Volunteer-Matching Organizations

If you have projects that might attract widespread enthusiasm, try getting in touch with organizations dedicated to matching volunteers with nonprofits in need of services. Most of these operate through the Internet. In fact, studies show that the Internet has become second only to word of mouth in its effectiveness at bringing in volunteers. Some national sites worth looking into include:

- **The Clearinghouse for Volunteer Accounting Services (CVAS), at www.cvas usa.org.** This group matches accountants with nonprofits in need of their professional services.

- **Idealist and Action Without Borders, at www.idealist.org.** Nonprofits can enter their own profile and update it to mention events and volunteer opportunities.

- **Jesuit Volunteers, at www.jesuitvolunteers.org.** The Jesuit Volunteer Corps' long-term volunteers, mostly recent college grads, accept one-year placements where they provide direct services to economically poor or socially marginalized people. (Your organization doesn't have to be Catholic or religious to use JVC volunteers.) The program pays travel costs and provides other support, while your organization pays for food, a monthly stipend, daily transportation, housing, and medical insurance.

- **Make a Difference Day, at www.usaweekend.com/section/MDDAY.** This is an annual (October) event sponsored by *USA Weekend Magazine*. Volunteers seek out projects for one-time work. Nonprofits as well as individuals can register project ideas.

- **One Brick, at www.onebrick.org.** An all-volunteer organization operating in (at last count) seven U.S. cities, One Brick mobilizes its volunteers around one-time events, with the added incentive of meeting to socialize afterward.

- **Taproot Foundation, at www.taprootfoundation.org.** This organization places professional volunteers, with expertise in technology, marketing, fundraising, and human resources, in nonprofits that have successfully gone through a service grant application process. Grant applications are reviewed quarterly, and you can expect the volunteer—or team of volunteers—to work with your organization for up to six months.

- **Volunteer Match, at www.volunteermatch.org.** This site not only offers matching services, but information and webinars on such topics as getting companies involved in group volunteer efforts, virtual volunteering for people who want to work online from home, and attracting volunteers online.

Matching Volunteers' Skills to Your Needs

Unfortunately, there's often a wide gap between what nonprofits hope volunteers will do for them and how the volunteers envision their roles, not to mention the volunteers' actual ability to follow through. The demands of daily life, kids, and so forth can derail even the most well-intentioned. What that means for your volunteer placement efforts is that you'll need to get organized, by:

- creating defined positions with (brief) job descriptions, based on both your needs and volunteers' motives

- holding individual meetings with prospective volunteers, and

- asking every volunteer to fill out an application form.

Further below, we'll address the related topic of how to screen out those few prospective volunteers whose criminal or other record indicates that they shouldn't be allowed anywhere near your organization. This is particularly relevant if your group will be placing volunteers in positions where they'll be working with vulnerable populations such as young, disabled, or elderly persons.

TIP

"Things go wrong when you don't know your volunteers' gifts and talents." That's the lesson Helaine Isaacs learned after years working with nonprofits, adding, "If you ask someone who's introverted to knock on people's doors or ask for money, it's not going to be successful. That's why I always meet with people during the screening process to determine their skills and interests."

Create Volunteer Positions

There's no faster way to burn out a volunteer than to ask the person to show up regularly without any idea of what tasks lie ahead—especially if the person ends up standing around waiting for assignments. Brainstorm with your core fundraisers and leaders about the volunteer positions that would both help your group and create meaningful opportunities for community participation.

If you need skilled help, create positions around that. Unless you make your needs and wishes clear, the people who want to offer their skills will pass your group over, assuming that their time will be ill-used pasting stamps onto envelopes. Groups that think of their volunteers as marginal participants whose time must not be very valuable get the very type of volunteers they visualized.

Once you've decided what needs doing and by how many people, draft brief titles and descriptions (a few sentences is fine) explaining each position or committee. Go easy on use of the word "fundraising"—it scares some people off. Vivian Shnaidman, for example, an active member of her synagogue in Princeton, New Jersey, remembers, "The last thing I thought I wanted was to join the fundraising committee. But when they told me my job would be to create posters with a photo and a little biography of each of the people to be honored at our dinner dance, I realized, 'I like to write, I can do that.'"

TIP

Businesses may offer paid staff as volunteers. While they don't get a tax deduction for providing free service, they do get goodwill, an opportunity for employee bonding, and an investment in their community. We'll talk more about partnering with businesses in Chapter 4.

Find Out and Cater to Volunteers' Motives

Your most likely volunteers will have some existing connection to your cause. They may be patrons of your library, parents of kids at your school—or the kids themselves—members of your religious organization, or adopters of one of your rescued dogs. And they may really care about your success.

Yet those sentiments alone may not have been what convinced them to contact you about volunteering. After all, plenty of other people know about your group's needs, but elect to spend their time in other ways. It's a fair bet the volunteers who do sign up have additional driving motivations. Perhaps they're looking for an opportunity to meet new people, develop skills, feel needed, put some variety into their daily routine, or in the case of kids, feel more grown up.

In an article by Marjorie Ingall called "What goes around comes around," from the December 2008 issue of *SELF* magazine, she proclaims, "I'm not proud. I'll admit that I started volunteering, in part, to meet men." She cites other benefits, from the endorphin lift to the free Oreos she gets after giving blood. But she was also happy to report that she eventually started dating a fellow volunteer. If you ask such a volunteer to go into a back room and sort garage sale donations for three hours, what are the odds of seeing that person again?

Fortunately, there are relatively simple ways to satisfy volunteers' needs and interests. Creating positions with an eye toward satisfying the most likely motivations, and writing up the descriptions to make clear what the volunteers can expect to gain from the experience, is a good start. Talking to volunteers personally is also useful, as we'll discuss below. Another great approach, if you have regular volunteers, is to schedule them so that they overlap and can talk with one another.

With volunteers who offer professional services, realize that some start out with good intentions, but can't maintain their commitment over time—especially if the work involves ongoing meetings, initial proposals, drafts, and final results. Some may use volunteering as a way to launch their business or establish their reputation. If paying customers start filling their time, your project may get pushed to the back burner. Also be careful about accepting free services that the provider wants to leverage into a paid relationship. Lay out your agreement and mutual expectations in a written letter at the start.

> ☼ **TIP**
>
> **Don't expect all volunteers to lend you their job skills.** It's common for volunteers to want a break from whatever they do at work all day, whether it's computer programming, grant proposal writing, or sewing. No matter how much you could use those skills, you'll have to respect the fact that some people want a break—though it's okay to ask them for occasional bits of advice.

Ask Volunteers to Submit Applications

Wouldn't it be a bit much, asking your fellow PTA parent or that charming widower who's been coming to your temple for years to fill out an application —and perhaps even provide references—before giving you free help? Not necessarily. A written application—even a short one—helps create a good match, perhaps by discovering skills, leadership experience, and interests that you may not have known the person had, even if it's an old friend. You do need to be evenhanded in this process, asking everyone to fill out the same paperwork, in order to avoid appearing unfair or discriminatory.

Most people won't object to filling out an application and providing references. In fact, they'll appreciate being treated professionally. If the person has an up-to-date résumé handy, ask to see that, too. Below is a sample volunteer job application, which you can tailor to your group's needs. If you really have no interest in knowing whether the person has a criminal background (and therefore in following up with the screening procedures described later in this chapter), delete that question too. You'll find a blank version on the CD-ROM at the back of this book.

We'll discuss how to handle "Yes" answers to the question regarding criminal history under "When and How to Run Background Checks on Volunteer Applicants," below.

Sample Volunteer Application

Volunteer Application: Bosc Hill Elementary School PTA

Preferred volunteer position: _Auction Planning Committee Member, Bosc Hill Elementary Annual Auction_

Applicant's name: _Mia Musashi_

Address: _444 Orchard Court, Bosc Hill, PA 23456_

Telephone: _212-123-4567_

Cell phone: _212-555-4567_

Email: _miam@schoolmail.com_

Education, skills, and interests

Highest level of education achieved: _MSW, Social Work_

Other training or certification: _CPR_

Other hobbies or skills (such as editing, calligraphy, Web design, photography; artistic, musical, or performance abilities, etc.): _video editing; playing recorder; baking_

What clubs, organizations, or associations are you involved in? _Early Music Ensemble_

What languages do you speak? At what level? _Japanese—basic conversation_

Have you had CPR or first aid training? Please state type of training and dates completed. _Yes, CPR and First Aid certification, 2004_

Are you hoping to pick up any skills by volunteering for us? Please specify: _Hoping to maintain community contacts before reentering job market_

Employment

Have you been employed within the last three years? ❑ yes ☒ no .
If so, please list your employers for the past three years, starting with the most recent:

Employer's name: _____

Employer's address: _____

Employer's telephone: _____

Nature of job: _____

Dates worked: _____

Reason for leaving: _____

Employer's name: _____

Employer's address: _____

Employer's telephone: _____

Nature of job: _____

Dates worked: _____

Reason for leaving: _____

Employer's name: _____

Employer's address: _____

Employer's telephone: _____

Nature of job: _____

Dates worked: _____

Reason for leaving: _____

Past volunteer experience

Please list any volunteer experience over the past three years, starting with the most recent:

Organization name, city: _____*KidsAtPlay   Bosc Hill*_____

Nature of job: _____*Making videos for Facebook page and events*_____

Dates worked: _____*2007-2010*_____

Reason for leaving: _____*The work required too much time away from home*_____

Organization name, city: _____

Nature of job: _____

_____

Dates worked: _____

Reason for leaving: _____

Organization name, city: _____

Nature of job: _____

Dates worked: _____

Reason for leaving: _____

Driving

Do you have a driver's license? (list the number) _____ 92 000 123 _____

Do you have a car that can be used while volunteering? (make, model, year) _Yes; Toyota Camry,_
_____ 2005 _____

If so, is your car insured? (list insurance company) _Yes; Amica Insurance._

Please provide us a copy of your proof of insurance.

Health

Do you smoke? _Rarely_

Do you have any physical limitations that would affect your ability to do this work? Please describe
_____ Can't lift more than 20 pounds _____

Do you have any allergies to pets, scents, or food? Please describe. _No_

Are you willing to make a minimum one-year commitment? _____ Yes _____

References

Please provide names and contact information for two references who are familiar with you
personally or have worked with you on similar projects:

Reference's name: _Toby Krohner_

Reference's address: _876 Wyndhill Road, Bosc Hill, 23456_

Reference's telephone: _212-987-6543_

Reference's name: _Abby Taperwick_

Reference's address: _545 Magnolia Court, Bosc Hill, 23457_

Reference's telephone: _212-575-8910_

Criminal history

Have you been convicted of a felony? ☐ yes ☒ no

If so, provide details (date, offense, sentence): _____

Signed: _Mia Musashi_

Date: _September 3, 2011_

Meet With Prospective Volunteers in Person

Soon after a prospective volunteer submits an application, your volunteer coordinator should meet with that person. This is a good chance to develop a friendly, mutually constructive relationship. It's fine to keep the meeting informal, perhaps holding it in a coffee shop or at the volunteer's home—but make clear that you need to obtain some information in order to make sure there's a good match between the prospective volunteer and your group's activities.

Here's a list of potential questions (some of which you can skip if, for example, the person won't be driving a car or working with children):

- *What interests you about volunteering here?* This is your chance to find out about the person's motivations.

- *Which volunteer position are you interested in, and how do your skills match that position?* This might also be a good time to discuss whether the person has additional skills that your group might be able to use, even if you haven't yet created a position using them. Don't waste the chance to bring in high-level skills.

- *Can you provide your own computer and work space, or will you need space?* Consider what you can provide, or where you want your volunteers to work on office or other type projects.

- *Are you comfortable driving, and have you had any car accidents?* As discussed below, you'll be able to confirm the accident record with official sources.

- *Do you smoke?* Smoking isn't a solely private matter. A regular smoker who agrees to refrain while volunteering—assuming this is what you require—will in all likelihood be undergoing withdrawal pangs. That can either put the person in a bad mood or drive him or her out for a cigarette break.

- *What's your opinion of the use of drugs and alcohol?* Asking outright, "Do you use?" is likely to get you a "no" answer. But many people will respond to a request that they express their opinions. Whether their stated positions match their personal practices is another matter, admittedly.

- *Do you have any health problems that affect your ability to do the tasks involved?* Be very clear on the physical requirements of the volunteer position. You can't just ask "How's your health?" without impinging on the applicant's privacy. But you do need to make sure that the volunteer is aware of any challenges and is ready, whether the task involves sitting in a chair, typing, hauling boxes around, or accompanying kids on a backpacking trip.

- *Do you have experience working with children (if relevant)?* Any volunteer whom you'll ask to interact with children should have previous experience, at least with members of their own family.

> **TIP**
>
> **Request a commitment.** After putting in all this up-front effort, you've got a great interest in ensuring that volunteers stick around. If you're recruiting for a one-time or short-term effort (which can be great for getting volunteers started), ask them to commit to seeing the project to completion. For longer-term volunteer positions, you might ask for a commitment to a certain number of hours per week or month. Some volunteers will still drop out, but you've done what you could to emphasize the importance of the responsibility they're taking on.

Perform Reference Checks

Asking for at least two references can a good idea for any volunteer with whom you aren't already familiar. Talking with someone who has worked with the volunteer will hopefully not only yield a positive endorsement, but you'll get to know the volunteer's strengths and weaknesses before assigning him or her to particular tasks. If you don't feel that's worth your time, at least check references for any volunteer position that involves dealing with money, children, or other at-risk populations, or one that involves regularly driving a vehicle. Ask references questions like:

- *How do you know this person, and for how long?* A three-month friendship five years ago could be a sign that the person lacks other, more recent references.

- *If this was an employer/employee or volunteer relationship, how did the relationship end?* If the person seems to have flaked out on past obligations, ask for detail.

- *If this was an employer/employee or volunteer relationship, what were the person's responsibilities?* In particular, ask not only about the volunteer's ability to do the work you'll be asking for, but how he or she dealt with any responsibility for handling cash, interacting with children, maintaining confidential information, driving a car, or any other sensitive tasks that you'll need.

- *Do you know whether this person has had any financial difficulties, or history of drug or alcohol abuse?* Some references might protest that they can never know for sure, but any hesitation is a red flag.

- *Have you ever ridden in a car with this person driving?* Ask for more than a thumbs-up or down, but a description of the person's driving abilities and whether the reference had any concerns as a passenger.

- *Can you describe situations where this person was trustworthy and reliable— or not?* The reasons for this one are self-evident.

- *Have conflicts arisen between the two of you, and how were they resolved?* Basic communications can be a common source of stress in any environment.

- *Is there anything else I should know about?* Be alert to the reference's tone of voice, and any hesitation.

After checking references, you'll hopefully feel even more excited about having the volunteer on board. But if something doesn't check out, you may need to either turn the person away altogether, or at least suggest a different project. Unlike paid positions, people generally have no legal right to hold a volunteer position. As a result, organizations often have greater leeway in determining who is a good fit, as long as their criteria are not discriminatory or otherwise illegal.

When and How to Run Background Checks on Volunteer Applicants

For a few, sensitive volunteer positions—or when the person states on the volunteer application that he or she has a felony conviction—it's worth taking your intake process up a notch, by requiring screening beyond the written application. In fact, some states' laws require background checks for volunteers in certain positions, such as those involving children, disabled, and elderly persons. And if your team or group is part of a national organization, it too may have a policy requiring screenings.

Background screening helps avoid uncomfortable situations like, "Mavis told us our new finance committee chair has a theft conviction—now what?" Screening can involve everything from checking references to getting a credit report, to ordering a comprehensive background check concerning the person's general character, including criminal, employment, and education history. As a general rule, however, you should collect the minimum amount of information needed to make an informed decision about signing up the volunteer.

Attorney Sandra Pfau Englund offers this analysis: "You do not have to screen or do a background check on all volunteers—certainly no federal law requires it, though state law may in certain limited situations. And the value and accuracy of background checks can really vary. In fact, it's virtually impossible (or too expensive) to do an absolutely thorough background check on someone, going back over the person's entire life, in every U.S. state and every country in the world. What's more, your liability as an organization may increase if you give the public a false sense of security based on your use of background checks, because you're raising expectations that your volunteers are safe. If someone relies on that and gets injured as a result, you could face a lawsuit."

Given that, how do you develop an appropriate policy—that is, an easily explained position and practice on when you'll screen volunteer applicants? Start with the obvious, and identify situations where, because the volunteer position involves driving or working unsupervised with vulnerable or at-risk populations or perhaps working unattended with large sums of money, screening is legally required or advisable for every applicant. Beyond this, Sandra Pfau Englund advises nonprofit clients to both check references and, if they're concerned about the possibility of a criminal record, add this question to the volunteer application: "Have you been convicted of a felony?" If the person checks yes, or there's another reason for concern (such as unexplained gaps in the person's work history, or a complaint by another group member), run a background check, as described below.

You can't perform such checks secretly—in fact, you'll need to comply with a whole host of federal laws regarding privacy and allowable access before delving into someone's background, particularly if you're using a third party to do the screening—which we do recommend, for the sake of ease and completeness. A reputable service will provide you with a form for the prospective volunteer to sign proving consent to the checks and providing a Social Security number. The service will comply with, or advise your group on complying with rules concerning the applicant's rights (described below).

Some volunteer applicants will be insulted at the very thought of having their background checked. To prevent this problem, and otherwise comply with your obligations to protect privacy, assure all applicants that your request is based on an across-the-board policy and mention any applicable state legal requirements. Explain exactly what information will be collected, over what time period, by which company and what method, and how often the checks must be repeated; who within your group will have access to the information; and how it will be kept confidential and properly disposed of. Explain to the applicant that his or her rights also include receiving a copy of the report, being notified of negative information within the report before you take an adverse action (such as refusing to let the person volunteer for your group); the chance to dispute the information in the report; and the assurance that your group will use the report only for the purposes for which you ordered it. (These are the same protections that regular employees would have in such a screening process.)

If the applicant's refusal to consent to the screening means you won't consider the application—which is a sensible measure, if you felt that screening was important enough to require in the first place—explain that, too.

Unfortunately, not all screening services provide the same thing. Ask for recommendations from other groups in your area, or check the National Association of Professional Background Screeners website at www.napbs. com. Ask the providers for a complete rundown on what records they check, and what information they'll give you, then compare.

> **CAUTION**
>
> **No background check is failsafe.** Not every court or agency maintains up-to-date, accurate information, and in some cases, only convictions that resulted in state prison time make it into the records. Some experts have reported a 40+% error rate.

Once the results to a background check come in, only people who need to know should have access. For example, Sandra Pfau Englund explains, "I handle the background checks for one of my clients. Once I obtain the results, I report to the head of volunteers only either, 'Yes the person is eligible,' or 'No, not eligible' based on the client's policy and rules for when someone is not eligible to volunteer. I don't disclose the actual results." If you've got a lawyer on your board or among your volunteers, that's the obvious person to choose.

What if the results come back showing a criminal conviction? Sandra Pfau Englund notes, "You need to develop a policy to deal with this. It shouldn't just say something broad, like, 'If you've been convicted of any felony, you can't be our volunteer.' A person who has served time is supposed to have paid a debt to society, and it's not good social policy to say, 'Your life is over.' Maybe the person only stole a pizza at age 19. But you could exclude volunteers whose background includes any conviction involving a child, violence, and so forth."

> **TIP**
>
> **Really can't afford a service?** Ask volunteers to bring in copies of their driving and police records, at least from within your state, and their credit report (which can be obtained for free at www.annualcreditreport.com); do your own

check of your state's online sex offender registry (every state has one—search online for "Megan's law" and the name of your state); and search for the person's name, in all possible permutations, in Google and other search engines.

If you're offered pro bono services by a professional, such as an attorney, architect, or masseuse, you might also want to check that the person is actually licensed. Your state probably has a professional association that can confirm this for you.

RESOURCE

Need more information? See the Privacy Rights Clearinghouse's "Fact Sheet 16d: Volunteer Background Checks: Giving Back Without Giving Up on Privacy," available at www.privacyrights.org.

Training and Supervising Volunteers

Volunteers work more effectively if given the right tools and instructions from the get-go. A group training can be a timesaver if you're gearing up for a major effort such as a fund drive or special event. For example, you can coach volunteers on how to approach businesses for sponsorships of an upcoming dinner event, how to make phone calls encouraging people to buy tickets, or how to process the winning bidders' payments at your auction.

If some of these sound basic, don't forget that you may be teaching people new skills. For example, if you'll be asking kids to call adults and request donations, this may be their first exposure to basic telephone manners. You'd want to provide scripts and ask them to practice with each other. If you'll be asking volunteers to contribute weekly updates to your group's Facebook page, you'll need to turn on the computer for some, guide them to the page, demonstrate how it works, and give examples of appropriate posts (and posting etiquette).

If you've got working professionals on your volunteer team, schedule trainings outside of business hours—and serve food if they'll be coming straight from work.

Choose the Right Person to Conduct Trainings

Training people is a specialized skill. Just because a person has the requisite expertise doesn't make him or her the best one to convey it. Rather than choosing your most experienced volunteer to conduct trainings, you might choose the person who has teaching experience, an animated manner, the ability to keep others' attention, and competency in communicating with the age or cultural group most of your audience members belong to. In fact, choosing a team of two trainers lets them complement each other's abilities and give independent perspectives on how the trainings can be improved over time.

Create Written Training Materials

To support your trainer, develop written training materials. These should start with a reminder of your group's mission and goals, and the important role of volunteers. If they'll be playing a role in fundraising—particularly in soliciting money from individual donors or businesses—it's crucial to educate them about why the group needs money and how you're going to effectively use it. Show them your case statement. Ready them with a brief "elevator pitch," such as, "Tax revenues cover only a quarter of our library's budget. We need to raise the difference not only to maintain existing collection and services, but to respond to numbers of patrons that have doubled in the last ten years, and to take advantage of an exciting matching grant opportunity that will allow us to modernize our computer system."

Your materials should cover such basic rules and logistical matters as:

- whom to call when they'll miss a meeting or be unable to fulfill an obligation
- oversight guidelines, such as the need to have your group leader review appeal letters or other written communications before they're sent, as well as approve any new fundraising initiatives
- ethical guidelines, such as the need for confidentiality regarding who in the community has donated how much, and
- policies such as personal use of group property, limits and required advance approvals on spending (for example, on lunch with a prospective donor) and how to claim reimbursements.

Add special instructions and policies when training people for specific activities such as a garage sale, car wash, or other event (based on our tips in the relevant chapters of this book).

> **TIP**
>
> **Will your volunteers spend unsupervised time with children or other at-risk populations?** If so, and even if you've already run background checks, it's worth mandating that two adults are always present. Imagine the fallout if, for example, a volunteer drives a minor to the store to buy balloons for your fundraiser—and the minor later claims that something inappropriate occurred? Such issues are far less likely with two adults present.

Mobilize Your Volunteers for Campaigns or Projects

For campaigns or projects, assemble your volunteers and give them a combination of information and pep talk. You'll probably have a lot to organize, so getting everyone thinking clearly about their responsibilities, operating on the same schedule, and communicating appropriately will be crucial. (Promising food never fails to boost attendance!)

Give people solid information and tools, such as how many "Yes" answers they can expect for every "No" if they'll be doing direct asks for donations; and how the money will be spent. If appropriate, supply telephone scripts or letters on group stationery that they can hand to business owners or others. Consider breaking the class up into small groups for role-playing exercises.

Provide Feedback

If you're in a leadership position, be ready to tell volunteers how they're doing—including constructive criticism as well as positive reinforcement. Volunteers who are trying to develop job skills, or will eventually ask you to serve as a reference, especially need this information.

In organizations with long-term volunteers, it can be helpful to tell the volunteer during the initial training that you'll periodically sit down for a review, for example, after six months. Make clear that the volunteer will then have a chance to give you feedback on the volunteer experience and what would make it better.

No matter what, you'll also need to provide feedback along the way, or simply follow up, perhaps with questions like, "Were you able to visit those five businesses that we are hoping to get donations from?" Unfortunately, because volunteering for your group is probably not the first thing on peoples' minds, they may need some prodding. Deep down, they'll appreciate the reminder.

What if a volunteer can't seem to get it together even after extensive feedback? Helaine Isaacs explains, "If you can reassign the person to another task, great; but that doesn't always work. We've had some volunteers at the hospice who were just too chatty. No matter how much training we provided, they found it difficult to just 'be' with a dying person, potentially in silence. In such cases, I candidly explained that while their hearts are in the right place and they have many talents, the needs of the role and their skill set did not seem to be a good fit. A nonprofit shouldn't feel obligated to keep someone around just because they're not being paid."

Create Incentives for Success

Offering incentives and revving up people's spirit of competition can work wonders toward helping volunteers fundraise effectively. For example, in a phonathon, you can keep people revved up throughout by loudly announcing who has won awards for things like being the first person to get three donations, the first one to get a donation over $100, and the one to raise the most by the end of the evening. The awards don't need to be huge—a T-shirt or even a candy bar will do it for the minor prizes. Try to get something significant for your biggest prize, like dinner for two donated by a local restaurant.

Keeping Volunteers Interested

Keeping volunteers around for more than a day or two, and managing them effectively, can be a challenge. If you're in a leadership or decision-making position, and expect to inspire other volunteers to provide you with free service over the long term, you'd do well to:

- Introduce your volunteers around. Make sure they know who their fellow volunteers are, as well as your board president, head librarian, and other key staff or board members.

> **TIP**
>
> **Name tags can help.** Few people will approach a nameless stranger. But if your volunteers wear tags or badges indicating their identity, others will feel warmly toward them and may say "Hello."

- Make ongoing volunteer service convenient. If the mechanics of volunteering for your group are difficult to work into a busy schedule— for example, the volunteer has to call someone who's hard to reach, or take time off work to attend a training—it creates another reason to drop the obligation.

> **TIP**
>
> **Online volunteering is on the rise.** Some people have just enough time to sit down at their keyboard and tap away for a cause. Take advantage of this trend, for example by posting online volunteering opportunities at www.volunteermatch.org.

- **Make volunteering satisfying and fun.** Although no one has time to make it a party for them, volunteers won't come back unless moments of drudgery are leavened by moments of satisfaction and shared purpose. Try having them work directly with people, or make them feel like they're part of a special club, perhaps even with perks attached. For example, many Friends of the Library groups give their members discounts at book sales. At the Southeast Steuben library in Corning, New York, volunteers receive a special newsletter highlighting their activities and accomplishments, congratulating those who've put in the most hours, and mentioning special incentives, like a raffle for dinner for two at a local restaurant that volunteers can enter for free every time they come in to help out.

- **Never leave volunteers idle.** Here's how Cameron describes why he stopped volunteering for an organization whose cause he'd felt quite committed to: "They sent out this desperate email saying they needed people to help with their dinner and silent auction, but when I got there, I was assigned to be one of four greeters, two at the bottom of the stairs, two at the top. The guests looked confused at getting all those greetings! And by the way, I'm a professional grant writer. I could have drafted up a whole proposal for them during those hours." Your point person or event coordinator must make sure that volunteers have a clear idea of what's needed at any given time, and what to do next after a task is done.

- **Show appreciation.** Every volunteer wants to know that he or she is making a difference and advancing the cause. And it's your job to tell them that, early and often. Groups with large numbers of volunteers sometimes create T-shirts or pins identifying people as volunteers, or recognizing them for having reached milestones in hours of service. But you certainly don't need to give people a steady stream of material gifts. Studies have shown that most volunteers prefer recognition, plain and simple. Listing their names in your newsletter or website, or profiling particular volunteers, gives them a nice boost. (Check first, in case some prefer anonymity.) An annual volunteer party will also be well attended, or you might invite volunteers to your group's other events, such as a holiday party, lecture, or donor picnic.

- **Recognize—and deal with—burnout.** In spite of your mighty efforts to recruit and retain volunteers, you may find that some helpers have just had enough. According to *The New York Times* ("Frazzled Moms Push Back Against Volunteering," December 1, 2010), overextended mothers of school-age children are increasingly reaching their saturation point. If they have a reasonable household income, you can still make a pitch for a straight donation (as described in Chapter 6). Also plan ahead for smooth transitions to replace key leadership, by always having more than one person familiar with each essential volunteer job. It's a real bonus to have a thorough written description of the job, its timeline, and a lot of helpful hints.

Working With Young Volunteers

You'll hear every sort of generalization about bringing young people into your volunteer corps—they're either energetic, enthusiastic, and more fervently committed than your average jaded adult, or they're irresponsible, disinterested, and can't exercise good judgment.

The truth is probably somewhere in between, especially given that children develop intellectually at different rates, may not all wake up to the benefits of altruism without a transformative outside influence, and may have different motivations for volunteering—among them, a school requirement to put in a certain number of community service hours.

In any case, there may be excellent reasons to involve kids as volunteers in your fundraising efforts. If they're the ones you're fundraising for—as members of your school band, your local sports league, your church's Young Life group, or users of the children's section of your library—then getting them involved is a natural. Even without a direct connection, their energy and connectedness to a different constituency can be valuable, and you're helping them develop lifelong philanthropic instincts. (Plus, they really do grow up fast, and may become donors before you know it.)

Obtaining Parental Consent

When children younger than 18 are involved in any of your group's activities, you'll need to get parental consent. Your permission form will document not only the parent's permission for the child to partake in your activity, but should also have a promise that the parent will not sue your organization in the event that the child is injured as a result of the carelessness of your volunteers or participants.

The actual effectiveness of parental waivers is a fraught topic in the law. When challenged, some do not hold up—their effectiveness depends on the law in your state and the way the waiver was written.

Below is a sample parental waiver. We haven't included a blank waiver form in this book for you to use, simply because it's impossible to create one that will do the trick for all states and for every fundraising activity. You really should bite the bullet and hire a competent local lawyer for advice and drafting help.

Sample Consent and Waiver

Sports Connections
for Kids

Parental Consent for Child to Volunteer

Sports Connections for Kids, a 501(c)(3) nonprofit dedicated to facilitating organized play among children of all ethnicities and demographics, encourages and appreciates the efforts of volunteers under the age of 18. Before a child begins volunteering, however, we require consent from the parent(s) or legal guardian(s). To consent, please read and sign the form below. Thank you, and don't hesitate to contact us with questions.

If a child has more than one parent or guardian, singular references should be read as plural. Both parents/guardians must fill out and sign this form.

Child's name: _____

Child's date of birth: _____

Child's age: _____

Parent/legal guardian's name: _____

Parent's address: _____

_____

Parent's home phone: _____

Parent's work phone(s): _____

Parent's mobile phone(s): _____

Alternate contact in case of emergency:

Name: _____

Relationship to child: _____

Home phone: _____

Work phone: _____

Mobile phone: _____

By signing this form, I, the parent or legal guardian of the child named above, consent to the child's participation in volunteer activities organized by *Sports Connections for Kids*. I understand that the child will be provided with orientation and training necessary for the safe and responsible performance of the volunteer duties and will be expected to meet all the requirements of the position, including compliance with *Sports Connections for Kids'* policies and procedures. I understand that my child will receive no monetary compensation for this work.

I also understand that inherent risks may be associated with volunteer activities, including but not limited to broken bones, contusions, sprains, concussions, paralysis, and death, and will not hold *Sports Connections for Kids* accountable or liable for any injuries that unintentionally result from the child's participation, or that arise during time spent volunteering due to any underlying physical condition.

_____

Parent/Legal Guardian's Signature(s)

_____

Date

My child has the following health limitations: _____

_____

Medical Treatment Authorization

Parent(s)/Guardian(s), initial one of the following:

_____ I/we give

or

_____ I/we do not give

Sports Connections for Kids permission to authorize medical care for my child, _____

_____ *(child's name)* _____ if, in the reasonable judgment of *Sports Connections for Kids*, the need arises.

Such medical treatment shall be provided upon the advice and supervision of any physician, surgeon, dentist, or other medical practitioner licensed to practice in the United States.

_____

Parent/Legal Guardian's Signature(s)

_____

Date

> **TIP**
>
> **Purchase adequate liability insurance.** Even if you use a custom waiver prepared by a competent attorney, you'll still want the assurance of an adequate liability policy.

> **TIP**
>
> **Will you be scaring parents by laying out the risks in a consent form and waiver?** Don't worry, most parents would rather know what's possible than be surprised later, and will understand that this type of language is legally required. Adviser Sandra Pfau Englund explains the reason for such language: "The more specific a waiver is regarding the actual risks that the child, student, or other volunteer will be exposed to, the more likely a court is to uphold that a valid waiver of liability was made."

Training, Supervising, and Working With Kids

Keeping in mind the general suggestions for working with volunteers laid out earlier in this chapter, let's look at special ways to work with young volunteers.

- **Have kids recruit other kids.** Your initial recruitment efforts will probably need to come from adults (perhaps parents), but you can also tell kids that their friends are welcome. Give them suggested messages for their Facebook pages (in conversational, not stilted jargon-laden English), or ask them to make a pitch, perhaps while at an event at their house of worship or in school.

- **Hold young people's trainings separately from the adult sessions.** You'll be speaking to different audiences, and will naturally address them in a different way. In fact, try to minimize the amount that you'll be speaking, and elicit participation early on. Young people tend to get more pleasure from sharing experiences with peers than with a bunch of boring grownups.

- **Think logistics.** Kids probably can't just hop in the car and arrive at a meeting. Instead, they'll either need to have parents available or a carpool arranged for them. It's important not to unwittingly limit volunteer activities to those with available parents, which might mean those from upper-income families.

- **Provide one-on-one mentoring.** Respecting kids doesn't mean assuming they know how to handle certain tasks that we take for granted, or act in a businesslike manner. That's where having a buddy, either an older youth or an adult, can be critical. That person can note where further training is needed, and provide input and feedback, preferably in private. (Kids are easily humiliated.)

- **Serve food.** Anytime, anywhere. They'll feel happily rewarded. But don't go overboard on the sugar—healthy snacks like bagels, fruit, juices, and granola should be in the mix.

- **Keep it real.** Kids have a supersensitive baloney meter, and will know instantly if you're talking down to them or not taking their views seriously. Trainers and supervisors should be truly committed to the kids' involvement, value their opinions, and be ready to make them equal partners in your efforts.

- **Provide incentives.** Kids already play games regularly, so turning a team effort into a competition gives them a chance to impress their friends and prove themselves.

- **Show tons of appreciation.** Kids even more than adults need reassurance that they're doing a great job and making a difference in the world. (Okay, a few will be naively sure of those facts anyway, but they'll still be happy to hear kind words from you.)

- **Explain the benefits of doing their volunteer work well.** High school students, in particular, may be focused on impressing college admissions officers, so you might mention your willingness to serve as a reference or write a letter of support for those young volunteers who've earned it.

- **Talk to experienced, well-liked teachers about techniques for maintaining discipline and order.** You neither want to be the kids' "best friend" nor their prison guard. Unless you already have experience and a knack for working with kids, you may find yourself leaning in one direction or another in order to deal with some high spirits or boundary testing—and you won't like the results.

RESOURCE

For further reading on how nonprofits can effectively use volunteers: See *Recruiting and Training Fundraising Volunteers*, by Linda Lysakowski (John Wiley & Sons), which provides detailed suggestions on involving volunteers in specific tasks like capital campaigns and major donor asks.

Planning Your Group's Fundraising Strategy

Meet Your Adviser

Jan Masaoka, Editor of *Blue Avocado*, a free, nonprofit online magazine containing practical, jargon-free advice for community nonprofits.

What she does:	"I talk to people daily about how to start new nonprofit groups, and how organizations like school booster clubs can operate legally from the start."
Earliest memory of taking part in a charitable activity:	"Collecting money on Halloween for UNICEF. I think we carried a separate little box—along with our candy bag, of course—and said, 'Trick or Treat for UNICEF.' Also, my parents were active in the Japanese American Citizens' League, so I went to a lot of their fundraising events as a child; like bowling tournaments and dinners. At the time, I didn't even know these were fundraisers."
Likes best about her work:	"Talking with real people in real community organizations doing real work. I see a distinct difference between them and those who do institutional philanthropy or participate in what I call the 'philanthropic consultant industrial complex.' Recently, for example, I enjoyed talking to someone who runs a child abuse prevention group in Missouri; another who runs youth programs on a Crow reservation, who explained how she's helped overcome local families' reticence to accept a free turkey on Thanksgiving (ironically enough) by sending the turkeys home with the children; and another who runs a Koreatown youth center in Los Angeles, who explained how they're now including Latino kids due to changing demographics."
Top tip for people new to nonprofit fundraising:	"Start with something doable. Make use of what you have, rather than looking at some textbook description of what's most successful or what's working for another organization. For example, I know of a school that has an amazingly successful fundraiser featuring top-tier rock music acts. Other people look at it and say, 'Why can't we do that for our school?' But what these people don't realize is that the school was founded by the wife of a major rock star, who simply calls on her close connections."

E very nonprofit group has some sort of fundraising plan, although it's not always a conscious one. Do any of the following "plans" sound familiar?

- Do whatever we did last year, even if it didn't raise a lot of money.
- Get a lot of people together and let them all try their own different things.
- Do a little bit of everything and hope it adds up.
- Just do something!

No wonder a number of nonprofits seem to limp along year by year, never getting ahead. But it doesn't have to be that way.

True, you've probably been asked to hit the ground running. Making a rational, conscious fundraising plan may seem like the last thing you and your fellow group members can handle. But take a deep breath and realize that your fundraising efforts will be much more efficient in the long run if you take time to gather information, brainstorm, and set priorities now—or lobby for your group leaders to do so.

This process can actually be fun! Developing a fundraising plan can be chance to rejuvenate your group's efforts, reaffirm what works and rethink what doesn't, set goals, and make a commitment to keeping an eye on the big picture. The key thing to understand is that there's no fundraising formula that works for every group.

For example, a community center that's one block away from a bowling alley might successfully raise funds with a bowl-a-thon. But another center that's 42 miles from the nearest set of lanes might better focus on a closer-to-home fundraising strategy. Every nonprofit group has its own assets, strengths, personal contacts, and unique position within the community it serves, and should play to those. Such assets may change year by year, as new members cycle in and old ones leave.

Here are the key tasks you'll have to tackle to create your fundraising plan, most likely for the next year, though some groups (especially the larger ones) plan for up to five years:

- clarify the needs your fundraising is meant to meet
- determine a reasonable dollar goal to work toward

- evaluate your group's greatest fundraising assets
- create a strategy that uses these assets to effectively reach potential funding sources, and
- write down your plan in a short, easy-to-understand memo.

Why Do You Need to Raise Money in the First Place?

Of course, your group needs cash in order to operate—the more, the better. But that's not manifestly obvious to the people, businesses, or foundations that your group might approach for contributions. In fact, they may consciously or unconsciously harbor thoughts like:

- "This group always muddles along without my help."
- "The group isn't that well organized—why throw good money after bad?"
- "They're doing the same old thing—what's to get excited about supporting?"
- "Aren't they already getting money from somewhere else, like the diocese or my tax revenues?" (These are particularly common public sentiments in the case of a school, house of worship, or library.)

People will keep on thinking such thoughts, unless and until you've done your background work and created what's called a "case statement" for support—that is, a summary of what you're doing and why.

You'll find that preparing one serves a variety of purposes, from helping crystallize your group's thinking, to providing a building block for communications with potential donors and funders. At its most basic, it allows you to have a ready—and better yet, inspiring—answer when someone asks you a question like, "Why do you need to raise money for the (school, library, club, etc.) anyway?"

Before you get worried about all the work this might involve, adviser Jan Masaoka offers some reassurance: "This isn't something to get hung up on. Simply realize how much more powerful your communications will be if, instead of saying, 'We're raising money for the PTA,' you and all your volunteers are ready to say something like: 'We're raising money to build a new jungle gym because we have two children in the school with cochlear implants. These kids can't play on jungle gyms made with plastic, so we need an all-metal one.'"

As suggested by Jan's example, it sometimes helps to break your case for support down into separate needs or projects. This is true even when addressing a seemingly loyal constituency. For example, Vivian Shnaidman, a member of a synagogue in Princeton, New Jersey, says, "I don't mind paying directly for an event, like a group outing to Hershey Park. But when we're paying big monthly dues, it bothers me when no one explains to us where the money goes. In fact, it makes me wonder about things like whether both the rabbi and the assistant rabbi really need to be there at all the services, and how high their salaries are." When Vivian isn't told why her money is needed, she may begin to question her continued support.

> **TIP**
>
> **"Donors like to fund change."** Those are the words of Craig Buthod, director of the Louisville Free Public Library and *Library Journal*'s 2010 Librarian of the Year. He explains, "Our donors are often inspired by the chance to contribute to rapid improvements or the evolution of the library—but not by filling gaps in government funding. One of our largest donors once said to me, 'Not a nickel for budget relief!' but he's extremely generous with more targeted initiatives, like a program that reaches out to new immigrants, helping connect them to library resources."

Your completed case statement—or statements—can be from a few sentences to one or two pages long. It shouldn't be a dry document that you stuff into a drawer. Instead, it should be a handy item for copying and giving to interested donors or funders, or a place from which to grab language for use in letters asking for individual support, grant proposals, and so on.

How Much Money Do You Need to Raise?

Every nonprofit group should work toward a particular fundraising goal. Ideally, setting the dollar amount of this goal should be a collaborative process, overseen by the group leader, with input from whoever handles your group's money matters; most likely the board, finance committee, or any other relevant participants. The resulting number will represent all of the income that your group brings in and all the expenses it foresees paying out along the way.

You might already have a minimum number in mind, such as "It will take $40,000 to avoid our library assistant being laid off." But that figure doesn't account for the expenses you'll incur along your fundraising path. In fact, arriving at your total income figure is—and typically should be—a more complex process, in which your planners look at:

- how much money is needed to meet the needs and goals you've identified as well as continue your group's work
- how much money was raised last year
- how much can reasonably be raised this year
- the absolute minimum your group can get by on to reach its goals, with appropriate pennypinching, and
- a reasonable dollar amount that will cover projected expenses.

Such predictions can be difficult. And your urge may be to simply say something like, "Well, we know we need to raise $8,000 for our marching band's new uniforms, so let's just keep trying to raise money until we get there." The problem with such a blind approach is that you may never get there. For one thing, some fundraising methods are simply so time-consuming and inefficient that anyone running the numbers in advance could predict they'd raise only a small sum. For another, aiming high can become a powerful motivator—while aiming low can turn into a self-fulfilling prophecy.

Take the case of Aileen, who isn't really sure what her church's overall fundraising goals are, but likes to help by organizing a yearly catered Thai dinner. A local restaurant provides meals for $15 a plate, the organizers spend about $25 total on drinks and utensils, and people pay $20 each to attend (she's afraid they won't be willing to pay more). About 25 people usually buy tickets, bringing the net profits to about $100. It's a fun event, and a surefire moneymaker given that they sell tickets in advance. But would you plan such an event if you were trying to raise several thousand dollars within a limited time? These are the kinds of issues worth considering as part of your planning process.

Does Your Group Have a Good Reputation With the People Most Likely to Support It?

Unless you and everyone involved in your fundraising efforts can say with pride, "I'm with that group!" you'll be hobbled from the start. Ask around in your community, search the Web for mentions, or even take surveys to find out whether the public considers your group vital, well-organized, and the provider of a valuable community service—or the opposite. (Do they know you exist at all?)

You may need to take steps or apply pressure to help solve your group's underlying public relations issue. An overnight turnaround may not be possible, but sometimes simple steps can attract positive notice—or any notice—such as:

- Improving the public's first impression of your organization, whether by pulling weeds near your front entrance and adding some blooming flowers, redoing your signage or website home page, or giving whomever from your group first interacts with the public some tips on friendly and helpful communication.

- Attending to the physical space where your group is located—for example, if it's a library, perhaps writing a small grant proposal to get new carpeting and lighting.

- Tooting your group's own horn, by announcing achievements, telling inspiring stories, or publicly thanking or recognizing the people within it. For example, you might put up posters on-site or update your group's Facebook page with mentions of what your volunteers have achieved, or send press releases to your local newspapers. You don't necessarily need to wait for news to happen—create your own, for example when a teacher, librarian, rabbi, or pastor has reached an anniversary date (whether one, five, or 50 years) of service with your group.

- Find something new to do, even if it's a small thing. For example, in James Swan's book *Fundraising for Libraries*, he describes how, by visiting schools and passing out flyers encouraging kids to get library cards, library usage as well as financial support increased, as people "discovered" the library.

Evaluating Your Nonprofit's Fundraising Assets

This section explains how to evaluate your group's existing assets, with an eye toward strategically deploying them as part of your overall fundraising plan.

An organization's assets come in all shapes and sizes. The reputation you build by being a visible part of your community is an asset, because it can help inspire donations. A building is an asset, because you can hold events or meetings there, or collect fees from others who do so. That's one way the Palos Verdes Public Library in California responded to recent drops in its funding, by starting to charge rent to for-profit organizations that reserved its rooms.

If your group has numerous members who work for a company that generously matches employees' charitable contributions, that's definitely an asset to follow up on.

A member's connection with a celebrity is another asset, if the celeb can be persuaded to perform at your gala dinner, undergo dunking at your carnival, or have lunch with the highest bidder at your silent auction. Objects, skills, people, connections, and experience can all be assets.

Of course, deeper issues may plague your organization—this isn't uncommon. These will have to be separately addressed, and as a fundraiser or volunteer, you can't do it all. But you can impress upon those in charge that a vicious circle gets created when a dysfunctional group isn't able to impress the public. Someone's got to break the cycle.

The key thing to realize is that different assets have different fundraising uses. Some may give you ideas for fundraisers that your group—or perhaps any group—has never tried before. But for the most part, you'll be matching your assets to the tried-and-true list of fundraising methods for small groups (as discussed throughout this book), which include:

- outreach to individual donors
- outreach to businesses (including sole proprietors, such as real estate agents or dentists) and corporate donors
- special events (dinners, fairs, lectures)

- sales of goods and services (such as sales of baked goods or scrip, and car washes), and

- grant proposals.

As your group grows, you may want to add a few things to this list, such as a separate program to solicit donations from major donors or gifts via donors' wills or estates. Larger groups commonly also institute a direct-mail program to attempt to bring in donors from outside their original membership base. And if your group works to support a publicly funded entity like a school or library, you'll eventually want to engage in the political process in order to lobby for continued or increased funding. These methods are not covered in this book. If you believe that any of them might already be useful for your organization, please see *Effective Fundraising for Nonprofits*, by Ilona Bray (Nolo), and, for advice on taking political action, more specialized products such as *Political Advocacy for School Librarians: You Have the Power!* by Sandy Schukett (Linworth).

> ⚲ **TIP**
>
> **"We turned a parking spot into a fundraising asset."** So says Jackie T., after serving as auction chair for her church school in California's East Bay region. "People love to be able to come to church at the last minute and find an open parking spot. So we auctioned off the right to a reserved spot on Sunday mornings. The bidding was getting hot, with two people close to $500. I had a quick word with the church secretary, and we agreed to offer two spots, 'double or nothing.' It worked: We brought in $1,000."

To better understand how to strategize based on existing assets, consider the following list of potential assets that a small, volunteer-led group might have. These assets vary from the standard to the wacky, yet each one is valuable in its own way when it comes to fundraising.

Fundraising Assets and Uses

If your group has:	You might use it to:
A built-in membership, such as schoolchildren and their parents, or members of a church, temple, or other religious group.	Solicit individual donations, and ask members for names of other people who might also be approached for donations; create internal competitions to raise money (for example, among school homerooms); and recruit volunteers and participants for fundraising events.
An extensive mailing list.	Ditto the above. Mailing lists are every organization's treasure—guard and update it carefully, and add names of interested people whenever you can.
A pulpit or other forum for a religious leader.	Ask the leader to honor and encourage giving, for example, by thanking the committee that's raising funds for the new roof and reminding everyone that donations are still needed.
A committed corps of fundraising volunteers, with strong leadership and interpersonal skills.	The sky's the limit—but think first about having these folks maximize your outreach efforts to individual donors, including building long-term relationships with people capable of making large donations, and making personal, targeted asks to those donors. Don't forget to ask the volunteers to donate, too! Volunteers are also crucial for planning and staffing events.
Numerous members with common interests.	Plan events around a theme, such as a group trip to a Shakespeare play to support a school theater group, or an authors' night to support the library.
Access to numerous members of the public (such as on a street with lots of passersby).	Sell passersby goods (such as at a garage sale or bake sale where interest in your mission isn't key to interest in buying).
Location in a walkable area where people are mostly willing to open their doors.	Door-to-door solicitations for donations or sales of goods.
Office space and a personal phone line available to fundraising staff or volunteers.	Make calls to individual and business donors, including thank-yous, progress updates, and actual requests for donations. A librarian, for example, can do this in between other work projects.
A front desk or area where members pass or congregate.	Put out a donation jar, flyers explaining projects that need funding, a barrel to collect used books or goods, and special appeals like a Christmas tree covered with slips of paper containing your organization's wished-for donations.
An empty basement or large storage area.	Collect donated used goods or books for a big annual sale.
Personal connections with a wealthy person.	Solicit major donations or names of other wealthy or influential people who might support your cause.

Fundraising Assets and Uses, continued	
If your group has:	**You might use it to:**
Personal connections with a member of a service club, such as Rotary, Kiwanis, or Lions.	Approach the local club for volunteer help, or to propose a joint project.
Personal connections with a business owner or manager.	Solicit donations of cash, office supplies, auction or raffle items, or other goods or services; line up employee-volunteers to help advise your group on legal or accounting matters or participate in fundraising events; borrow office space or parking lot for events. (You don't need a personal connection to make such requests, but it helps.)
Members or donors whose employers match employee donations.	Encourage people to find out whether their employers will match donations, and to follow up with individual donations.
Large hall or outdoor area, or members with access to one (consider unusual venues, too, like an airplane hangar).	If your group owns the venue, rent it to other groups. Use it for fairs, carnivals, dinners, garage sales, games, tournaments, and other events.
A wall, new construction, or other area where you can add engraved plaques, tiles, or bricks, hang a quilt, or place a bench.	Offer naming opportunities, in which donations are made in exchange for placing the person's name on a tile, brick, quilt square, plaque. Or, donors can make a gift in someone's memory. Librarians can also put bookplates in books in return for donations.
Members who are professional fundraisers.	Ask first whether they'll join the fundraising committee—but if they're already overwhelmed by a day job, see whether they'll consult on a limited basis. For example, you might ask them to sit in on an initial planning meeting, read over a letter requesting donations, or suggest a venue for a special event.
Members with Internet skills.	Ask them to set up a website, Facebook page, and email outreach program for communicating with members and requesting donations.
Members who own or have access to a nice home, club, boat, or other facility.	Use these for house parties (a fundraising strategy described in Chapter 6), other fundraising events, or as part of an auction or raffle prize package.
Members with writing skills.	Ask them to write letters requesting funds, newsletters for ongoing communications with members, and grant proposals.
Members with cooking skills.	Ask for contributions to bake sales, community meals or food festivals, or raffle or auction prizes (for example, a customized cake).
Members with artistic, construction, or graphic design skills.	Ask them to create publicity posters or flyers, other publicity materials, and items for auctions or raffle prizes. Recently, popular items include decorated fiberglass animals, playhouses, birdhouses, doghouses, and more.

Fundraising Assets and Uses, continued	
If your group has:	**You might use it to:**
Members with makeup, hairdressing, or massage skills.	Organize a "makeover" or women's spa day fair.
Members who own farms, cows, or horses.	Plan outings or rides for kids. Organize cow or horse patty bingo games!
An innovative idea for a new project.	Attract interest from foundation or corporate grant funders.
High-profile personality who is willing to undergo public humiliation.	A dunk tank at the carnival, anyone? Seriously, both kids and adults will pay to see people in authority made to look silly—such as dressing like a turkey on Thanksgiving.
Unique expertise among your nonprofit staff.	Hire them out for speeches, tours, or other events. Draft articles for your group's website and license the content to other websites.

A Hotel Director Becomes a Fundraising Asset

The Parents' Club of the Belmont Oaks Academy in Belmont, California, holds an annual fundraising auction. Kaleo Waxman, a parent who served on the auction committee, describes how they came up with some items that had the bidders going crazy:

"One of the mothers in the group happened to be a director for a group of Ritz-Carlton Hotel properties. She arranged for the donation of not one, but two weekend stays at the Ritz Carlton in San Francisco—a luxury hotel in the exclusive Nob Hill area, with a spa and five-star restaurant. On top of that, she donated a surprise stay at a Ritz Carlton ski resort near Lake Tahoe to the winner of the 'Last Person Standing' contest." (For a description of Last Person Standing, see Chapter 9.)

Recognize Your Group's Weaknesses

In the course of considering what makes your group and its people great, you'll have to also consider what it lacks—gaps or weaknesses, personal or organizational, that might undermine the use of a particular fundraising strategy. Maybe your membership base doesn't have a lot of money, or your volunteer team could use more members or more professional skills among those members.

Fortunately, recognizing such weaknesses can help you figure out strategies to minimize them, or to turn supposed negatives into positives. For example, Debbie Essex, a mom and former PTA president active with the schools in Albany, California, says, "Because Albany is a very small city, we soon realized that we were asking the same local merchants, again and again, for donations and in-kind contributions. That forced us to get creative, for example by finding ways to sell intangible goods. One of our best auction items—which I myself placed the winning bid on—was a behind-the-scenes tour at an art museum in San Francisco, given by a parent who worked there as a restorer. We were fascinated, watching her take paintings off the walls to show where there was a scratch that she'd need to repair. And she showed us around her beautiful studio, where she did the actual retouching."

An increase in community need can feel like a weakness—but doesn't need to be. For example, when the recession hit, many public libraries were swamped with new patrons seeking job assistance, at the very same time that the libraries had to cut staff and hours. However, the smart libraries turned this new need into a fundraising asset, by demonstrating to donors and funders that the change in demand justified support for new training and resources.

List Your Group's Assets

As soon as you and your fellow group leaders or interested volunteers are ready, get together and brainstorm about all the relevant assets—whether people, property, or abstract qualities—that you can identify within your group. Write them on a chart like the one below. Next to each asset or strength, list the types of fundraising it could support.

Fundraising Assets Chart		
Category	**Specific Asset or Strength**	**Fundraising Uses**
People within the organization		
Contacts with people outside the organization		
Contacts with businesses		
Physical location(s)		
Know-how		
Membership or constituency		
Equipment		
Other		

During the brainstorming session, remind participants about the various tasks and activities involved in fundraising, and ask them to think specifically about what and whose skills and advantages might be helpful.

After you've completed your brainstorming session, transfer the information onto paper, creating a master chart of your organization's assets and their possible fundraising applications. You'll use this to develop your fundraising strategy, as described below. You'll also probably want to refer to this chart again during next year's planning process.

Basic Strategic Principles to Keep in Mind

You're almost ready to do some serious planning. But first, let's look at a few overarching principles about what tends to work for effective fundraising among volunteer-led or small groups—and what doesn't.

Consider Why Your Donors Give

Whole books have been written on the subject of donor motivation—which can probably be summed up as, "It's complicated." There are many good people in the world, and many of them want to support a cause. But not all good people want to support a cause right now, or your cause in particular.

Individual motivations can vary widely. For example, a group's donors may be motivated by some or all of the following:

- a wish to change the world
- an immediate and even personal need, such as to assure a child's continued participation in team sports or access to a local public library
- a feeling of debt to society or to a particular group that helped them in life
- spiritual training or practice
- a desire to affirm membership in a group of like-minded people
- friendship with the person who asked for a donation
- to attain social standing, for instance by having their name engraved on a building
- a desire to share the good luck they've enjoyed
- tax deductions, or
- something else.

You probably don't have time to survey or study your donors, but it's worth thinking through their most likely motivations based on what you already know about your mission, their common characteristics, and what you've learned in personal conversations. That allows you to play to those motivations when soliciting funds. Adviser Melissa Irish (whom you'll meet in Chapter 6) suggests considering the following questions to help understand the needs and motives of your donors:

- Who are your top three target markets (donor groupings)?
- What are some key demographics of each?
- What motivates them to give?
- What emotional needs are met by supporting your organization?
- What does your organization need to share about your results to be relevant to this target market based on these needs, demographics, and motivations?

Just remember, there will be variety even among your group's limited donor pool—for example, you might have one donor who'd love to see her name on every tile, quilt, or brick in town, and another who wants all her gifts to be anonymous.

TIP

Success motivates donors far more than desperation. Even a donor who's sympathetic to your cause might turn away from whining messages like, "Help, no one's giving us money; if you don't pony up a few bucks, we're closing down tomorrow." As Jose Aponte, Director of the San Diego County Library system (which has been subject to plenty of funding cuts) explains: "When I go out to Rotary Groups, Lions Clubs, and so forth, I go with a simple message: We're building the library of the future, and creating community in a world that has lost its connectivity. I point them to our efforts to expand, not contract our hours of operation, and show them how they can be integral to our success. And they listen."

Try for Thematic Consistency

Thematic consistency among your mission and types of fundraising activities helps draw in donors. For example, if your group is arts-related, you may be able to sell works of art or sculpture at a silent or live auction—but for any other kind of group, art sales tend to fall flat. (They're too dependent on both personal taste and existing home style or space.)

Silicon Valley Puzzle Fest Tournament Logo

Emily Shem-Tov, cochair of Silicon Valley Puzzle Fest, remembers abiding by this concept in the early days of planning this event: "I was on the committee to raise money for our new library at Morgan Hill, and people were talking about having a poker night, a bingo game, and various other events—none of which seemed library-related. So I suggested trying a crossword puzzle tournament, because the use of words seemed like a natural tie-in to the library. Some people were skeptical. In fact, I talked to one major crossword expert who said, 'Oh, it will never work west of the Mississippi, there just aren't enough crossword people there.' We've totally proven him wrong. We've got some of the best crossword writers, solvers, and competitors right here in the Bay Area, and the event attracted enthusiastic participation from the start. Our tournament is now in its fifth year."

> **TIP**
>
> **Avoid the old, "Let's just play golf!" syndrome.** Time and time again, we hear stories of groups whose missions range from suicide prevention to music education, telling the same story: Although golf has nothing to do with their mission, certain volunteers or board members (who, not so coincidentally, like to play) insist on organizing a golfing fundraiser every year. So, why is anyone complaining? Because this fundraiser seldom brings in a lot of money for groups with unrelated missions, and is even less likely to draw in new donors or volunteers—they just show up to putt! Meanwhile, the event can absorb a lot of the entire group's energy.

Fulfill Donors' Expectations—To a Point

If certain fundraising activities have withstood the test of time or become core to your group's identity, it's worth recognizing that. Don't feel that you have to drop a beloved, income-producing holiday-wreath sale or summer carnival—or even a golf game—just for the sake of thematic consistency or change. If your volunteers have become a well-oiled machine at putting on this event, so much the better.

Some donors plan around traditional fundraisers, thinking "I'll buy my greeting cards from X organization again this year, and take my friend Cynthia to Y's annual auction." Because it's easier to get donations from these long-term donors than from anyone new, there's a lot to be gained by meeting their expectations.

That said, there are times when you must make changes, because a fundraising strategy has outlived its usefulness, or takes more time than the resultant income can justify. And you're bound to encounter some resistance to making such a change.

When making changes, be up front with your group's members, and offer them choices when possible. For example, if you decide that mailing out a printed newsletter is too expensive to continue as a membership benefit, and that you'll switch to an online newsletter instead, tread gently. Warn members of the coming change, explain the financial and environmental reasons behind it, and perhaps give people the option of requesting a printed newsletter during a phase-out period.

Expect Special Events to Require Lots of Volunteer Effort

When you get volunteers together to think "fundraising," you'll often see most of the excitement and ideas generated around proposals for special events. Most people have more experience with bake sales, raffles, silent auctions, wine tastings, and so forth, than with any other kind of fundraising. And in the abstract, who wouldn't rather plan a party than write a grant proposal or call ten potential donors?

There's just one catch: When you figure all the time and energy that goes into them, special events are, on average, the least efficient or profitable form of fundraising. That doesn't mean you shouldn't plan them—as mentioned, they're the number one, most effective way to mobilize the volunteers required to keep a group like yours going, and the fun of both planning and participating in them makes for terrific community building. For these very reasons, much of this book is dedicated to special events.

That said, you'll need to keep your expectations realistic. Make sure the volunteers expressing enthusiasm at the outset will still be with you for the follow-through. And if you have certain volunteers or staff whose time and skills could be better used on more profitable fundraising activities, such as approaching individual donors, make sure you protect them from getting sucked into event preparation. Keep focused on the full breadth of group assets that might be turned to methods of fundraising beyond special events.

TIP

"It's our biggest fundraiser of the year—but still doesn't make much money," confesses Emily Shem-Tov of the Morgan Hill Library Foundation's Silicon

Valley Puzzle Fest. "We put a lot of volunteer work into this two-day combination of workshops and competitions, but it usually clears only a couple thousand dollars. We're continually looking for ways to maximize our profits during the event, like holding a raffle, selling food, and putting out a separate donation jar. But really, what keeps us doing it is our long-term goal of getting people to come in and love the library, and maybe leave us a gift when planning their estate. In the meantime, the people involved in this event are wonderful, and we have so much fun."

Try for a Mix of Fundraising Methods

A certain level of diversity among funding streams can be helpful, especially as your group grows—we all know the risks of putting all your eggs into one basket. If your carnival gets rained out (and you didn't buy insurance), your main corporate sponsor relocates to another town, or your $5,000 donor from last year is suddenly unemployed, you could have a problem. The idea is to have a manageably sized mix of stable sources providing the bulk of your budget, with some additional sources to provide balance, create future potential, and fill in the gaps.

Adviser Jan Masaoka suggests, "If your group has a small annual fundraising goal—in the neighborhood of a few thousand dollars, for example—your ongoing, reliable sources might include membership dues and scrip. In addition you might hold one or two events per year, such as a walkathon and a raffle."

Add Mini Fundraisers to Any Main Event

As long as you're going through the effort of planning a fundraising activity, why not make it do double duty? You may have attended fundraising events that followed this principle without your noticing; for example, a gala dinner that incorporated a silent auction, a bingo night at which food items were sold, a kids' event with a booth selling mystery grab bags, or a bake sale at which customers could place orders for birthday cakes.

Don't worry, such combo-platter offerings don't offend the donors. The evidence shows that most people don't mind being given another way in which to spend their money, especially if it's all part of the fun, not to mention for a good cause.

There are, however, two potential drawbacks to combining fundraising activities. First, if your event is already complex and your pool of volunteers stretched thin, you can easily overdo it by piling on more responsibilities. (Keep everyone to a strict schedule, and make sure, for example, that a silent auction ends before dinner starts.)

A second possible drawback is that combining fundraising activities can, in some situations, exclude potential donors. For example, at an Oakland, California, school, the former fundraising tradition was to combine a gala fundraising dinner with a raffle. But the fundraising committee realized that because many of the parents were low-income, they couldn't afford the relatively expensive dinner tickets—but would have been quite willing to buy raffle tickets. So, the two events were split apart, and overall parental donations increased as a result.

Always Plan Direct Asks to Individual Donors

Now, for the news that beginning fundraisers hate to hear: The easiest, most efficient way to raise money is simply to ask people for it. Therefore the one part of your fundraising program that you shouldn't even think of abandoning is outreach to individual donors (whether through mailings, phone calls, meetings, or a membership dues drive).

We know, asking directly for money can feel uncomfortable at first, and the very prospect may drive away potential volunteers. Again, that's why many of the chapters in this book discuss how to organize fundraising events. But eventually you, and they, will probably learn for yourselves that direct solicitations of donations can be both efficient and all-around merciful.

Kari M., for example, a mom in Orinda, California, says: "I recently attended a school fundraising event, wanting to show some support. I couldn't believe how over-the-top it was, with tropical decorations everywhere, and hired hula dancers. Did they think we were kids going to the prom? I ended up wishing they'd just asked me for a direct donation, rather than squandering my money on plastic palm trees."

Your members' feelings about how they'd prefer to be approached for money may go in cycles. Helaine Isaacs, an active volunteer and board member with a synagogue in Princeton, New Jersey, explains: "We've seen a pendulum effect. We've gone through phases of having lots of fundraisers, such as dinner dances, dessert receptions, concerts, special preconcert receptions with patrons donating at various levels, and so forth. But then people start feeling nickeled and dimed. Recently we switched to just having an Annual Fund for donations over and above our dues. The idea is that we can tell people, 'We're just going to ask you once a year, and that's it, the operating expenses will be covered.'"

In-Kind Contributions Can Substitute for Cash

Before rushing out to raise every dollar that your organization might need, consider whether you can supplement your fundraising with "in-kind" donations, where you're directly given new or used goods or professional services.

You've no doubt seen "wish lists" that other organizations place in their newsletters, event programs, and so on. They're often for major items of equipment, such as a computer or printer, a used car, or a costume for an event. But you can get as granular as you want. Some libraries, for example, post individual book or movie titles that they'd like copies of, or request flowering plants for their entry garden. And school parent-teacher groups often distribute long lists with everything from pencils to puzzles to beanbag chairs to microscopes. (You can make this process easier—and avoid duplication and gaps—by going to Classwish, a nonprofit website at www.classwish.org.)

These wish lists work. Though you can't count on receiving every item on your list, you'll get some of them—and quite possibly from supporters who wouldn't have given money. Some supporters may be more willing to part with a potted plant than with their hard-earned cash.

An alternative to the wish list is to approach local businesses with requests for equipment or supplies, either new or used (but still serviceable). This can yield donations of everything from refreshments to computers to printing services. We'll talk more about soliciting corporate contributions in Chapter 4.

Your organization should always be looking for new ways to get volunteers involved, as covered in more depth in Chapter 2. As you look at the budget, observe whether any discrete new volunteer possibilities emerge, particularly for professional services to replace having to hire or contract with someone.

Creating Your First-Draft Plan

Now it's time to make some important choices about which fundraising activities to pursue, based on your brainstorming. Don't ask one person to handle this alone. Instead, bring in some combination of your president or executive director, key board members, fundraising committee, and other relevant movers and shakers. Before you meet, however, ask someone to go over your brainstorming chart and do a little research into which strategies are actually viable, given the costs involved.

Create another chart, following the model shown below (there's a blank copy on the CD-ROM at the back of this book). Here, you'll prioritize the best fundraising activities for your group and make sure that these activities will help you reach your goal without draining your budget. You'll notice that we suggest subtracting the estimated expenses associated with each activity. At this point, you won't know precisely what the expenses will be, but using an educated guess will remind your group not to set the monetary goal too low. (Regular or ongoing expenses aren't included on the chart because we're assuming you set the overall goal high enough to cover these.)

As you go, keep a running total of the income amounts in the sixth column. Keep matching up your organization's greatest strengths and their corresponding fundraising uses, being sure not to assign more tasks to any one person than is realistic, until you reach or even exceed your goal.

Sample Fundraising Goal Worksheet: After-School Choir Program

Amount to Be Raised: $10,000					
Activity or Funding Source	New Expenses	Notes/Assumptions/Key Requirements	Who Will Lead	Estimated Income Reduced by Any New Expenses	Running Total of Net Income
Collect parent donations	None	$250 per member; aim for participation by 25 out of our 30 members; need ten volunteers for outreach and follow-up.	Karen	$6,250	$6,250
CD sales	CD graphic design and production; $4 per CD or $480.	Need one volunteer for production, at least one for marketing. Look for volunteer graphic designer. Assume sales of 120 CDs at $15 apiece. Prepare in time for selling at Holiday Sing-Along.	Fang-Li	$1,500 – $480 = $1,020	$5,500
Scrip	none	Need one volunteer organizer. Assume150 sales of $100 Safeway scrip cards ($15,000 worth), yielding 4% rebate total of $600; 90 sales of $20 Peet's Coffee scrip cards ($1,800) yielding 8% rebate total of $144; 40 sales of $25 Land's End scrip ($1,000), yielding 16% rebate or $160.	Greg	$904	$6,404
Holiday Sing-Along at the Mall	Buy Santa hats this year? Need to research cost	Proceeds depend on audience donations; usually around $360, but good for morale, visibility, and selling CDs.	Loretta	$360	$6,764
Raffle	Ticket printing at 2¢ per ticket (online), totaling $10.	Sell 500 tickets at $4 apiece. Need two to three volunteers to organize, solicit prizes, follow up with winners.	Sergio	$2,000	$8,764

GRAND TOTAL: $10,534

In planning who will spend time on each project, remember that your fundraising committee may have to take on responsibilities that don't raise money directly. Preparing a newsletter, setting up a new social networking presence, or planning appreciation events for members or donors frequently fall to the fundraising volunteers or staff, even in in fully staffed, larger nonprofits. Leave enough time or energy for someone to take care of these activities. Play around with the chart until you've found a way to raise all the needed money.

TIP
Seek buy-in from the people expected to participate in these efforts. Before finalizing your preliminary fundraising plan, it's wise to run it past any board members, volunteers, or staff who weren't at the meeting, but whose help you'll need to carry it out. Give them an opportunity to be heard, so that your core committee can, if necessary, adjust the plan based on their ideas.

Drafting Budgets to Support the Plan

In the course of creating your plan, you needed to make a number of assumptions regarding both income and expenses. At some point, you'll need to work these out in greater detail. Creating a fundraising budget doesn't involve higher math—just sitting down with an Excel spreadsheet or a calculator and listing every income source and expense that you can reasonably predict.

For example, a simple budget for the choir, from the example above, might look like the below; or could be split into separate budgets for each fundraising activity (with certain general expenses divided among them). Note that we've carried over the estimated income amounts from the previous chart—though these figures could also change, after you've had a chance to do some further research.

After-School Choir Program Fundraising Budget	
GROSS INCOME	
Parent contributions	$6,250
CD sales	$5,500
Scrip sales	$3,000
Holiday Sing-Along at the Mall	$360
Raffle	$2,000
Total income	$10,534
EXPENSES	
Office and miscellaneous supplies	$500
Hiring Web developer to build and maintain group website	$2,000
Postage and mailing expenses	$300
Printing (flyers, raffle tickets, etc.)	$50
Sing-Along permit fee	$50
CD production	$480
Total expenses	$3,380
NET INCOME (to cover program costs)	**$7,154**

Take a look at past years' budgets or fundraising-expense records from your group, if they're available. What were the biggest expenses? You might be surprised to notice, for example, that while renting space for last year's microbrew beer tasting was relatively affordable, the cost of hiring a professional bartender accounted for a large chunk of the expenses (and vow to find a member with bartending skills who will volunteer next time).

If you've already been involved with this group for a year or more, think about what will (or should) change. Was there enough money last year to order appropriate supplies? Did you have a large one-time expense, such as buying supplies for the newly instituted rubber duck race, which won't be repeated because a full supply of duckies is now waiting patiently in your storage closet?

Of course, no budget can reflect future income or expenditures with 100% accuracy. That's why, over the course of each fiscal year, it's important to keep an eye on how things are going, on both the income and the expense side.

TIP

Celebrate your fundraising progress. Reaching toward a particular goal can be a motivating force, and worth making public in a fun way. For example, you can put the classic thermometer in an entryway, or add regular reports to your group's newsletter or Facebook page.

Creating the Final Plan

You'll want to write down your fundraising plan, with supporting budgets, so that you and others can remember what you decided and refer to it later. But this isn't like school, where more pages get you a higher grade. Keep it simple, and choose a format that everyone will intuitively understand and want to look at. A memo can work well. Some helpful components to include in your plan are:

- **An indication of the plan's time duration.** One year is the standard, but it can also be helpful to include less detailed projections for the next few years.

- **A description of the overall plan.** For example, if it's to continue on your current course, say so—or if it's to get rid of the golf event and focus on scrip sales and collecting recyclables, describe that. Mention any goals that support fundraising indirectly, such as projects involving your website.

- **A budget reflecting the plan.** See the description and sample earlier in this chapter.

- **A calendar showing what your group will work on month by month.** This should including any planned sales, mailings, grant proposals, events, and whatever else was decided upon.

- **A breakdown of responsibilities.** Describe who will lead each task, and who else will be involved.

- **How you'll know you're on the right track.** Plan to revisit the plan every couple of months, to see how reality is measuring up to projections.

- **Descriptions of backup plans if risky strategies don't pan out as hoped.** The picture is sure to change over the course of the year, and keeping track of any "Plan B" possibilities you discussed is a great way to minimize any shock or need for new planning meetings.

Once you've written the plan down, email it or make copies for the appropriate people. Bring it to committee or board meetings. Ask committee leaders to report back on progress toward the various goals, including honest descriptions of what's working and what isn't. And plan on having someone issue individual reminders of tasks to be done.

Preparing a detailed fundraising plan once a year is a good idea. This doesn't mean reinventing the wheel or overturning your strategy every year. For people who stick with your group long-term, this process will get easier each time. And even if your group has high turnover, having a paper trail and a history of carefully considered action will help the new fundraisers pick up the reins and move forward.

Sponsorships and Other Support From Businesses

Meet Your Adviser

Gail Drulis, Executive Director of the Albany YMCA in Albany, California; Board Member of the Albany Education Foundation; and member of the Albany Rotary Club.

What she does: "I oversee the management of all the programs at the Albany YMCA, which include adult and senior health and wellness programs, a fitness center, childcare, youth and teen programs, and summer camps. The YMCA is a volunteer organization and I have the primary responsibility to work with our volunteer board of managers and board committees. I'm also in charge of fundraising. The YMCA strives to make its programs available to everyone in the community, so we raise funds to provide financial assistance for those who need it. Our primary fundraising effort is an annual campaign, where volunteers ask community members and businesses for donations. Over the years we've also raised money through special events such as a garage sale, a wine and food tasting, a dance-a-thon, a walkathon and a Halloween carnival."

Earliest memory of taking part in a charitable activity: "In high school, I volunteered to participate in a walkathon. I can't remember what we were raising money for, but I walked from 8:00 in the morning until well past dark. I walked much farther than most of my sponsors thought I would, so I raised a lot of money, but I could barely move the next day."

Likes best about her work: "I love working for an organization like the YMCA, because it makes a positive difference in the lives of people in our community. I enjoy the fundraising part of my job because that's when people are working together to help others, which at the same time helps them feel more connected to each other and to their community."

Top tip for people new to nonprofit fundraising: "Be careful about spending a lot of money in order to raise money. I've seen groups buy things like sodas, raffle prizes, T-shirts, or bumper stickers to sell, and then not sell enough to cover their initial costs! It's so much better when you get things donated, then a higher percentage of every dollar earned goes back to the organization. The donors are happier to hear that, too."

The businesses in your community have the potential to become your small nonprofit's best friends. Their financial assistance can fill the gap between the point where your group has tapped out its own constituency, and the future time when it's ready or sufficiently established to attract a reliable stream of foundation or other grants.

A business may have various motivations for helping a charitable cause. Perhaps the owner has a personal interest in your group's mission and goals; the company has made an express commitment to improving the community in which it operates (and from which its customers are derived); or, as expressed by Nini Curry, Marketing Director at Fenton's Creamery in Oakland, California, "Spending money that we might otherwise use on advertising is better spent on goodwill and gifting within the community instead."

TIP

They're not *all* flush with cash. Bear in mind that many businesses, small and large, struggle financially as much as your group—if not more. While you're with a nonprofit, they may be running a negative profit. Approach businesses respectfully, with an eye toward figuring out how a gift to your group can benefit their business as well, such as through your publicity efforts.

You can approach a business of any size for contributions to your cause. The larger, corporate ones, such as national chains, may already have a giving policy in place, and a designated amount of cash, inventory, or staff time set aside for whichever nonprofit groups present the best case for support. That makes it easy to know how to approach them, but there's a potential downside: You may face a lot of competition for the corporate personnel's attention, you may have to deal with a national office that isn't located anywhere near you, you may be ignored if your group has remained unincorporated and/or without 501(c)(3) status, and your group is probably small potatoes in terms of the amount of publicity it can give in return.

No wonder many nonprofits find that smaller, local businesses are actually their best bets for contributions. For example, Adviser Gail Drulis says, "I've found that many of the bigger businesses, with their separate corporate donation departments, lose their feeling of connection to the community. We held a dinner event where a major national beverage chain declined to give us anything, but a small store right around the corner from us donated two cases."

How exactly might a business help you? Through the myriad of ways described in this chapter, including:

- Making cash or in-kind donations, perhaps as a named sponsor of your special event or team.

- Providing volunteers from its own staff to help you with your work or serve at a fundraising event.

- Splitting profits, such as when a restaurant agrees to collect a share of the proceeds from anyone your group sends to eat there on a certain night.

- Paying your group's members for short-term work (like serving food at festival booths).

- Paying your group for toner cartridge, cell phones, and other items that you've collected for recycling.

SKIP AHEAD

Selling goods provided by for-profit businesses, as well as applying for grants from corporate foundations, are discussed elsewhere in this book. This chapter focuses on instances where you directly approach a particular business, which is in turn at least partly motivated to help you by charitable purposes. We'll discuss the many opportunities for reselling goods provided by businesses, such as scrip, wrapping paper, magazines, books, and more, in Chapter 5. And we'll discuss applying for grants from corporate foundations in the bonus chapter on the CD-ROM.

Requesting Donations or Sponsorships

Just as you can request cash or in-kind donations from individual donors, you can request them of businesses. The basic principles for doing so successfully include:

- Start with a little background research on likely businesses.

- Think creatively about what you'll ask for or accept.
- Prepare written materials.
- Send letters in advance.
- Make a personal request.
- Be specific about what publicity you'll offer in return.

TIP

Soliciting in-kind donations is an excellent task for reluctant fundraising volunteers. It feels easier for most beginning fundraisers to ask a business for, say, some food or supplies, than to ask an individual for money. And the volunteers will likely hear enough "yes" answers to become energized by their success.

Background Research

It's certainly possible to trudge up and down your local streets, stopping at every business to ask for donations. But you'll get better results with a bit of advance planning. After all, you'll feel a bit sheepish if you stop at a business that informs you that its website clearly states that all requests for donations must be in writing, with two months' advance notice.

Start by creating a master list of local or likely businesses. First on the list should be any vendors or suppliers that you personally, your group, or its members, either regularly use, work at, or own. A connection within the business can make all the difference. For example, Lisa Handley, Community Responsibility Manager for the law firm Orrick, Herrington, & Sutcliffe LLP, says of their firm's philanthropic grantmaking, "Having one of our lawyers or staffers involved in a particular nonprofit, either through rendering pro bono legal service work or as a board member or volunteer, is the key criterion for us in considering a grant request."

Expand your list with businesses in your neighborhood that you've walked past, or ones you've identified, using online sources such as your local chamber of commerce or MapQuest. (If you enter an address, the resulting map gives you an option to find nearby businesses.)

If (as is optimal) you're working with a team of volunteers, divvy up the names of the businesses on the resulting list. Each volunteer should maintain responsibility for the businesses on his or her list from start to finish, carefully tracking all contacts and results. (Showing up at a business that got solicited by your fellow group member only yesterday doesn't exactly look professional.)

Next, Google as many of the businesses on your list as you have time for. Check their websites for any established giving policies or application procedures (otherwise known as red tape, in some cases). Watch out for deadlines, especially if there's a cutoff date for that year's giving requests. If you've missed the date for a cash donation, you may still find the same business willing to give something in-kind, perhaps for your auction or food tasting, or even office supplies. These come from different line items in their budget than cash gifts. (Make a note of when their deadline is, for next year.)

If you're not getting the information that you need online, call, introduce yourself briefly, and ask to whom you can address a letter requesting sponsorship or a donation. Don't be offended if they try to put you off—they haven't seen your letter yet (we'll discuss these letters below).

Also research whether the business has made the headlines with anything relevant, such as "Impending Bankruptcy" (in which case a donation is unlikely) or "Owner Indicted for Child Pornography" (in which case you don't want a donation from them in the first place). Even if a business hasn't made the news, consider whether its activities—such as selling junk food— are antithetical to your group's aims.

TIP

Here's how the big-league nonprofits do it: Helaine Isaacs, Event Director of the Parkinson's Unity Walk (PUW; www.unitywalk.org), says, "I never approach a company without figuring out how it would benefit them to sponsor us. I do advance research about the appropriate timing for our request, what's going on in their business, who their competition is, and how they're performing. If we're not up to speed and savvy enough to talk intelligently, others will be."

Don't overlook the businesses that don't have storefronts. A dentist once told me: "I'm surprised at how rarely I'm approached by local schools. If I were to get, for instance, a handwritten note from a schoolkid explaining what supplies were needed in their classroom, of course I'd give!"

Think Creatively About What You'll Ask for or Accept

Cash is the most obvious donation to request, especially in instances where a company has committed to giving a certain percentage of its profits to charity. Closely related to this is asking them to buy tickets to your event, perhaps a whole table's worth at your gala dinner.

But many businesses are more agreeable to donating their goods (anything from samples of their products to office supplies), services (such as a gift certificate for a free haircut or legal consultation), or a private tour of their facility (which doesn't cost them a thing, other than staff time). These may be plenty useful for your group, to perhaps fill the plates at a food event or add to the selection of items at an auction.

With the tough economy, businesses may be especially willing to part with an item that it has overstocked or discontinued. (Remember, they most likely bought their goods, or the ingredients for their goods, at wholesale prices.) Or they may offer "space available" gift certificates for unused hotel room space, concert or theatre seats, or classes. Donations of magazine subscriptions can also benefit the publisher, which hopes that the recipient will sign up to renew when the free subscription is over. If day-to-day sales activities are slow, a business's staff may also have some free hours to donate to your efforts.

Besides, every business has to pay for marketing in some form, and if you do your publicity job right, low-cost marketing is exactly what it will get—a win-win situation. If you're featuring the business's products, it may also gain direct access to potential new customers. Kim Litland, Director of the Brookfield Public Library in Illinois, describes capitalizing on this strategy while helping to organize the library's annual "Taste of Brookfield" event: "We ask all the restaurants in our community to donate items of food for the event. Because it's just a tasting, none of them has to take on a big part of the responsibility. Part of the fun is the variety that comes in—from Thai food to pizza to donuts, plus a keg of Guinness from a local Irish restaurant. In keeping with the theme, our only limitation has been that the donations come from a business within the village of Brookfield, but in this past year we've relaxed that rule a bit. These donations end up covering around 85% of our overhead."

Loans of materials, rather than outright donations, will cost the business even less. Gail Drulis says of organizing a champagne-and-chocolate evening, "In addition to donations of food, drink, and flowers, we got use of tablecloths from a local event venue."

It's best to have a clear idea of what you'd like from the business before approaching it. If it's the local garden shop, for example, decide ahead of time what your dream donation would be—a cash sponsorship, a private tour of the growing areas by their head gardener, centerpieces for your event, or a gift certificate to include with one of your raffle prizes. (You can always suggest a couple of alternate possibilities.) Be flexible, of course, if the business comes back with suggestions you hadn't thought of.

Adds Library Director Kim Litland, "There's almost no business we won't approach—everyone can give something. If it's small, we'll combine it with other things to make a basket for our auction. We often do themed baskets, such as a romantic 'take your spouse to dinner' one, with bottles of wine and a restaurant gift certificate, or 'pamper your mom,' with a basket featuring a free massage at a local spa as well as restaurant gift certificates."

Large businesses may be downright eager to give you sample sizes of their products, such as mini-moisturizer bottles or individually wrapped candies. These, too, can be useful for creating or filing the gaps in gift baskets or grab bags.

TIP

Outright gifts are best. Some businesses may want to offer you discount coupons, such as "two-for-ones," or discounts on services, in which case someone has to buy something to get any benefit. As a last resort, one or two of these can be used to fill out a gift basket, but they're really not going to wow the recipients.

Prepare Written Materials

If you were to walk into a local wine store empty-handed and say, "Would you give me a case?" the business owner might easily suspect you of trying to perpetrate a fraud. You'll avoid that problem, not to mention appear more professional, if you can present official-looking written materials. The right materials will also make your group's cause, or the upcoming event, seem real and exciting.

Here's what to prepare, either for mailing or for in-person visits (both of which we'll discuss below):

Albany YMCA Event Poster
Designer: Doug Donaldson

- **A short letter on your group's letterhead.** In this, you'll request a specific donation and provide a quick explanation of your group's mission and how you'll recognize the generous gift. (More on the letter below.)

- **A printed flyer with more information on your group.** If you have one, that is—a flyer is a handy thing for any group to have. If you don't, just make sure to cover the basics in your letter. Or you could come up with something else illustrative, such as a copy of your recent newsletter or a positive article in the media about your group or the upcoming event.

- **Any graphic materials that have been created around an event that you're soliciting for.** Gail Drulis recalls, "A graphic artist, Doug Donaldson, did a beautiful poster for our chocolate and champagne gala, with delicious images of truffles and fluted glasses sparkling with bubbly champagne. Just looking at it seemed to get our potential business donors intrigued." Alternatively, samples from past years would work.

Send Letters in Advance

By sending a letter before you visit a business to request a donation, you can make sure to say everything you want to—without having to memorize it as a speech. One page is enough. You'll see an example below; you can write your own using the form, "Letter to Business," found on the CD-ROM at the back of this book. Note that the form provides an alternative section if you're asking for a donation not for a specific event, such as a dinner or auction, but to support your group's actual goals or ongoing activities (for example, with donations of office or schoolroom supplies).

If you can't offer a way for the business to make an online contribution or response, include a stamped, self-addressed envelope, with a form they can fill out to say who they are and (if their donation is not something that can be slipped into the envelope) what they'll offer, and who to call to arrange pickup or other logistical matters.

Sample Letter to Business

Village Green *Rejuvenation Society*

_____April 22, 20xx_____

Dear_ Store Manager at Wild & Wacky Cakes _:

I'm a volunteer, writing to you on behalf of the _Village Green Rejuvenation Society._
We're a nonprofit, 501(c)(3) organization committed to working toward ___the restoration of the
duck pond, band shell, and natural features of our town's historic green space___

Currently, we're planning our _____annual Community Picnic and Silent Auction,_ which will raise
money for the important goal of _hiring the professional landscape firm of Green and Greener,
which has generously agreed to provide its services at a deep discount_.

We'd like to invite your business to donate an item or gift certificate for the upcoming
_Community Picnic and Silent Auction. The customized sheet cake, made as a representation of
our Village Green that you supplied for our silent auction last year received the highest bids of
any item, and we'd be thrilled if you'd repeat that contribution!_

This exciting event is sure to be as big a hit as ever. _We expect upwards of 200 attendees, and the
Town Evening Times has already expressed interest in sending a reporter and photographer for
coverage. It will take place on June 24, 20xx at—where else?—the Village Green._

We will be happy to recognize your business's contribution on all promotional materials,
including _in the event program, on our website_, and in later reports on the event in our
newsletter, website, or other communications to the public.

I will follow up with you within the next two weeks to discuss your possible contribution. Thank
you for your consideration.

Sincerely,

Zenobia Calfalon

Community Picnic Volunteer Chairperson
Village Green Rejuvenation Society
555-101-4545; zenobiac@email.com

Sample Business Pledge

Village Green *Rejuvenation Society*

Business Pledge

To make a donation or pledge to help the *Village Green Rejuvenation Society with its Community Picnic and Silent Auction,* please give us the following information.

Business name: *Wild & Wacky Cakes*

(Please use the name by which your business would like to be recognized for its donation.)

Business contact's name: *Cassandra Baeker*

Title: *Store Manager*

Business address: *8765 Center Ave., Historia, LA, 12345*

Contact's email: *cbaeker@email.com*

Contact's phone: *555-123-1234*

For monetary donations

This donation of $ _____ will be paid by:

❏ Check or money order (make check payable to the *Village Green Rejuvenation Society*)

❏ Credit card. ❏ MasterCard ❏ Visa

  Cardholder's Name: _____

  Credit Card #: _____ Expiration Date: _____

  Billing Address (if different from above): _____

  Cardholder's Signature: _____ Date: _____

  Card Verification Number (three digits on back): _____

For goods, services, or gift certificates

Our business pledges the following goods, services, or gift certificates: *one custom "Village Green" sheet cake* The approximate retail value of this item or items is: $ *145*

❏ Special instructions regarding pickup or handling: *Please advise customer to give us at least three days' advance notice of desired cake*

Thank you! We will contact you to follow up. After processing or receiving your contribution, we will also mail you a written receipt for tax purposes.

What will happen next? You're likely to get some immediate responses, even with no follow-up—but probably not as many as you'd like. (The response rate will likely go up over the years, however, for regular events if the business was satisfied with its interaction with your group.) Plan to make personal visits to the businesses that haven't answered, as we'll discuss below.

Offer Plenty of Publicity

Offering classy, abundant publicity is your part in that win-win situation we described earlier. Both in your letter and in person, it's wise to be completely up front about how your group will publicly recognize the business's sponsorship or contribution. And this means more than just casually saying, "We'll be sure to thank you." (On the other hand, you'll need to stop short of providing actual advertising, which can complicate matters tax-wise. To be on the safe side, avoid "calls to action" such as "Buy Your Next Bike at Ray's!")

Brainstorm with your group ahead of time to come up with all of the ways you can offer publicity to your business donors, whether in your newsletter, website, event program, auction catalog, on banners, on T-shirts, and so forth. Gail Drulis says, "We held a casino night at which we asked businesses to sponsor each blackjack table for $500 apiece—and then we'd put the business's name right there on the table." Emily Shem-Tov, co-chair of Silicon Valley Puzzle Fest (which benefits the Morgan Hill Library Foundation), says, "In addition to mentioning sponsors on the website and in the registration packets for Puzzle Fest participants, we create a big poster with our sponsors' logos and information that participants see as they walk into the library for the tournament. Our sponsors can also hand out materials or set up a little table in the entryway if they want. For example, the bookstore that provides many of our prizes sells books, and the International Institute for Mathematics, which provides some cash prices to the young participants, sets up a table with information about their own events and classes."

For formal sponsorships, it's helpful to set predetermined levels, such as, "We're looking for a $1,000 lead sponsor who will be mentioned on our banner, T-shirts, and all online and written communications about the event; five $500 table sponsors, who will be mentioned on the blackjack tables and online and in written communications about the event; and another

five $250 sponsors, to be mentioned in the written and online materials."
(Note that the dollar figures in this example are deliberately low, in keeping
with what a small, grassroots group might expect. Large, established groups
planning a major event like a citywide marathon or star-studded gala might
ask for lead sponsorships in the neighborhood of $50,000 or more.)

Make Personal Requests

After waiting about ten days for responses to your letters (except in cases
where the business has a lengthier, formal application process), it's time
to put on your walking shoes. Kim Litland explains, "If businesses don't
respond to our letter, I visit in person. In fact, I take a second person from
our volunteer group with me. It seems harder for them to say 'No' to two
people standing right in front of them."

It's best if you've already researched whom to speak to, so that you don't
have to repeat your pitch a few times over. If you haven't, quickly explain
your cause, and ask the front-desk person to direct you to whomever handles
charitable donations. (Pitching to the bored teenager who sells the movie
tickets, for example, isn't likely to get you anywhere.)

When you've got the right person, mention any previous letters or contacts
from you, and review the basic points in your letter. Then highlight any
special reasons they should choose your group for a donation. For example,
Gail Drulis says, "There's one local grocery store that always seems to say no
to our requests. But for our champagne and chocolate tasting, I really wanted
to include this store's brownies. Why? Because I'd been at a Rotary Club event
that included a 'best chocolate desert' contest. After a tasting of 15 items,
and a unanimous decision as to which one was best, the winner confessed in
embarrassment that she'd entered store-bought brownies—made by this very
grocery. So I personally went to the store manager and told him that story. He
immediately said, 'Well, our brownies need to be at that chocolate tasting.' If
I'd done nothing but write a letter, I'm sure we would have received nothing.
The personal touch plus the story made all the difference."

Your demeanor is important here—conveying excitement about the
successful event or activity that you're working toward is much more likely
to get good results than desperate begging or attempts to guilt the business

owner into opening the coffers. If your organization or its key members are regular customers of that business, be sure to mention that—with statistics, if possible.

> **TIP**
>
> **Tell them which high-profile businesses are already on board.** If you can mention that a certain fancy restaurant has already promised to provide appetizers, or that a prestigious company will be a lead sponsor, you enhance your group's credibility and the prospect that your event will be a smashing success.

Hopefully, your visit will lead to an immediate "Yes." But it could also lead to a "Maybe," or "We'll think about it." Don't give up—you may have to follow up multiple times with a business before your request makes it to the right person and that person feels ready to make a decision. In any case, think of this as part of your relationship-building efforts. Even if this year's gift or sponsorship doesn't work out, you're laying the groundwork for a possible one next year.

Arranging Gifts of a Percentage of Profits

Here's a way to take the win-win aspect of corporate-nonprofit partnerships one step further. You encourage customers to patronize a certain business, and it in return gives you a cut of its proceeds, usually over a set period of time (from an evening to a month to the entire time the customer uses that business's customer card). Some businesses will even credit your group with a percentage of the proceeds from all customers for the designated time period—but of course, it's still in your mutual interest for you to publicize the arrangement and recommend that everyone you know shop there.

For example, as adviser Gail Drulis describes, "A new pizza place near us recently agreed to give a percentage of its proceeds, one evening a month, to a local education nonprofit. The first night there was a line down the sidewalk! Passersby must been thinking, 'Wow, that must be a great place to eat.'"

A surprising array of businesses offer such programs, from large grocery chains to local specialty stores. Fentons Creamery, in Oakland, California, for example, creates a featured monthly sundae on behalf of a nonprofit

Fentons Employees Pitch in at the Alameda County Food Bank

group. In August, 2010, if you'd gone into a Fentons and asked for the "Adoptalicious Sundae," the Berkeley East Bay Humane Society would have received 25% of the proceeds. Existing customers play a role in which groups get chosen for this benefit.

Checking the websites of your local businesses, talking to store managers, or even noticing when, in a checkout line, you're asked which charity you'd like a portion of your payment to go to, are all good ways to find out where such percentage programs are offered. You could also design your own mini-program of this sort, if there's an item or service you think many of your members might be interested in. For example, you could ask a photographer to donate a percentage of every family portrait done for people who mention your group.

How much will you earn? The percentages are often small, so it really depends on your ability to get the word out. Send emails to friends, grandparents of schoolchildren, and anyone else who might not make an outright donation to your cause, but who'd readily sign up to have their shopping dollars do double duty.

💡 **TIP**

Repeat, repeat, repeat your request. Debbie Essex, a former PTA President in Albany, California, says: "At the beginning of the year, when the PTA puts registration packets on each kid's school table, we include a form for parents explaining how to register their Safeway card so that the school gets a percentage of what they spend. But busy parents of little kids need more than this. So we send out reminders on our email tree and set up tables at school open houses. I even sat in front of a Safeway once, asking people from the community to register. They don't care if Safeway makes a donation, because it doesn't cost them anything; and Safeway doesn't require that school parents be the only ones to sign up."

"Shop to give" websites are another way that businesses share their profits. These usually require that the shopper access the business's website through an online charity mall or the nonprofit's own website. See, for example, iGive.com or dogreatstuff.com.

Although well-intentioned, this model hasn't lived up to expectations, because the percentage given to the nonprofit is usually minimal, typically 2.5% to 10%; and the merchants don't usually tell your group the identity of the shoppers, which prevents you from building a deeper relationship with these donors.

Does this mean that you should avoid these online giving sites? Not necessarily—for very little work, you might see a little boost in your budget. In fact, small groups with minimal fundraising staff, who can mention this opportunity in their newsletter or other publicity materials, tend to be happiest with these services, because the rewards are significant relative to their overall budget. Just do your research before choosing a service—ask other nonprofits about their experiences.

Requesting Volunteer Help From Company Staff

You should approach a business in search of volunteer help in much the same way you'd ask it for any other kind of donation. It's easiest if you've got a contact there, and important to be specific about what you want, whether it's a one-time legal review of a contract with your caterer, some willing hands to help you paint your office space, an EMT for your marathon's First-Aid booth, or a regular source of advice or help.

In addition to businesses' usual motivations when contributing to the community—such as their desire to help out, gain publicity, and introduce people to their products—those that supply volunteer help may do so to boost employee morale, give them a break from their regular work routine, and make them feel that their employer is an important and active part of the community. Nini Curry, for example, describes ways in which Fentons' staff have enjoyed the mutual benefits of volunteering: "After we helped Ken Korach, the Oakland A's play-by-play announcer, with his Community Fund's effort to build the new ball field at Oakland Tech High School, he thanked us by inviting two groups of our staff into the broadcast booth last season. A totally unique experience! And we'll soon be on the USS *Hornet*, where we've donated our Rocky Road ice cream for the unveiling of the Mars Rover 'Rocky' exhibit. As a thank-you, the Hornet Museum has invited our staff to come onboard with their families to the event."

Maybe you can't duplicate this type of a thank-you, but you can be mindful of the need to make the experience positive for the people who come to help. Also look for creative ways acknowledge the business's contribution of its staff time. Let's say, for example, that a local business agrees to send over its staff to paint your offices. You'd want to be ready with not only paint and brushes, but a camera to document the event—for a later writeup in your newsletter, press release to your local newspaper, or mention on your Facebook page.

Lending Your Volunteers as Paid Staff for Business Events

Keep your eyes and ears open! Opportunities to have your volunteers act as temporary paid staff for a for-profit business come along periodically—like the following one, reported in *The Sacramento Bee* in August, 2010:

Volunteer and nonprofit groups looking for fundraising opportunities are sought to operate food and beverage booths at the California Capital Airshow. The groups will share in a percentage of the booths' gross sales during the air show Sept. 11-12. All booth workers must be working on behalf of a nonprofit group; no paid positions are available, according to a news release.

Such events will typically have the booths and food already set up. That way, all your volunteers need to do is to show up, pay attention (or in some cases attend an advance training), and do the job required. You may need to do some quick communicating with volunteers in order to assemble the required number. It's often one nonprofit per booth, so if you can't muster up the number of people required, you're out of luck. In fact, signing up an extra volunteer or two in case of no-shows would be wise, to make sure you're welcomed back next time.

In a few situations, such as with local parades or fairs, your group may be asked to bring its own booth, as well as food or beverages. That involves more work—but someone has written a whole book on this, called *Food Booth; The Entrepreneur's Complete Guide to the Food Concession Business*, by Barb Fitzgerald (Carnival Press).

Although this type of opportunity is most often in connection with a special event, it can also be part of some regular occasion. For example, Golden Gate Fields, a horseracing track in Albany, California, holds "Dollar Days" on Sundays. The public pays a dollar for entry as well as for hot dogs, beer, and sodas. Golden Gate Fields invites nonprofit, community organizations to staff the hot dog and beverage booths on Dollar Days, in return for a flat donation of $1,000. Jerry Aldaroty, Director of Sales and Hospitality at Golden Gate Fields, explains, "It's a nice way for us to give directly to the community, and a very popular program—there's always a long waiting list for participation. Of course, nonprofits planning to sign up for this type of activity have to realize that it's a serious responsibility, as most do. For example, we require that the nonprofit supply ten people over age 18, with five of them over age 21 for beer-pouring purposes, and that they don't drink the beer. A group that has too many no-shows or is otherwise unable to meet our criteria wouldn't be invited back."

Collecting and Selling Recyclables for Mail-Back Programs

You've probably visited charities whose front entrance held a donation box for empty or used printer inkjet and toner cartridges, cell phones, MP3 players, batteries, and possibly more. Here's how it benefits the nonprofit. Services such as eCycle Group (www.ecyclegroup.com), Recycle4Charity (www.recycle4charity.com), and GreenPhone Recycling Program (www.greenphone.com) buy these items (if they're in undamaged condition). They are able to reuse them. The price paid depends on the item; less than $1 is common for toner cartridges, but an Apple iPhone might fetch around $75.

The nonprofit is responsible for packaging the items up, but shipping is often free. The service typically sends the charity a monthly check if and when a certain threshold amount of dollars or items is reached. Read the fine print, however—if you don't reach the minimum amount in a particular month, the amount you're owed may be given to another charity.

This is an easy program for volunteers to manage, but you'll of course need some storage space, preferably in an area where no one minds if a little toner leaks out. You'll also need to communicate this program to potential donors on a regular basis. The first (or second or third) time they hear about it, they may have nothing to get rid of, and soon forget. Unless you can eventually bring in a steady stream of donations, this program isn't worth your time. But once you get your members in the habit of dropping off their recyclables with you, the program can become virtually self-sustaining.

For more information and to compare details and prices, ask other nonprofits which services they've been happy with, see the websites named above, and search for others using the term "mail-back recycling."

TIP

Keep your eyes open for other programs suited to your organization. This chapter can't cover every possibility out there! Schools, for example, can earn revenue by collecting "box top" logos from qualifying products; see www.boxtops4education.com.

Selling Goods and Services, New or Used

Meet Your Adviser

Edie Boatman, Director of Fund Development for SHARP Literacy in Milwaukee, Wisconsin, and board member of the German Immersion Foundation and several other nonprofit organizations.

What she does: "During the day, I raise funds to support SHARP Literacy, a nonprofit enrichment program that helps urban Milwaukee schoolchildren learn to read and write using the visual arts as the primary tool. In the evenings, I volunteer on several local boards that serve women and children through education and/or the arts. I serve on fundraising committees and also on marketing/communication committees doing everything from writing appeal letters, drafting fund development and marketing plans, updating websites, writing newsletters, and filling in wherever help is needed."

Earliest memory of taking part in a charitable activity: "My childhood friend Debbie and I going door to door to collect money for the Jerry Lewis Telethon for Muscular Dystrophy. We were only asking for change, so everyone gave—from which I learned that if your expectations are reasonable, you're polite, and you have a good cause, people will respond. However, when the contents of our cans were dumped out and counted up, it wasn't nearly as much as we'd thought it would be!"

Likes best about her work: "The cause I'm representing gives me a door to meeting with some of the most fascinating, generous people in my community. Even when, perhaps after a breakfast meeting, I find out that my organization isn't a good fit with a prospective donor's interests, I usually walk away feeling like it was a great experience. And of course it's even better when it is a fit! The more I get to know people, the more I see how many of them want to pitch in, often as actual participants in philanthropy, not just passive bystanders."

Top tip for people new to nonprofit fundraising: "If you're passionate about your cause, people will catch that zeal and want to support it. The converse is also true—prospective funders can see in an instant when someone doesn't believe in the cause he or she is attempting to represent. That gives volunteer fundraisers an advantage, because everyone knows that you're not simply being paid to ask for contributions."

From calendars to cookies, there's probably no one in America who hasn't either bought or sold something on behalf of a nonprofit. Selling goods and services is particularly valuable for small groups trying to attract support from people outside their membership. People don't need to feel strongly about your cause—or even know much about it—in order to willingly pay for a car wash, baked good, raffle ticket, or garage-sale find. For example, Edie Boatman says, "One of the schools supported by the German Immersion Foundation takes advantage of the fact that it's used as a polling place, by holding bake sales on voting days. It makes a good amount of money from people with no connection to the school, who are just standing in line and think, 'Yum, I'd like one of those.'"

As explained in Chapter 1, it's perfectly legal for a nonprofit group to sell goods at a profit—even an exorbitant profit, if you can get people to go for it. The only limitations are your group's willingness to pay taxes (under certain circumstances), and the IRS requirement of 501(c)(3) groups that their sales activities not take over the purpose of the organization. (Review Chapter 1 for details.)

This chapter will cover some general principles regarding successful selling, including tips on particular types of sales.

Is Selling Goods or Services Right for Your Organization?

Practically any nonprofit can sell something, and many do. Sales are an especially good way to add to the proceeds from other events or activities. Sales aren't necessarily the community builder that some special events are, but they often take less creativity, and can mobilize more people.

In fact, fundraising sales work best if you have a large corps of volunteers willing to divide up the labor and reach out to their networks of friends and relatives. For example, Marcia Eaton, a parent who volunteers as President of the Band Boosters group at College Park High School in Pleasant Hill, California, says, "We hold an annual raffle, and ask each of our 185 students to sell 12 tickets (at $10 each). That's a manageable amount; just a little something they can do to help take charge of the program, since the fundraising directly benefits them. We do need to give them lots of encouragement and reminders, however."

Your group's sales efforts will be enhanced if you have some or all of the following assets:

- **Space.** For events such as garage sales, a large storage space at your disposal, and a good, easily seen and accessed area (such as a playground or auditorium) in which to hold the sale.
- **Network.** Connections to experts who create certain goods, provide services, or market or perform other business functions.
- **Home-team experts.** In-house expertise or resources that can be turned into something salable. For example, some libraries have delved into their archives for old photos of local homes and neighborhoods, then sold reproductions to interested homeowners.
- **Connections.** A contact who could offer you discounted items, or lend you commercial space for a short time period.

Of course, a brilliant idea for a new product that everyone will want or need can't hurt either—but you're unlikely to stumble upon it. Better to focus on selling things that large numbers of people in your area already buy.

> **TIP**
>
> **Look for corporate sponsors.** Even for a small-scale sale like a bake sale, lining up just one sponsor, who's willing to, for example, match up to $500 in earnings in return for its name being displayed on your banner, can give a big boost to your efforts.

Avoiding Leftovers, or a Garage-Full of Unsold Stuff

First, the good news. People like buying things for a good cause. In fact, according to studies by Cone Inc., 79% of consumers say they'd be likely to switch from one brand to another of the same price and quality, if the brand is associated with a good cause.

Now, for the bad news. Selling goods rarely comes with the profit margin you think it might. If you'll be selling used goods, such as at a garage sale, you'll have to sell them relatively cheaply. The object is to get everything moved out before the end of the day (and reduce the load you'll need to haul to, say, Goodwill), with profits to be made on a volume rather than per-item basis. If you're selling new goods, such as wrapping paper or wreaths, you'll probably have to pay more than you might like to buy them yourself—and then will need to sell them for above-market prices, which reduces the number of people interested. And with the economy down, fewer people than ever are making impulse or luxury purchases.

What should be your strategy, given all this? Below are our top tips.

Don't Invest Too Much Up Front

The less cash you can lay out in advance, the better. Of course, the ideal is to get donated goods to resell, but that's not likely to happen with new goods on a volume basis. More likely you'll have to pay, either up front or as a percentage of what you sell.

Up-front investments can be problematic. As Debbie Essex, former PTA President at an Albany, California school remembers, "We tried selling candy one year, including Easter baskets. But we had to buy it ahead of time, and sales went slowly. For a while, every time we had a school open house, someone would be selling that candy."

Similarly, more than a few nonprofit groups have had the bright idea of designing their own greeting cards, cookbooks, or calendars, and have had 1,000 or so printed up in order to take get a volume discount—only to end up with closets full of unsold stuff.

Given a choice between buying something nonrefundable or entering into an arrangement where you take orders and pay for the goods only after you've lined up customers, the latter is usually your safest option. Unfortunately, this advice may deliver you straight into the hands of various commercial outfits that specialize in charging high percentages to nonprofit groups that market their goods. As we'll discuss below, however, the convenience offered by these companies is, for some nonprofit groups, worth the markup.

Consider Who Your Buying Audience Will Be

No matter how good your cause, people aren't going to buy things they don't want. Some of the worst-selling goods or services include car washes in cold weather, old clothing at a garage sale, and increasingly, wrapping paper to people who have too much of it already.

Think like a businessperson when choosing what to sell on behalf of your nonprofit. Keep an eye on your audience's tastes and buying habits, and when you aren't sure, arm yourself with samples and ask around. Edie Boatman also advises, "Remember that people—parents, in particular—are bombarded by a whole array of fundraising requests, whether at work, from their school, by their kids' soccer team, and so on. If you can sell something unique, that helps."

Rather than buying random consumer items, your members might be more interested in something thematically consistent with your mission or shared interests. Edie Boatman describes how she made this work for the schools supported by the German Immersion Foundation: "When I was PTA president, sales through a particular catalog were a regular fundraiser for us. But then someone suggested a company that sold strudel, which was frozen and ready to bake, and was really good. This seemed like a good fit, given that we're a German-language school. Many of the parents' first reaction was, 'Please don't make us do another fundraiser!' But I urged them to give the strudel sales a try, and it went over very well."

Know How You'll Market the Goods

Many nonprofits' sales efforts fall down when it comes to marketing. It's easy to think, "Everyone will sell some to their friends!" or "I'll take some down to the corner shop and they'll set aside a little space on their counter for these." But will they—whoever the "they" is in your ideal scenario—really follow through? It's best to ask questions ahead of time, and get actual commitments (verbal, at least) as well as estimates of numbers.

Create a Basic Budget

You'll want to run a few numbers to figure out whether your sales plan will work. Jackie T., a parent volunteer with her daughter's Girl Scout troop in the Bay Area of California, describes what happens if you skip this step: "Our troop came up with the idea of setting up a fingernail-painting booth at the local elementary school's fall carnival. We thought, this will be great, everyone will bring some nail polish, and our middle-school age kids will have fun painting the elementary-school kids' fingers, charging $2 apiece. Lots of moms got involved in the coordinating, and we all bought new nail polish so that it was considered sanitary. After five hours of work at the fair, with ten youth volunteers and five adults, we made only $38—and I'm pretty sure we spent more than that on nail polish."

To avoid such scenarios, figure out your likely:

- **Up-front and fixed costs.** These are the costs that you'll have to pay regardless of how much you produce or sell, such as a hall or booth rental, and basic supplies such as a sign, cash box, and other equipment.

- **Variable costs.** This means how much each item will additionally cost to buy or make. For example, if you'll be selling baked goods, you might need to add up the costs of ingredients, and ribbons for wrapping them up nicely.

- **Price.** Settle on a price that covers your variable costs plus a cushion— limited by how much people will be willing to pay. (Of course in some cases, where you're following the dictates of a catalog vendor, you'll be told what price to charge.)

Before you set the price in stone and forge ahead, however, figure out how many you'll need to sell, at an absolute minimum, in order to break even. The formula for figuring this out is:

$$\text{break-even sales} = \frac{\text{Average fixed costs}}{(\text{average per-unit price} - \text{average per-unit variable cost})}$$

So, for example, if you were planning to sell brownies at a carnival, charging $1 for each, your fixed costs (booth, gas, and sign) were $50, and your variable costs (ingredients, packaging materials, and napkins) were $60 for every 200 brownies (or 25 cents per brownie), your break-even calculation would look like this:

$$\$66 = \frac{\$50}{(\$1 - 25¢)}$$

Stand by Your Price

The DAMAYAN Migrant Workers Association came up with a fundraising idea that its volunteers and new members were excited about: to set out a table at the Asia Pacific American Festival in Union Square Park, New York City, and sell home-cooked Filipino treats. (DAMAYAN is a nonprofit membership organization that organizes Filipino domestic workers in the New York area to fight for their rights and welfare; www.damayanmigrants.org.) Here's how Amanda Vender, former board member, describes the event:

"It was a beautiful, sunny day. We unfurled our newly painted green banner, propped up the photo display of recent events, and put out stacks of brochures. Most of the table was filled with trays of cassava cake, biko rice cakes, and empanadas—all on sale for two dollars each. Festivalgoers flocked to our table.

"When the time came to pack up, the organizers found the food trays empty and the brochure stack mostly full. And when all of the cooks were reimbursed for the ingredients, we found that we had only broken even. What happened?

"It turned out that a few festivalgoers had negotiated down the price of our sweets and empanadas, saying that they were cheaper at other tables. And as the day went on, two dollars apiece became $1.50, then $1.00, then 50 cents, then finally four for a dollar!

"We'd obviously forgotten an important element: to sell our organization, not just the empanadas. With the help of a fundraising consultant, we learned that we should have been telling customers: 'Your donation of two dollars helps to support our organization. We organize Filipino domestic workers—some of the most isolated and exploited workers in the city—to know their rights and to fight for better conditions.'"

If selling 66 brownies at $1 apiece sounds doable, that's a good start. But realize that you'll need to move well beyond that point to make a worthwhile profit. And if you fail to sell some of your inventory within the allotted time, you'll have to subtract the costs of producing it from your profits. Not to mention the fact that we're assuming that all the labor is volunteer—but as Jackie alluded to in the example above, your time is valuable, and spending hours at an activity that makes less money than you could have earned by say, clipping a coupon or bringing your lunch to work for a few days, can feel pretty ridiculous. If the numbers don't look promising enough, rethink your sales plan, or at least your price.

Organize and Motivate Your Sales Force

No matter how great your items to be sold may be, you've got to have someone doing the selling, or showing up to wash the cars, sit in the booth, and so on. This can be difficult, either in spite of people's good intentions, or because some aren't all that interested in helping in the first place. Marcia Eaton, for example, has noticed that, "By the time students get to high school, they've got other things on their minds besides fundraising, and their parents are getting tired of it as well. We created a candy sale last year in support of our band's trip to New York that we thought would get good participation, because we allowed students to put the earnings into individual accounts to offset their costs. But out of 185 students we had maybe 25 students partake, and the rest were coming back to our organization wanting us to give them money!"

See Chapter 2 for basic principles on mobilizing volunteers. A group training can be a good start, where you cover important issues like the following:

- How to approach buyers, reminding them that the sales support your cause, and giving them a brief pitch about what that cause is.

- Basic rules and best practices regarding making change, what forms of payment can be accepted, how to provide receipts, and, if you'll be sending out a bunch of people to sell individually, how best to collect money and transfer it back to your group without losing it along the way.

- What's in it for the volunteer salespeople. For example, you might invite them to a celebratory party at the end of the sales period, or give prizes to whoever sells the most.

> **TIP**
>
> **It's all in the pitch.** Christy Fell, who helps the German American Society of Tulsa put on its annual Christmas market (called "Christkindlmarkt") says, "I'm usually posted near the front door, selling tickets to a quilt drawing. At first, I wasn't that careful about how I'd phrase my pitch—sometimes I'd say, 'Would you like to enter a $1 drawing for a quilt?'; other times, I'd say, 'Would you like to make a $1 donation to the German American Society, and be entered in a drawing for a quilt?' But I started noticing that many more people bought tickets when I mentioned the donation, so I switched to that line alone."

Publicize and Advertise

You'll help your individual salespeople if you build some buzz around your sale, with signs, advertising, and email notifications to anyone who might be interested. In fact, although one benefit of fundraising sales is that they allow you to reach out beyond your membership base, don't forget that your base is an excellent starting point. For example, Kyung Yu, who helps fundraise for her children's hockey teams in Paoli, Pennsylvania, describes: "Last year, we held our annual car wash at the end of September, and the weather was terrible—40° and raining. Ironically enough, that drew out all the team parents, who'd been notified of the car wash, and felt sorry for the kids. They paid a lot to have their cars washed! The following year the weather was great, but the team parents didn't show, so we made less money overall."

When drafting emails, do so with the idea that they may—and hopefully will—be forwarded, to people's friends, relations, and so forth. Provide enough explanation of your group, and how sales of your product will help it, that even Grandma in Peoria will get enthused enough to buy.

Chapter 7 contains further information on getting and creating publicity.

The ultimate decision about what's appropriate should probably be left to the parents, with your group simply accepting their decision. We suggest not exerting undue pressure on parents who don't want their children to participate, and keeping some balance in your choice of fundraising methods, with some spearheaded by adults, without kids' involvement.

Is It Okay to Turn Your Kids Into Salespeople?

PTAs and other groups with young members need to be aware of the ongoing debate about whether drafting kids as salespeople is acceptable. Depending on who you talk to, it's either a way to teach young people important business skills while they raise funds for causes that directly benefit or interest them—or it's an unfair and exploitative burden to place on their small shoulders.

At least it's not likely to violate any child labor laws. Paul Irwin, attorney in Arlington, Texas, explains: "As long as your group isn't overworking the children, you shouldn't run afoul of any laws; and some of the child labor statutes actually contain exemptions for charitable efforts. I would advise, however, getting parental consent before the kids get involved."

To some degree, what's okay probably depends on the child. For example, Margo Palmer says, "Our daughter was already used to selling Girl Scout cookies, so by the time school fundraisers came along, she didn't seem to have a problem with them. We found that, in addition to how to make change and do other basic math, one of the most important things she learned was how to take 'No' for an answer. This can be hard for kids! We turned the fundraising sales into a game, to see how many no answers she'd typically get for every yes. Then we'd encourage her with the thought that, if she'd already gotten five 'No's,' a 'Yes' must be coming along."

Selling Goods From Companies That Cater to Nonprofits

Let's start with the fundraising method that everyone loves to hate, or hates to love: selling candy, wrapping paper, popcorn, wreaths, gifts, tchotchkes, and yes, even strudel, under the auspices of a company that manages such sales for nonprofit groups. Jackie T., who helps her kids' school in California with fundraising, nicely sums up the sentiments of many volunteers: "It can be such a game with these vendors, many of which make a ton of money off of nonprofits. A few seem downright exploitative, like one magazine company that pestered our buyers to renew their subscriptions until eternity, and sold their names to mail order companies. But I have to say, if you find the right kind of company, it solves a lot of problems for you—providing food that meets health code requirements, helping deal with tax rules, providing slick flyers and websites, and all-around making it easy to orchestrate the sales process."

Debbie Essex, former PTA president in Albany, California, adds, "We sold wrapping paper and magazines to raise money for the middle school music program. This was good for getting out-of-town relatives to buy something; I'd email them. But by the second and third year, within my family at least, no one was interested."

Laura Reichgut, with the South Mountain PTA in New Jersey, says that part of the motivation for their "No Frills" campaign, described in Chapter 6 (in which they dropped some of their more complicated fundraisers and went straight to parents for individual donations) was that, "I was ready to take a break from gift wrap." She says that their PTA has, however, continued selling school supplies through a company: "The profits are small, but at least we're selling something people need."

The lessons here are pretty obvious, if you're still interested in selling new products: Ask around to get recommendations on companies, choose a product that won't have people rolling their eyes, and look carefully at your profit percentage.

Also consider whether you can offer an immediate alternative to people to whom you're attempting to sell a product, but who say, "I don't need any [chocolate, wrapping paper, or other good] right now, but can I make a straight donation?" If, for example you're selling things at a booth or are going door to door, having donation receipts on hand in order to satisfy such requests might both raise your profits and please the donors. Unfortunately, in cases where you've got kids doing the selling, and they're trying to win prizes from the vending companies based on the amounts they sell, you'll have to realize that they're not going to be happy to offer this alternative.

> **TIP**
>
> **Look for locally generated sales possibilities.** For example, in the San Francisco Bay Area, many nonprofits sell the *Chinook Book*, containing up to $3,000 worth of coupons to environmentally friendly local vendors. The book retails for $20, and the nonprofits keep up to $10, depending on volume sold.

Selling Scrip

If you're a parent, you've probably already heard of scrip. If not, here's what it is: Various stores, in particular the national chains, sell nonprofits what amounts to gift certificates, at a slight discount. For example, your group might pay $95 for a grocery store certificate worth $100. You then sell the scrip certificates to your members and others, for the full $100. The scrip buyers aren't out any money, because they're spending the exact amount they would have at the grocery store regardless—or at the gas station, coffee shop, restaurant, drug store, or department store.

Scrip has allowed relatively small organizations to raise tens of thousands of dollars. It's especially useful in cases where your members are feeling tapped out, but can help you by doing the exact same shopping, at the same stores, as they would anyway. You can either go straight to your members' favorite stores to arrange for your scrip, or use a website such as www.escrip. com, Great Lakes Scrip Center (www.glscrip.com), or www.scrip.com.

> **TIP**
>
> **Will your scrip buyers get tax deductions?** Potentially; but only for a portion of the discount—that is, the difference between the face value of the scrip and the amount your group paid for it—and only if you actually offer the buyer the option to be given all or part of that discount, and the buyer confirms that they'd prefer to donate the amount to you. For example, if your group offers a $100 card with a $5 discount, you'd want to ask your donors, in writing, something like, "Please choose between receiving a $2.50 rebate on your scrip or donating this amount to our group." (Your group probably wouldn't want to offer donors the full $5 back, so as to cover your own expenses in administering this program.)

Holding a Garage or Used-Book Sale

Garage sales and used-book sales are winners for almost everyone involved: The donors get to clean out their shelves and closets, low-income buyers get needed goods at affordable prices, buyers of every income level get to satisfy their bargain-hunting urges, the environment benefits from reduced material in landfills, and your group makes money with very little up-front spending.

> ⚠ **CAUTION**
>
> **Will your donors of used goods get tax deductions?** Potentially; but the IRS says that old clothing, household goods, or furniture must be in "good or better" condition for the donor to qualify for a deduction. You can help donors by providing filled-out receipts stating the products' condition, though few organizations have time for this. Experts also advise the donors themselves to take photographs of the goods in case of an audit.

If you've got a dedicated storage space, and plan to make your sale an annual event, you can collect goods year-round. (Not everyone cleans out their houses on the same schedule.) For example, some Friends of the Library groups place large barrels for book collection in the libraries' front entrances. If you don't have storage space, it's best to publicize to your members that you'll be collecting goods for a period of time leading up to the sale, such as one week. Try to avoid having people bring items on the day of the sale—your volunteers will be overwhelmed sorting and pricing them.

Although garage sales are most commonly a warm-weather, outdoor activity, adviser Gail Drulis notes, "At the Albany YMCA, we hold our annual garage sale indoors, at our facility. And we've found that holding it in winter attracts big crowds, because it caters to the garage sale junkies who won't find many other options at that time of year. We typically open our doors at 9 a.m. to find an average of 85 people lined up in front. The place is full for at least the first three hours."

Used-good and book sales offer a chance to bring in volunteers beyond your usual corps, by offering them an incentive: the chance to shop before the general public gets in. Gail Drulis notes, "We bring in about 60 to

70 volunteers to start setting up at noon on the Friday before the event. They put in two-hour shifts, and we're done by about 8 p.m. We allow the volunteers to shop as soon as their shift is done, and to buy all they want. In fact, there was a time when we'd make as much money the day before the event as the day of. I think many volunteers are motivated to help because they know they can shop early."

Here are some other tips on making used-goods or book sales profitable. Every item should have a price tag on it, so that buyers don't have to find someone to ask. Ideally, all merchandise should be reviewed in advance by an expert, who can help you figure out which items might be antiques or first editions and worth setting aside in a special area at a higher price.

Your experts can also help you identify which items are junk, and should either be rejected before the goods donor drives away, sold at a very low price, or disposed of immediately. If you don't recognize and deal with the junk well in advance, two bad things happen. First, the worthless items tend to pull down the prices of the more valuable property. Second, your trip to Goodwill or the Salvation Army at the end of the day—an inevitable part of the event—will be an even bigger endeavor than you'd anticipated. Gail Drulis notes, "Even places like Goodwill and the Salvation Army are placing tight restrictions on what they'll accept these days. We do our best to stream the items we can't sell, or haven't sold, to places where they'll be most needed. Animal shelters appreciate used bedding or towels, some international charities like to receive warm-weather clothing, and the Friends of the Library takes leftover books. Also, we're affiliated with a HeadStart program, and invite their families to come and take whatever they want after a certain hour—which helps get rid of some of the stuffed animals, for example, which many other thrift shops won't accept."

For the rest of the goods, price them to sell—without giving them away entirely. Pricing is an art. Instead of dividing this task among several volunteers, it's best to have one or two "pricing czars," who are familiar with the garage sale scene and visit thrift shops to remind themselves what people normally expect to pay. These mavens should be available at the sale itself to answer questions and deal with customers who want to bargain you down.

Assuming you've priced things well, you'll probably want to hold fairly firm to those prices for at least the first half of your sale. Reminding customers that this is a fundraiser will help deflect some of the more persistent bargainers. However, you'll also want to decide in advance when to start dropping prices, to make sure you aren't left with too many unsold goods.

CAUTION

Decide how you'll deal with earlybirds. First, you'll have to decide whether to sell particular items to a professional antiques dealer or bookseller, and to your other volunteers who've no doubt been eyeing things they'd like, in advance of your sale—this will bring in guaranteed profits, but it also diminishes the public's perception of the quality of your sale. One option for dealing with this is to let the professionals pay a fee to come early, or else place bids on the items they want, and tell them that unless someone is willing to pay $x more for it within the next X hours, it's theirs. Next, you'll need to be ready to deal with the semiprofessional bargain-hunting community. They're likely to show up at your sale well before it's open, demand to start shopping, and scarf up all the good stuff before you've even begun. Be ready to put up ropes and post no-nonsense volunteers until you're ready to open.

Displaying the goods nicely is also important. Avoid leaving things stacked on the floor or in boxes. Bring racks for clothes, easels for artworks, and shelves for books, if possible. If you don't have bookshelves, it's best to arrange books on tables in low boxes or box lids, spines facing outward and aligned for easy scanning. Sort items thematically; for example, kitchen goods, decorative items, children's toys and clothes, and so forth.

Holding a Car Wash

Car washes are another standby of grassroots nonprofit efforts, particularly among schools, scouting troops, sports teams, and band groups, with lots of energetic young people ready to do the actual washing. (Fifth graders through high schoolers tend to be best suited for washing cars.)

One perennial issue, however, is that it takes a fair amount of time and fresh supplies to properly wash a car. This can mean either that the nonprofit doesn't make much money, or that customers end up dissatisfied when soap bubbles dry into spots on their windshields. To ensure efficiency and quality, practice car-washing techniques with your volunteers, and explain to everyone what you expect. Most groups don't go for fine detailing or interior work: As Jackie T. describes of her children's Band Boosters' car wash, it's usually "a quick rubdown with a soapy sponge, a hosedown, and then you clean windows with squirt-bottle cleaner, finishing with paper towels or a squeegee. Just make sure to have constant parental supervision, to deal with things like the occasional arrogant driver who's looking for imperfections in the wash job or the kids' overly enthusiastic hosedowns that erupt into horseplay."

Volunteers should work in teams of four or five (so that cars move in and out quickly) and put in two-hour shifts. It's hard work! Bring refreshments to reward and motivate your volunteers. Also consider making some extra money by selling refreshments to the people waiting to have their cars washed.

It's essential to use an appropriate space, preferably one loaned by a gas station, car mechanic, tire company, barber shop, or other place with lots of hose hookups. (In many areas, certain businesses are required to drain their outdoor wash water to the sewage treatment system rather than through the storm drains to local waterways, which makes them an environmentally friendlier choice for you, as well.) Kyung Yu describes their hockey team's annual car wash in Paoli, Pennsylvania: "We arranged to use the parking lot of a local McDonald's. They let us hook up our hoses into their kitchen. That meant that we got customers from people who were stopping anyway, and I think they got customers from people waiting to have their cars washed."

How much should you charge? From $5 to $10 is typical. However, many groups do as Kyung Yu describes: "Instead of setting a fee, we've done it on a donation basis for the last couple of years. This has worked surprisingly well, with people donating an average of $10 to $20. Of course, we're on Philadelphia's 'Main Line,' a relatively affluent area where it usually costs $20 to get your car washed anyway. You have to know your audience before going with this plan."

Holding a Bake Sale

Bake sales or other food sales are guaranteed crowd-pleasers. They're an easy way to involve people outside your usual volunteer pool, who will willingly bake up some of their specialties, usually without asking to be reimbursed for ingredients. The sales can be varied up with interesting themes, such as Valentine's Day, St. Patrick's Day, "Recipes from Grandma," or "Pies You've Never Heard Of."

Holding the actual bake sale can be done with as few as three people, for setup, customer interaction—including injunctions not to touch the goodies before committing to buying them—and cashiering.

> **TIP**
> **Want to reduce the time spent returning plates and baking tins to volunteers?** Ask them to bake with, or transfer their baked goods to, disposable plates and holders.

You have, however, probably seen some of the problems that can reduce bake-sale profitability—such as stingy or overgenerous portions, or too much of one type of good and not enough of others. Also, with allergies and vegetarian or vegan diets increasingly on the minds of the U.S. public, you need to be prepared for probing questions about what your food items contain—if not outright prohibitions. Some schools, for example, no longer allow bake sales within a certain radius of the campus.

Your first step must be to check for any relevant school or health codes (call your local health or food service department). A surprising number of cities and counties—from Albuquerque, New Mexico, to Champaign-Urbana, Illinois, to Lewiston, Maine—require nonprofit groups (and others) to get a permit before holding a bake sale.

Not all areas charge for the permit, and the majority still let you go ahead without one. But even the no-permit areas are paying increasing attention to the health issues surrounding selling food to the public, and expect bake sales to comply—for example, by individually wrapping all goods.

CAUTION

Beware the cream pie! It's frequently found on official "DO NOT SELL" lists, even for groups that have a permit for their bake sale. Apparently all the milk and eggs make a lovely recipe for not only custard, but for bacterial growth when left outside a refrigerator.

If you don't find any rules that clearly apply to your group, you'd nevertheless be wise to include the following in your bake-sale plans:

- Take steps to avoid being the cause of health problems, such as reminding your bakers to be extra careful about cleanliness in the food prep process, wrapping or covering everything in plastic at the sale, and serving with tongs.

- Ask bakers to create labels with full and accurate lists of ingredients, in case buyers have allergies. (Peanuts, nuts, wheat, eggs, and milk or butter are common concerns—try to stock at least a few items without these.)

- Whatever you do, don't sell cream, pumpkin, or meringue pies.

TIP

Keep track of who's baking what. We don't suggest actually assigning people to certain baking jobs, which might stifle their creativity. However, it's worth asking volunteers to tell you what they're planning ahead of time—and then suggest alternatives if you discover that everyone plans to bring chocolate chip cookies. For the sake of good health, consider including granola bars, cheese bread, and other healthier or nonsweet temptations. And for the sake of customer excitement, have someone with an artistic bent bring colorful cupcakes or decorated cookies.

Pricing is again a key decision. Fortunately, most people have become accustomed to paying at least $1 for a cookie and $2 for a cupcake or slice of cake or pie. Some groups have found that asking for donations works just as well—and offers the added convenience that customers typically won't ask for change. Also think beyond the immediate appetites of your customers. Some might, for example, be interested in buying a "value assortment" of cookies or a whole cake or pie to take home. Figure out and post these prices in advance.

An attractive display is also important. Bring a nice tablecloth, put up a large, friendly sign or banner, and be ready to wrap the sold goods with pretty cellophane and ribbons. Rotate the goods on the table every so often, so that everything gets its time in the forefront of the audience's attention.

Running a New Book Fair

Selling new books, in partnership with a bookstore or company, is another standby for schools and some churches—though its profitability has unfortunately decreased in recent years, as books have been declared "dead" in the face of online information and electronic entertainment. Nevertheless, children's books remain the strongest of any sellers within the book industry. Plus, book fairs are low-risk, can be fun, and may have an important tie-in to your group's mission regarding education and literacy.

The basic idea is that the bookstore or company sends a selection of books (some of which you've requested in advance) for you to sell on a certain day or days. Your volunteers handle the promotion and sales, and your group receives either a percentage of the cash profits or a credit toward future book purchases. And all this with almost no up-front expenses!

"Book fairs were pretty steadfast and manageable fundraisers for us," confirms Margo Palmer, a parent volunteer who has chaired many book fairs on behalf of her children's elementary and middle schools. "We'd start planning them about six to eight weeks ahead of time, using ten to 12 volunteers, doing two- or three-hour shifts."

If your school or other nonprofit group needs books, opting for the credit toward future purchases is usually the best deal, because it's calculated as a higher percentage than a cash reimbursement. How much you earn will probably be pegged to sales levels. So, for example, if you were to sell at least $2,000 worth of books, you might be given a choice of receiving either 10% of the proceeds in cash or a 15% credit toward books.

Start by selecting a vendor. Scholastic, Inc., is hugely popular. It's been doing book fairs for decades, and is known for sending selections of books that will please all possible members of your buying audience—children, teachers, and parents—and for making the process easy, for example by providing promotional posters and flyers, theme suggestions, prizes and bonuses, and scanning technology.

Scholastic isn't without controversy, however. Debbie Essex, in, California, says, "One issue with the Scholastic book fair is that they send lots of tchotchkes along with the books, and parents get upset when the kids spend their book money on these. One year, we just hid them behind the counter." Margo Palmer confirms, "Students sadly spent a lot on impulse items, like gag gifts and goofy calculators."

Parents and teachers have also noted that, because Scholastic orders its own inventory well in advance, and mostly deals in paperbacks, it may not have the latest, most exciting books on hand, or hardback versions of books, when you're ready to cash in your credits and perhaps expand your school's library collection.

If you're lucky enough to have local independent booksellers in your area, they may provide a fine alternative to the larger book-vending companies, offering flexibility and access to the latest publications. For example, Luan Stauss, owner of the Laurel Bookstore in Oakland, California, says, "We do regular book fairs, and can style them to whatever works best for the school—anything from a two-day fair at a preschool featuring only young children's books, to the more typical week-long, on-site fair at a school with a wide variety of books, to an in-store benefit where, for example, a certain percentage of a weekend's sales go to a certain school. We also do single-copy sales, where the school sets out only one copy of each of a wide variety of books, and then takes orders—that model is a lot easier on volunteers, because there's less to shelve and keep track of. Parents also seem to appreciate the fact that they can come to my store ahead of time to look over and choose books for the fair, which I'll supplement based on both my knowledge of what's likely to sell, and the records I keep of that school's sales in previous years. Or if the school is focusing its studies on a particular theme, like oceans, I can send them ocean-related books."

After choosing a vendor, your next step is to set a date, or more likely a series of dates. Think about when you'll get the most traffic by people who are buying for themselves, buying gifts, and buying books as donations to fulfill the teachers' and librarians' "Wish Lists." Margo Palmer says, "At the middle school, we ran the fair for a week, right before the winter holidays. Most days, we just held the fair open during lunches, but we'd pick one day to keep the fair open all day—before, during, and after school—as well as one night when there'd be an evening concert, which attracts parents and grandparents. That also gives the kids a chance to pressure their parents, and what parent doesn't like to buy a child a book?"

Be sure to coordinate with teachers and librarians in order to create the Wish List before the sale. You can circulate flyers with book descriptions provided by your vendor, as well as hold a preview after the books have arrived but before the book fair opens. Inviting kids to the previews to create their own wish lists can also be a good strategy, allowing them to go home and ask their parents to send cash or a check back with them.

> **TIP**
>
> **Keep shoplifters in check.** Staffing your fair with enough volunteers that their presence is felt will go a long way toward heading off theft. Margo Palmer says, "You always need more volunteers at the middle school, because there's more of a problem with shoplifting." She also suggests, "Think about your layout. We set up book carts in horseshoe shapes, then set rules saying that nobody could loiter outside the carts. That avoids kids passing stuff over the carts or kicking books through. Also have a talk with the librarian beforehand, for tips on which kids should be kept an eye on." Requiring that backpacks be left outside the shopping area is also a good idea.

As alluded to above, rounding up a sufficient number of volunteers is crucial to making the fair a success. The volunteers' basic tasks will include helping with setup, assisting children and other customers to find and select books and figure out how much they can afford with their pocket money, cashiering, and breakdown/cleanup. If you want to amp up the fun factor, find volunteers to do short readings or dress up as favorite book characters. Luan Stauss notes, "One of the most common mistakes I see is not having enough volunteers. Just by having someone there who's regularly straightening books and seeing what's selling can make a big difference to your profits, because if you're working with an independent bookstore, you can immediately call to see whether more copies of the top sellers are available. (For the top sellers, sales of ten to 20 books are typical, though most books sell only one or two copies.) It's also good to have a volunteer put a bookmark in the last copy of each book, for the same reason."

> **TIP**
>
> **Kids don't understand sales tax.** Margo Palmer explains, "This can lead to disappointment, when kids discover they can't buy as much as they'd thought. At the middle school level, we had the teachers build the concept into their math lessons. But younger kids need a lot of hands-on help. We also tried to make sure that every kid who wanted a book could get one, whether or not they could afford it, by reallocating some of our profits. To my mind, these fairs are about promoting literacy, not just making money."

It's important to build up anticipation of the fair within the student body. Start putting up posters approximately two weeks out. Send flyers home with the students. You can also request sample books to put in a display case ahead of time.

Holding a Raffle

Raffles—in which you sell tickets and award prizes to the winners in a random draw—are a favorite fundraiser for groups of all sizes, and don't take long to plan or carry out. In fact, I know someone who says, "All you need is three kids and a mountain bike." She's been known to simply arrange with a sports store to buy the bike at cost, post some kids and the bike outside the store, sell raffle tickets until they've earned enough to cover the bike plus a healthy profit, then let some lucky ticket holder pedal off into the sunset.

With a little more planning, however, you can line up donated goods and spend more time selling tickets. That lets you earn even more, by setting an ambitious goal and assigning a certain number of tickets to each volunteer ticket-seller. Not incidentally, it also gives you time to be sure you're complying with your state's laws on raffles, discussed under "What Does Your State's Law Say About Raffles?" below.

A raffle is a common add-on to an event like an auction or carnival. As Edie Boatman explains, "At every silent auction with which I'm involved, we try to have at least one, if not several raffles. If you do only an auction, and someone doesn't win anything, chances are that person will go home with money he or she would have otherwise given you. With a raffle, you increase the chances that your group will get at least some of that money. Or, if you're holding an event that's expected to be more of a friend-raiser than a fundraiser, a raffle can put you over the breakeven point."

A well-run raffle can earn between $2,000 and $15,000. In order to pull that off, however, you'll want to arrange for some fabulous prizes (usually between one and five), and set a ticket price that seems fair (and sufficient to make it worth your investment of time and/or money).

What Does Your State's Law Say About Raffles?

Many states regulate raffles—for example, by limiting the number of raffles you can have per year or the total value or type of items you can raffle (with liquor and firearms often limited or prohibited); requiring you to file a report when you're holding a raffle; or dictating whether you can sell tickets in advance. Check with your state nonprofit-regulating agency for more information. Many of them display helpful information online, which you can access via http://rafflefaq.com.

Because of the variation among states' laws, be cautious about following general raffle "rules" that you may read online or in other guides to fundraising. A rule that one author takes as gospel may simply reflect the laws where he or she lives. For example, California requires that you make raffle tickets available to anyone who asks, whether the person has paid or not—while in Washington, giving away free tickets is prohibited. As another example, in California, kids can sell raffle tickets if they're supervised by someone over the age of 18; while in Minnesota, it's fine for kids to sell raffle tickets, but the winners must be 18 or older; and in Washington State, ticket sellers must be 18 years old unless the primary purpose of the group is youth development. (Speaking of Minnesota, it has special rules if you combine a raffle with an ice fishing contest!) Everyone, however, must heed the federal tax law that prohibits raffle ticket buyers from deducting their cost.

What Makes Good Raffle Prizes?

Particularly if you've got inexperienced volunteers selling tickets, they'll do best if your prizes have an instant "Wow" factor. Jackie T. notes, "Lining up prizes for a raffle can actually be harder than collecting for an auction. For auctions, you can hit donors up for a haircut, a book, a day of raking, or other small-time prizes. But with a raffle, the prizes need to be exciting to a wide audience, like a vacation (with airfare and hotel), or a dinner cruise. What's more, you'll sell the most if the prizes can be delivered remotely, as in to grandparents in other states."

If you're hoping to line up a vacation package as a first prize, one of the first issues to think about will be how to arrange for airline tickets. Edie Boatman says, "If an airline flies out of your city, you may have luck getting it to donate vouchers for tickets." Or, in rare cases, you may find a group member with transferrable frequent flier miles. But many raffle organizers find they simply have to pay for airline tickets. This presents some logistical issues. You can't just buy the tickets in advance, because security regulations require you to supply the passenger's name. So you'll need to either wait until you know who the winner is to buy the certificates (but do your research about the likely price ahead of time), or give the winners a gift card with which to make their own reservations (Southwest Airlines, for example, makes these available in local grocery stores or at www.southwest.com).

It's also worth trying for donations of other prizes. For example, check whether members have time-shares, and would be willing to part with some of their unused days. In the end, however, you may end up having to pay out of pocket for other major prizes. Your next best bet is to find a corporate sponsor to underwrite the cost of the prize, then give it advertising space on your raffle tickets or other publicity materials. Jackie T. notes, "One year, when DVDs were fairly new, we got someone to donate a DVD player for a second or third prize—that was a big deal then, and easy to ship."

If you end up not having any big prizes, another way to hold a successful raffle is to display a number of raffle prizes, most likely in conjunction with your silent auction, and then put individual baskets in front of each item. People who buy tickets can choose which baskets to put the tickets into. If they have their heart set on a particular prize, they'd put all their tickets into that basket.

Carrying Out a Raffle

With just a few volunteers, you can take care of the primary tasks of lining up raffle prizes, getting tickets printed, promoting the raffle, organizing the ticket sellers, holding the drawing, and distributing the prizes.

Of course, you'll do best with a small army of ticket sellers, most likely kids (if that's legal in your state). Marcia Eaton notes, however, that, "You can't always count on the kids to sell as many tickets as you need to. One of our best years was one in which the band director got really excited about the Band Boosters raffle, and continually reminded and encouraged the kids. A later year's band director didn't do that, and sales dropped off markedly. We've also tried to supplement sales by putting up tables in front of Trader Joe's stores for a couple of weekends."

Be sure to give your sellers a deadline, such as, "Bring your money and ticket stubs back to the band room by [a certain] date (four days before the auction)."

> **TIP**
>
> **Sales going slow? Play that fact up!** As Jackie T. explains, "I like to remind buyers, 'We have to sell 2,500 tickets to make this worthwhile, and we're not there yet, so you have a great chance of winning.' One year, sure enough, my parents won a wine country tour, including a fancy picnic basket with wine, china, and more. They loved it. In fact, another year, they won a trip to Maui!"

By most state's laws, drawings must be held in public, with a neutral person doing the drawing, and people must be able to win regardless of whether they're present. "Add a little drama to the drawing," notes Jackie T. "That makes it part of the entertainment."

Planning Tickets and Sales Prices

Logistically speaking, you'll need to create tickets with a stub for the buyer and a portion for you. The buyer should ordinarily have space to fill in his or her name, address, and email. (The names and addresses you collect are yet another source of potential new members for your mailing and email lists.) Check your state's law on what else needs to be printed on the ticket and stub. The rules can be complex and very specific, and may require you to hire a professional printer. For this reason, we don't provide a sample in this chapter.

How much should raffle tickets cost? This will partly depend on how much you've paid for the prizes. Ticket prices of anywhere from $2 to $25 are common, with discounts for buying several at a time. For example, Edie Boatman says, "We sold three tickets for $25, or an arms' length worth of tickets for $100—that means that you hold a line of tickets up in front of the person with his or her arms spread out, and that's how many they get."

Variations on the Raffle Theme

Although a raffle is plenty fun by itself, there are a myriad of ways to vary it. For example, Edie Boatman says, "We did something called a 'wine pull,' where people pay $10 to reach into a box and pull out a number (printed on a cork), with each number corresponding to a bottle of wine. We sold out all 30 bottles in the first 25 minutes, probably in part because people knew they'd get something for their $10, even if they didn't know what kind or quality the wine would be. All the wine was donated, so this turned into an instant financial success."

Another variation is the so-called "50-50 raffle," where you sell as many tickets as you can, and the winner gets half the pot. The other half goes to your group. You're guaranteed to earn some money!

A cakewalk is popular at carnivals and festivals—it's sort of a mix between musical chairs and a raffle. Volunteers donate cakes, you set up a path or a circle of numbered squares, people buy tickets, you play music for about 30 seconds, and then when the music stops, you draw a number from a hat (with the numbers in the hat corresponding to the ones on the squares). Whoever is standing on (or closest to) the number that was drawn gets to choose a cake to take home. As Hilary Cooper, a parent-volunteer says, "We have a cakewalk at the Piedmont Harvest Festival. Last year, about 150 cakes were donated—including one by my daughter, featuring hot pink frosting and butterflies—and we sold around 400 tickets at $1 apiece. Many people bought multiple tickets, like my daughter, who was so determined to win a cake she reentered ten times." Of course, you could substitute any type of prize for the cakes. Make sure whoever runs this event is prepared to watch the action carefully, and act as judge in the event of a dispute over who was standing on the winning number!

Kaleo Waxman, who volunteers with her children's school in California, describes a playful way to hold a raffle during an event: "We stuffed blown-up balloons with gift certificates, and sold them for $5 to $15 during the cocktail hour at our school's silent auction. Balloon sellers circled the room, and the excitement built up as the balloons were popped and people saw what they'd won—things like the latest iPhone, a certificate to Barnes & Noble, or dinner for two at a local restaurant."

Rubber Ducky, You're the Winner!

While we're on the subject of games of chance, who can resist a rubber duck race? The idea is to choose a local stream or small river with a decent current, sell tickets for every duck (at $5 or $10), print numbers on the ducks, release all the ducks at once, then award prizes to the ticket holders whose ducks reached the finish line first, second, and third.

This type of event is, however, regulated by raffle laws, so check your state's rules first.

Requesting Donations From Individual Members

Meet Your Adviser

Melissa Irish, MBA, a fundraising consultant, former nonprofit staffer, and volunteer with her children's PTA and other school fundraising efforts.

What she does:	"I've spent the last 16-plus years focused on helping Bay Area nonprofits raise funds, particularly through major gifts as well as individual and corporate giving programs."
Earliest memory of taking part in a charitable activity:	"My mom was an English teacher and super civic-minded, so we always took part in charitable activities. When I was about six, for example, she was teaching a population of Hmong immigrants, and brought me in as her helper, to work with the kids. She showed me that I had something to offer even at that age."
Likes best about her work:	"I'm so lucky—I get to work with people who do amazing things and make a difference in the lives of others. Whether they're volunteers or staffmembers, they've made a life priority out of helping others."
Top tip for people new to nonprofit fundraising:	"Set boundaries—understand what you can and can't do. People get into trouble because they think they can do more than is realistically possible. It takes both time and money to make money. Allow your spark of inspiration to grow gradually, rather than rushing in and getting disillusioned early on."

The question for most small or volunteer-led nonprofits is not whether to directly ask people for donations, but how to most effectively go about it—especially given one uncomfortable reality: Making personal asks is the very last task that most fundraising volunteers will sign up for. Yet making these asks is not only the most efficient method of fundraising ever invented, but one that every volunteer eventually comes to appreciate—especially around midnight, when cleaning up after a special event that raised a modest amount of money after an incredible amount of work. This chapter will address both subtle and more direct approaches to approaching individuals for support, including:

- getting your group's house in order first
- creating incentives for giving
- drafting and sending appeal letters
- making one-on-one, personal requests
- holding phonathons, and
- approaching major donors.

Should Your Group Ask Individuals for Contributions?

In a word, yes. As long as you've got interested members who can spare even a little money, and the ability to contact them in writing and in person, you can practically start using this fundraising method this minute. For example, at the Harmony Project, a Los Angeles-based nonprofit providing year-round music lessons, mentoring, and ensemble participation to at-risk youth in underserved areas, Development Director Gretchen Lightfoot explains that asking recipients of the organization's efforts to help out not only raises money, but results in a feeling of buy-in that they might not otherwise have: "We've started including parents, alumni, and the families we currently serve on our solicitation list. Although they've got very little to spare, there's a known tendency where, if people get something completely for free, they start to feel entitled. The response has been very touching. Sometimes we'll open a reply letter and see ten $1 bills."

Timing might be an issue, depending on where your group is in its annual fundraising cycle. If potential donors are feeling tapped out by various smaller fundraisers—perhaps a car wash, raffle, and community dinner—now might not be the perfect moment to ask them to start writing checks. But wait a bit, and you might find that they're actually relieved to support your organization in a way that doesn't tie up their calendar, and where every dollar given goes directly to the cause.

Harmony Project Brochure

That's how donor sentiment has cycled at South Mountain Elementary School in South Orange, New Jersey. PTA copresident Laura Reichgut describes, "We sent out a survey last year to get a sense of how the school community was feeling about fundraising, programming, and so forth. A lot of the feedback suggested that parents had had their fill of the various smaller fundraisers, such as giftwrap sales or walkathons. So the PTA decided to eliminate some of those this year—or at least take a break from them—and replace them with what we call the 'No Frills Campaign.' We sent out a simple letter asking for donations and including a reply envelope. Our pitch was that this is an opportunity to support all the great work of the school with 100% tax-deductible donations."

At least one parent was thrilled: Nancy Schwartz, (who happens to be a nonprofit professional, providing marketing planning and implementation services to nonprofit organizations and foundations nationwide) commented, on her blog: "Frankly, I didn't even know how tired I was of candy bar and cookie sales, car washes and bake sales, until I saw the ad for the No Frills Campaign in our school e-newsletter. My take on why it works is that everything—including giving—is so complicated these days, and offers us so many options. Once in a while it's gloriously refreshing to go plain vanilla." (For more nonprofit marketing guidance from Nancy Schwartz, subscribe to her Getting Attention e-update at www.gettingattention.org/nonprofit-marketing/subscribe-enewsletter.html.)

In fact, a mere week into the campaign, the South Mountain PTA had already reached its minimum monetary goal for the No Frills Campaign, and the donations continued to come in during the following weeks. Laura Reichgut adds, "The majority of donations were paid by credit card—I think being able to offer this payment option was a huge benefit to us."

Before Asking for a Dime: Preparatory Steps

Your efforts to fundraise directly from individual donors will be both more efficient and more sustainable if you get a few ducks lined up first. For starters, we're assuming you've read Chapter 1 regarding setting up payment systems that make it easy to give, tracking donations, and thanking donors right away. Make sure all your volunteers understand these principles. Then look into implementing the steps below.

Review Your Case Statement

As described in Chapter 3, you need to have a clear idea of who your target donors are, and how you can match up what your group does with the donors' interests and values. Melissa Irish reminds us, "People are inspired by results and success, not needs and wants. Your messaging needs to pass the 'so what' test. Why should the prospective donor care enough to give? I try to personalize the message whenever possible. For example, I worked with a fabulous foster care program whose funding results were lackluster, despite being located in an affluent community. In our solicitations, we started trying to give people a tangible idea of what life is like for the foster kids— they arrive at their new homes with nothing more than a plastic bag with one coat, two pairs of underwear, and some socks; and then they're attending school with the prospective donors' kids, many of whom have everything they could want. The donors responded very positively."

Figure Out Who Your Members Are, and Grow the List

One of the most precious resources of any group, large or small, is its list of members and donors. Such a list helps you set goals based on likely donation levels, build relationships with prospective donors, and reach out for donations or other help when the time is right. Large and established nonprofits keep extensive databases that track their donors.

If you can afford a database, or if someone in past years has started one, great. (The commercially developed ones go by names like DonorPerfect and The Raiser's Edge.) If not, guess who gets to start one (assuming that your budget can't handle purchasing one of the commercial ones)?

Use whatever computer program you and your fellow leaders are comfortable with. Create fields for members' and donors' names (both spouses or partners, if they're in a couple), all possible contact information (name, address, phone numbers, email), committee assignments and other volunteer involvement, gifts made (by date and with reference to whether the gift was in connection with a special campaign or came with restrictions), records of thank-yous or any other letters sent, calls made, or other contacts between someone from your group (enter the name) and the donor, along with miscellaneous notes.

With any luck, you'll be able to start with an existing list, at least showing this year's team or club parents or church members. (Unfortunately for libraries, cardholder records are usually off-limits for fundraising purposes.)

Your next task is to try to widen your group's circle of contacts, now and on an ongoing basis. Adviser Melissa Irish counsels, "It can be hard to think about donor acquisition when you're in the middle of everything else, but I recommend that every group set aside time, at least once a year, to consider how to reach out to prospective new members. If you don't, you're likely to find your numbers dwindling, through attrition, or perhaps as elder members pass on. A church, for example, might strategize how to reach out to new people who've moved into the neighborhood."

Also ask everyone you can think of to go through their memory banks and address books and provide names and contact information of people with some connection to your group who aren't already on your list. Collect names of alumni or past coaches, teachers, troop leaders, and other volunteers; grandparents (or doting aunts, uncles, and friends); homeowners in the neighborhood (who may recognize the importance of your work or just love being able to walk to a carnival or auction); local business owners and their staff who've volunteered with your group; and so forth. You'll be happy to have such a list, as you watch support levels grow over time.

At any event that you hold or participate in—whether it be an arts or entertainment event, lecture, crafts fair, walkathon, petition drive, or annual dinner—you have an opportunity to inspire and bring in new donors (say, friends of friends who just came along for the fun of it). At the Louisville Free Public Library, Director Craig Buthod explains, "Our library foundation occasionally holds free author events, where it asks people to call in for tickets. The tickets are mailed out along with a solicitation, saying something like, 'If you enjoy programs like this, please consider making a donation to the library foundation.' If that person responds, then that's another name we can add to our mailing list."

Remember also that personal checks you receive from ticket buyers and others usually have addresses on them. Don't cash these without first scanning them or making photocopies, so that you can enter the information into your records.

Recruit a Core Group of Volunteers

As you recruit volunteers (using the principles laid out in Chapter 2), keep an eye out for any with a willingness to or affinity toward making direct asks for donations. It's usually the person who readily makes friends, listens well, puts others at ease, and can express desires or thoughts that others might struggle with in a calm, often gently humorous manner.

> **TIP**
>
> **You're not looking for arm-twisters or speechmakers.** Rhona Frazin, President of the Chicago Public Library Foundation, explains: "You definitely want your fundraising solicitors to have a passion for your cause, but that doesn't mean they have to be loud about it. The most dramatic cases I've seen where reluctant fundraisers grew to love their role were among quiet, thoughtful, people, many in the religious community. As is common, they started out worried that their task was

to talk someone into making a gift. But it's virtually impossible to convince someone to give money against their will. And even if it were possible, it's no way to make a donor or a friend for life. It's the volunteers who can communicate their personal passion, and think of what they're doing not as asking for a gift, but as spreading the word, who wind up becoming the most effective."

Any volunteer willing to help ask for individual donations should be quickly recruited to this task, then carefully protected, lest other, less productive committee work draw him or her in.

Reaching out to individual donors is easy work to divide up, as it involves discrete tasks like sending personalized letters, making phone calls, meeting with others in person, and having house parties. (Try to have your volunteers communicate and follow up with a given list of donors, in order to achieve continuity in relationships.) If everyone ends up with a list of ten friends whom they'll ask to support a cause or project they all believe in, that can't be too bad, right? (Well, okay, half the people asked will probably refuse to make a donation. But knowing that, the "no" answers shouldn't sting so much.)

Open Up Lines of Communication

Shouldn't people already realize that the library wouldn't have that new carpet without money from the local Friends' group, the school wouldn't have a music instructor without funds raised by the PTA, or that your group has been working its tail off to achieve and continue providing great benefits to them and others? No, not unless you tell them. In fact, says Melissa Irish, "I've seen this issue come up a lot, even in school settings. The PTA tends to assume that 'everyone knows' how underfunded the school is, and how important their contributions are. But when you're talking, for example, to parents who are living on a shoestring, it takes more than generalities for them to understand why they're being asked to contribute a substantial sum, in the hundreds of dollars."

Communication is the key, and preferably two-way. How does a small nonprofit begin this process? First, figure out how great the information gap is. You could informally poll people within your group's membership, asking questions like, "Would you tell me your impressions of what this group actually does? Did you know about 'X' project? Would it interest you to hear more about it? How would you like to find out more—perhaps in a regular email update or via a social networking page?" Then create broader initiatives based on what you've learned. Melissa Irish adds, "For the PTA, we've found that it often helps to show parents actual budget numbers of what the government is and isn't paying for, and to vividly describe what their children's experience would be like without the programs the PTA or school foundation is supporting."

Starting a Facebook page is an obvious early step. (Or use whatever social networking site may have overtaken Facebook in popularity by the time you're reading this!) There's been a lot of buzz over Facebook in the fundraising world, with experts trying to figure out how to turn it into a direct fundraising tool. So far, the consensus is that it's not going to result in donations from every viewer who takes a look, and rarely results in big donations, but that it can perform a crucial role in developing the ties and conversations alluded to above.

The basic idea with Facebook is that you create a page for your organization (easy, at www.facebook.com), then post regular—even daily—status updates, just a few lines long. Anyone on Facebook who signs up as your group's "friend" will see these updates as part of a regular news scroll when they log in. This being "social" media, the tone should be casual—no one wants to hear that your group has, "successfully implemented its strategic plan for corporate outreach and met its 20xx sponsorship goals." But if you're "excited that Main Street Wines will be donating a rare bottle of champagne to our silent auction," that might get readers' attention and follow-up comments.

Better yet is to create some dialogue, by asking questions like, "What's the best thing you ever bought—or wish you had—at a silent auction?" Before long, you may have some regular readers—and their sense of attachment may increase their likelihood of donating or volunteering.

If someone in your group is tech savvy, set up a website for your group. Include information on what your group does and how to get in touch. Work toward making this a place where people can register for events, donate or pay for things online, enjoy photos of group activities, view copies of newsletters, and otherwise connect.

Ensuring That Readers Appreciate, Not Resent, Your Emails

Here are a few guidelines to remember when sending email:

- **Confine your mailings to people who have expressed an interest in receiving email communications.** And give them a chance, in every message, to opt out.

- **Make your subject line brief and catchy, yet specific and clear.** Even existing members have to be convinced to open the message.

- **Don't get caught in a spam filter.** First, beware the "content filters," which are set to prescreen the spammers' latest favorite words or tricks. Though these are ever changing, surefire trouble words are any that sound remotely sexual, strings of capital letters or punctuation marks, and mentions of debt, baldness, or popular health remedies, and even the words "free," "limited time," or "opportunity." Second, try to avoid "volume filters," which interpret all messages sent to large numbers of people as spam. You can get around these by breaking up your list and sending limited numbers of emails per hour or per day (though unfortunately, no one knows the exact limit).

- **If a particular message is likely to resonate with a wide audience, encourage recipients to forward it to friends.** But be sure to date the message, and to tell people about any deadlines for action. You don't want your email to bounce around the Web for years.

- **Include enough information that someone who's never heard of your group will see who you are and understand what you do.** Your email may be forwarded beyond your immediate supporters.

- **Keep messages short and readable.** A few paragraphs, with lots of bullet points, is plenty. If you have the capacity to put the message in html format, great. If not, use a large font, put spaces between paragraphs, and review the text from the viewpoint of someone who will open it and give it a few seconds' quick scanning.

Also look for volunteers to take photos or videos to add color to your Facebook page or website. At the Louisville Free Public Library, for example, the Library Foundation created a video for online viewing. Craig Buthod, Library Director, explains, "It describes the many ways in which our library system serves the community—providing books, Internet access, job-search help, community meetings and seminars, and even financial support to people studying for the GED—and how, with the help of donor funds, we're pursuing a master plan for improvements in services and public access."

Regular newsletters or news updates (via print or email) are also good ways to keep your members and potential donors informed. Emails are particularly good for quick updates.

When and How to Use Email

Email can rarely be relied on for major fundraising, but it's good for keeping up regular communications, such as quick updates, alerts on issues requiring member action, or requests and reminders for volunteer help and upcoming special events.

This type of email doesn't directly ask for money. However, there's no harm in adding a "how you can help" link within the message, ideally taking readers to your website's donation page.

Proofread All Written Materials

Good writing and careful editing of emails, letters, and Web content is a fine way to emphasize your group's professionalism. Any writer will recommend against sending out communications right after having written them. Try to have a second set of eyes look over the work, particularly if it will be distributed publicly.

Creating Incentives for Giving

People don't give to charity solely because they know they'll get something in return, whether it's their name mentioned in public or a thank-you gift. But offering some sort of incentive can help push donors to act right away, instead of waiting until … well, until they forget, in many cases. For example, in order to drive membership, some parent-teacher groups promise a party to the homeroom that gets 100% of its parents to sign up by a certain date.

Offering Thank-You Gifts

Offering some benefit for giving, like a T-shirt or tote bag, is a common nonprofit strategy. But as Melissa Irish says, "I've never found these gifts to be important in driving donors to give. They can help brand your organization, but shouldn't be too valuable—donors will rightfully question why you're spending money on that." Also, be sure to give donors a chance to opt out of receiving the gift. Some want to know that every cent that they give will go to straight your group. Think about homemade alternatives to the standard thank-you gifts, such as drawings by children, or DVDs of a favorite speech or performance at your last special event.

Arranging Matching Gifts

Lining up matching gifts is another way to motivate donations. As explained by adviser Gail Drulis: "During our annual fundraising campaign at the Albany YMCA, we've had luck arranging for various local businesses to match donations made on a certain day—usually a day when large numbers of members come in to work out."

If you doubt the power of matching gifts, consider that the Seattle Library Foundation announced in 2010 that it had reached its goal of matching a $500,000 anonymous donation. According to reports, 4,438 people contributed, in amounts ranging from $35 delivered in coins to $50,000 from a longtime supporter.

Also look for instances where the donors' companies match gifts to charity. Adviser Cherie King, whom you'll meet in Chapter 10, says, "Lining up company matches has been a key part of our fundraising efforts at the Mary Lin Education Foundation (in Atlanta, Georgia). If one parent donates $500 and it turns into $1,000, that's a major boost. At the bottom of our campaign letter, we've added the question, 'Does your company match donations?' and we offer to help them with any necessary paperwork. We've also put on our website a list of local companies that match donations. This year, one of the folks who donated knew two other people at the school who worked at the same company. So he sent them an email basically saying, 'Hey, I just donated to the foundation, our company matched it dollar for dollar, and it was easy, here's what you need to do.' One of the two people he contacted then donated as well."

Creating Donor Recognition Opportunities

Though a few donors wish to remain anonymous, they tend to be in the minority. At the other end of the spectrum are a few donors for whom heightening their reputation as a philanthropist, impressing their peers, or being part of a "club" is a major motivation for giving—and even giving large amounts.

Should you make that acknowledgment public? That depends. At South Mountain Elementary School, Laura Reichgut explains, "We don't give public recognition, even for the larger gifts—it doesn't seem appropriate in a school district where some parents simply can't afford to make large gifts, and others are putting in long hours volunteering (as a way of contributing without the financial burden). Still, our donors have our eternal gratitude!" Religious groups also struggle with whether maintaining donor anonymity is the best way to emphasize equality and a dedication to spiritual values among its membership—or whether honoring giving helps create a good example for others to follow.

At most nonprofits, however, including many houses of worship, public recognition of donors is all but expected. Groups that issue an annual report, for example, commonly list the names of all donors of large amounts (such as $500-plus), and as many other donors as space will allow. Newsletters or event programs are also good places to thank donors by name, or perhaps focus on a particular gift and what it helped to fund.

Popular ways to recognize and name donors, depending on how much they gave or for what purpose, include bookplates (at the front of a library book) tiles on your wall (or a "naming scroll" in the sanctuary of a synagogue), a metal plaque (perhaps on a new piece of playground equipment), or squares on a quilt at your front entrance. The Task Force of the Davidson Library in North Carolina, for example, working to raise enough money to keep the branch open for another year, renovated a patio area with bricks upon which donors could have their choice of message engraved. (The cost was $100 for a 4' by 4' brick and $500 for an 8' by 8' brick.)

Drafting and Sending Appeal Letters

A gentle way to reach out to your mailing list of prospective donors is with an appeal letter, reminding them of what your group does, highlighting current goals and projects, and requesting donations. You can either prepare a standard letter in the name of your group, or divide up your mailing list and have volunteers send out personal letters based on a sample you provide.

How often should you send out appeal letters? Established organizations send a new one every two to three months. However, if you're part of a group where members interact frequently anyway, perhaps because they see each other in church, at parent-teacher events, or at your fundraising events, such frequent mailings might be seen as either intrusive or impersonal. Set a schedule that makes sense in terms of your cycle of activities and the degree to which you'll follow your letters up with personal contacts (as described below).

TIP

"Never miss the opportunity to do a calendar-year-end mailing." As Rhona Frazin explains, "Many people put all their requests from charitable organizations in a pile, and make decisions at the end of the year. You don't want to be left out."

Writing a Compelling Letter

With people's attention spans steadily declining—and because too many groups send out long, heavily underlined pitch letters—an appeal letter that's limited to one or two pages is the most likely to get read. Mike Maxwell, a nonprofit professional with 20-plus years of direct-mail experience, reiterates: "Today there's greater-than-ever competition for donor dollars. Many donors seem to appreciate you getting to the point in an honest and forthright fashion."

> 💡 **TIP**
>
> **This is a personal letter, not a college essay or academic paper.** Use personal pronouns, and ditch overly long words or flowery language. The letter should address the reader as "you," and be written in the honest voice of the "I" who will sign it—perhaps your board president, executive director, or fundraising chairperson. Better yet, according to adviser Melissa Irish, is if you can "create different letters for different segments of your donor population—for example, a special letter for alumni, so they feel you're really addressing their interests directly."

The most important elements to include in your letter are:

- **A personal story or hook.** For example, a student or library patron could describe looking forward to the new books that will result from your current fund drive.

- **A defined project or event.** This is your reason for writing. For example, a holiday gift drive, in which you collect and wrap gifts for low-income children, would both make for a good story and provide an understandable reason for sending a separate letter.

> 💡 **TIP**
>
> **Drop-dead dates are great motivators.** For example, former PTA president Cindy Shelby, from California, explains, "We'd always send out a letter in September requesting donations. But, to give parents a sense of urgency about replying soon, we'd often explain that we needed to raise a certain amount by a certain date in order to continue something—for example, an after-school chess program."

- **The financial challenge you're facing.** Be clear about the costs associated with the project, and how donations of specific amounts can make a difference.

- **A reminder of your group's overall mission and how your current appeal fits into it.** Tie your appeal to your group's purpose and goals.

- **A request for a donation (as well as for volunteer help, if appropriate).** Tell people what they can do to make this project or event happen. You may want to refer to the amount of the donor's most recent gift, and ask to increase it by a certain amount. Describe other ways to support your group's work.

- **A "P.S."** This isn't required, but it's a nice added touch—especially if you can get volunteers to come in and handwrite a personal P.S.

If, after fitting all this material in, you see that your first draft is longer than two pages, review it and eliminate any extra words. Put it aside for a day. When you come back, read it to see where your attention starts to wander, or ask a friend to do the same.

After having at least two people check your final draft for typos, boring bits, and other issues, print the letter on your group's letterhead. No need to have it professionally printed, unless you've got a connection with a printer and an unusually large mailing list.

Packaging Up the Appeal Letters

Along with the actual letter, you'll want to include both a reply card and an envelope in which to send the reply back.

The reply device. To make the giving easy, include a reply card (or preprinted sheet of paper) allowing donors to indicate how much they're giving and by what means (check, credit card, monthly installments, or whatever you're prepared to accept). You've seen a thousand of these reply devices—the format is fairly standard.

The biggest decision you'll make is simply what gift amounts to suggest (for example, "❏ $25, ❏ $50, ❏ $100, ❏ Other"). Starting out with an amount that's too low may encourage people to take advantage of that option. On the other hand, I know of an organization that suggested $1, simply as a way of building its membership. Choose suggested donation levels based on your sense of your potential supporters' giving capacities and your ability to credibly ask for high amounts.

If people will receive something in return for particular gift levels (a T-shirt or baseball cap, for example), your suggested donation amounts should bear some proportional relation to the value of the return gift. (See Chapter 1 for a discussion of when the value of the gift is great enough that the donor will have to subtract it from any claimed tax deduction.)

If you have a website, be sure to list its URL on the reply card and indicate whether supporters can donate online.

The reply envelope. The reply card should fit neatly into a reply envelope (which has to be small enough to fit into your cover envelope). Your address should, of course, be printed on the front of the envelope. No need to provide return postage: Most people are willing to add their own stamp.

Optional inserts. You can include optional items in your direct mail package, such as a Post-it note with an urgent or "late-breaking" message, a relevant news clipping, or a "freebie" such as return address stamps or a bumper sticker. All of these will, of course, add to your costs, and it's fine to leave them out—particularly the freebies, which are getting so common that people feel less and less obligated to donate anything in return.

Sending the Letters

Depending on the size of your mailing, you may want to assemble a group of volunteers to prepare the mailing—perhaps make it a party. The volunteers will likely need to fold the letters, combine them with the reply cards and envelopes, place them in the mailing envelope, and put on labels and stamps.

Carefully train everyone in the assembly process. Letters should be neatly folded and placed in the envelope so that the greeting is the first thing the reader sees upon opening it, with the other inserts behind.

In theory, your nonprofit can take advantage of the U.S. Post Office's bulk mail rates. However, doing so isn't a project for beginners. For starters, you'd need to send 200 or more identical pieces of standard mail (same size and weight, up to 15.999 ounces, with no handwritten personal notes inside). You'd also need to get a permit (using Post Office Form 3624, *Application to Mail at Nonprofit Standard Mail Rates*). The bulk mail regulations are so tricky that staff members at established nonprofits usually attend trainings just to find out how to meet the requirements, or they hire outside mail houses. All of this makes the cost of a first-class stamp start to look pretty good. First-class mail can also be forwarded if the addressee has moved; bulk mail doesn't offer this advantage.

RESOURCE

Want more detailed information on bulk mailing? See:

- The U.S. Postal Service's website at www.usps.com. Be careful, however—many of the links lead you to for-profit business bulk mail rules, which are different. Look for Publication 417, *Nonprofit Standard Mail Eligibility*, by clicking "All Products and Services," then "Publications" in the alphabetical menu.

- The website of the Alliance of Nonprofit Mailers, see www.nonprofitmailers.org.

Follow-Up to Appeal Letters

If you've sent an appeal letter without results, or to a person who's been a loyal and important donor to your group in the past, it makes sense to follow up with a phone call. This is a good time to mobilize your core volunteers.

TIP

Will a phone tree work for this? After years as a PTA president in California, Cindy Shelby says, "I've tried practically every system for making follow-up calls. Sometimes I made all the calls. Other times I'd have a group of up to 12 volunteers doing so. We've also tried dividing up calls within our PTA phone tree, five per parent, but this tended not to work so well—many parents would (perhaps conveniently) forget."

Before dividing up the list between your volunteers, someone familiar with the names should see whether it makes sense to assign certain callers to make contact with certain members. Check your list for anyone who has made significant donations in the past, perhaps in the neighborhood of $500 or more. Such donors deserve extra attention, as described under "Working With Donors Who Can Make Sizable Gifts," below.

If your membership can be divided into obvious groups, such as classrooms or alumni years, it may make sense to divide up the calls among teams, or team captains. Melissa Irish explains, "This strategy led to a dramatic jump in giving for a nonprofit I was advising—a civic leadership group that has been around for about 65 years, and has alumni from every year. We recruited class captains from most of the graduating classes and had them personalize the letter to their class. Then we created a challenge among the classes, so that whichever raised the most was invited to share a table at the group's annual luncheon. Some class captains hadn't given in years, but loved the idea of reconnecting. Within the first two weeks, we'd already raised double the usual amount."

Advise everyone making calls of the subject matter of the appeal, and train them using the tips offered in, "What to Say in a Brief Personal Ask," below.

To give supporters an additional reason to donate when called, volunteers should remind them of what an early gift will mean—an immediate and needed boost for the project, and for the caller, freedom from future mailings about this particular effort! If you have a premium you can offer the first several donors, all the better.

CAUTION

The bad news about today's phones. While serving as PTA copresident, Debbie Essex in Albany, California, found that, "Making phone calls to request donations seems to be getting less effective, because more and more people list their cell phone number as the primary way to reach them. Then they'll screen the call and not pick up. You'll have to either keep trying, or be ready to leave a compelling message."

What to Say in a Brief Personal Ask

A personal ask for a donation can be done in a few minutes (such as over the phone) or, when working with major donors (described below), built up to over time—sometimes as long as a year or more. In groups where members see each other regularly (such as at PTA meetings or days of worship), these asks can be particularly informal, as friends see friends in the hallway, and take the opportunity for a quick reminder of what goals they're working toward.

The Psychology of Asking

To get yourself into a frame of mind that will allow you to survive—and even enjoy—the asking process, remember these simple rules:

- **Be yourself.** No canned script can give you the words to describe what excites you about your group's work. Ultimately you'll want to put the script aside and speak from the heart.

- **Be direct.** There will come a time when you simply have to say, "A gift of $x would provide a crucially important launch for our efforts." Once the words are out, the air becomes clear, and the other person has the opportunity to respond with equal directness.

- **Focus on the cause.** You're not begging for money for yourself—you're asking the supporter to partner with your group to achieve a mutually desirable result. Show excitement, not desperation.

- **Be ready to adjust to the donor's interests.** You'll find that some donors are just plain opinionated about how their money should be spent. You may hear things like, "No, I won't give one penny to area public schools—the whole system is a mess." At times like these, you'll have to think on your feet, and look for common ground. Perhaps the donor is particularly interested in a certain program, and you can point out how parental support for it sends a message that more public funding is needed.

Of course, there are certain people who just won't make charitable gifts, even if it's in their own, or their children's, interest. That's not a reflection on how you asked.

Of course, even the most casual encounter should be thoughtfully carried out, using the message you developed when creating a "case statement" in Chapter 3. For example, a phone volunteer's opening pitch might (after a few polite preliminaries) go something like this: "Hi, my name is Vera, and I'm a volunteer with Local Wildlife Rescue. Is this Nigel? That's great, I understand you've been a long-time volunteer with this group. Do you have a minute to hear about an exciting opportunity? I know you'll be as interested as I was to hear that we've been offered the chance to buy a plot of land where some of our animals can roam freely, at a cost of $50,000. I've already donated $500 to the project, a corporate sponsor has put in $10,000, and I'm hoping you can pledge $100 toward this goal. Can we count on your participation?"

After that, the volunteer should wait for an answer, offer to answer any questions, thank the donor, take down any credit card information if the person will be donating on the spot (or, if a credit card is not an option for your group or the donor, explain that a pledge confirmation form will be in the mail shortly), and sign off.

> **TIP**
>
> **Have you made your own contribution yet?** It's more powerful when you can assure a prospective donor that you've made the same commitment that you're asking for.

Phonathons

If you've got more people to contact for support than can be readily handled by dividing your list up among your volunteers, a phonathon (also called a phone bank) can help get the calls done. The basic idea is to arrange a location with a lot of phone lines, such as a real estate or law office (or just ask people to show up with their own cell phones); set a starting and ending time (with about three hours of total calling time), set a challenging but realistic financial goal, and create an atmosphere that's both organized and party-like.

Adviser Melissa Irish notes, "It takes a lot of time and energy to do a phonathon right. You might give each of your callers 30 names, with the expectation that they'll reach only two or three people. That's because one third of the numbers will likely be out of date, and many people will be away from home or unwilling to talk. So you really do need a long list!"

You also need a membership that feels close enough to your callers that they won't feel irritation at what they perceive as unwelcome calls. For example, Craig Buthod, Director of the Louisville Free Public Library in Kentucky, says, "We've given up on doing phone solicitations. For us, it wasn't effective. In fact, we got the sense that we were making the people we called mad, and thus giving up our good name."

But if your list is a long one, and your membership tight-knit, you may be able to make some major progress in a short time. As a PTA copresident, Debbie Essex, in Albany, California, found, despite all the barriers to reaching people, "Our spring phonathon was a major fundraiser. We'd ask people to sign up their credit cards for automatic withdrawals, explaining that $30 a month is no more than the price of a coffee every day."

A phonathon can be done either as an independent effort or as a follow-up to an appeal letter. Or, in a hybrid strategy, you can send appeal letters to everyone on your prospect list a few weeks before the phonathon, telling them the time and date that you plan to call, and promising to take their names off the evening's list if they send a contribution right away.

TIP

The best times to call: Phonathons tend to reach the most people when they're held on a Tuesday, Wednesday, or Thursday, between the evening hours of 6:30 and 9:30.

Preparing for the Phonathon

Start by recruiting enough volunteers to make 30 to 50 calls apiece, helpers (to collect pledge sheets and tally subtotals), a cleanup crew, plus some to write thank-you letters. Yes, you could leave the thank-yous until later, but bringing in more bodies during the phonathon enhances the festive atmosphere, not to mention that some people who were shy about calling might show up for letter-writing but get enthused as they watch others make the calls.

Get donations of food, drink, and prizes (discussed below). Assemble supplies, including pens, stamps, paper or cards for thank-you letters, and envelopes. Create written materials for use by individual callers. These should include:

- Call sheets; one for each prospect. There's a space on our sample call sheet to record the prospect's name and giving history, as well as the outcome of each call and the name of the volunteer caller. Fill this information in ahead of time, using your donor list and your computer. (If you end up having to contact the prospect multiple times, successive volunteer callers can record their outcomes.)

- Information sheets with sample scripts and key facts, such as what various donation amounts will achieve and news of any matching gift or thank-you gift opportunities.

- Confirmation sheets to send donors who pledge support but don't make an immediate credit card donation. Fill in the information about your organization and the purpose of the fund drive, then print lots of copies and give them to your callers. They will enter information about the donors as they talk. See the sample, below.

- Summary sheets with which to gather statistics from the evening based on the call sheets.

You'll see a sample Call Sheet, Pledge Confirmation, and Phonathon Summary Sheet below (blank forms are on the CD-ROM in this book).

Sample Phonathon Call Sheet

Happy Tunes Music Camp

Phonathon Call Sheet

Happy Tunes Spring Phonathon; May 2 – 3, 2011

Prospect's name: _LaBelle Flores_

Company: _InterWebbing, Inc._

Home Phone: _206-555-1111_

Cell Phone: _206-555-1235_

Home Address: _383 N.E. 42nd, Seattle, WA 98105_

Email: _LaF@geemail.com_

Recent Donor History:

1. Amount: _$ 20_   Date: _March 4, 2008_   Event: _Appeal Letter_

2. Amount: _$ 85_   Date: _September 22, 2009_   Event: _Auction ticket plus bid total_

3. Amount: _$ 35_   Date: _March 8, 2010_   Event: _Appeal Letter_

4. Amount: _$ 120_   Date: _September 24, 2010_   Event: _Auction ticket plus bid total_

Other facts to know about the donor:

Single mother of two kids, Eric and Hans, who have attended Camp Happy Tunes since 2006.

Works in executive-level position. Donated handmade candles to 2010 auction.

Call Notes

Date: _May 2, 2011_

Phone volunteer's name: _Carl Endevor_

❏ Yes   ❏ No   ❏ Maybe   ❏ No answer   ☒ Left message

Notes, amount: _____

Date: _May 2, 2011_

Phone volunteer's name: _Sondra Kales_

❑ Yes   ❑ No   ☒ Maybe   ❑ No answer   ❑ Left message

Notes, amount: _Too busy to talk. Willing to have us call back._

Date: _May 3, 2011_

Phone volunteer's name: _Marita Carson_

☒ Yes   ❑ No   ❑ Maybe   ❑ No answer   ❑ Left message

Notes, amount: _Pledged $30, but said she couldn't do more because her company isn't doing well, and layoffs are possible._

Sample Pledge Confirmation

Happy Tunes Music Camp

May 3, 2011

Dear _LaBelle Flores_ ,

Thank you for your pledge of _$ 30_ to support _Restoration of the dining hall_
at Happy Tunes Music Camp

To fulfill your pledge, please provide us with the following information:

Address: _____

Phone number: _____

Cell phone number: _____

Email address: _____

Payment method:

❏ Check (made payable to _Happy Tunes Music Camp_)

❏ Credit card

Card number: _____ Expiration date: __/__/_____

Security code (3-digit number on the back of the card): _____

Signature: _____

Today's date: _____

Send this form along with your payment to:

Happy Tunes Music Camp
554 Post Road, Walla Walla, WA 98765

Thank you very much for your support!

Marita Carson

Marita Carson, Happy Tunes volunteer

Sample Phonathon Summary Sheet

Happy Tunes Music Camp

Dining hall restoration

May 2-3, 2011

Phonathon Summary Sheet

Today's date: *May 3, 2011*

Volunteer caller's name	No. of calls attempted	No. of calls completed	No. of "yes" responses	No. of "maybe" responses	No. of "no" responses	Total amount raised
Marcie Davis	1	1	1			$50
Walter Harmon	2	1			1	$
Lia Samuels	2	0				$
Eric Garcia	1	1	1			$25
Sylvia Yee	2	1			1	$
						$
						$
TOTALS						$75

Holding the Phonathon

Making calls for money is inevitably a bit uncomfortable. That's why it helps to make the event fun, for example by:

- **Providing lots of support.** Start out with a brief training and encouragement session, covering the topics mentioned below. Give participants sample scripts; and have leaders on hand during the calling to congratulate, commiserate, and answer questions.

- **Creating thank-you gifts for volunteers.** Energy bars or nice pens will convey appreciation. (By now, you know the drill—try to get things donated!)

- **Fostering competition.** For example, you might award prizes not just at the end of the phonathon, but throughout, to whomever calls the most people within the first half hour, gains the highest pledge within a particular time period, or, at the end of the evening, has raised the most and gotten the most yes answers overall.

- **Cheering participants on.** Organizers should continually tally up statistics and call out information such as how close you are to your goal, the average pledge amount, and any interesting stories of caller interactions.

In the training session, explain to your callers that it's important to tell those at the other end of the phone that the callers are volunteers, not paid professionals. Emphasize that the calls should be friendly but short, and that volunteers shouldn't allow themselves to be drawn into debates or arguments. Callers should hang up after six rings, cross off wrong or disconnected numbers, and make no mark on the call sheet if they get a busy signal. They should speak only to the person whose name appears on the list. If some people sound particularly enthusiastic, it's worth asking not only for a donation, but whether they'd be interested in volunteering.

In response to successful pledges, send a handwritten thank-you letter—specifically stating the amount of the pledge—and, for donors who didn't already pay by credit card, a copy of the pledge sheet (the original version; keep a copy for your records) and an envelope with your address.

Do a final debriefing, where your leaders thank participants, share final statistics, award final prizes, and give volunteers a chance to share impressions and stories.

Don't forget to check back, two weeks later, on pledge fulfillment. Someone will need to make reminder calls to those who haven't yet sent in their pledge forms and payment.

Working With Donors Who Can Make Sizable Gifts

If you were in a large, established nonprofit, you'd have a staff person to track your donors' giving patterns, identify the ones who've made the largest gifts—or probably could do so, if asked properly—build ongoing relationships with them that will hopefully lead to ever larger gifts, and even make requests of potential major donors who aren't existing members of the organization.

On the assumption that your group isn't quite ready for that type of effort, we're going to give a somewhat abbreviated overview of how to create a program for cultivating major donors. However, that doesn't mean you should ignore your highest givers. By knowing who they are, and taking appropriate steps to acknowledge and establish meaningful communication with them, you'll go a long way toward continued fundraising success. In the short term, you may bring in some good-sized checks.

If you're with a school, library, or other group that relies on public funding in addition to individual donations, lining up major donors can also be critical to leveraging needed public support. Jose Aponte, Director of the San Diego County Library system, explains, "I always recommend leveraging your donations, or even pledges of donations. Let's say you're in a community of 20,000 people and hope to build a new library at a cost of $1 million. Very few major donors want to be first in line to fund such a project, and the politicians won't fund the whole thing until they find out, 'What's your skin in the game?' So if you can do as we've done, and say, 'We've got a rancher ready to contribute $750,000 after he sees the first shovelful turned,' you've got a shot at pulling together the entire sum."

What's Different About Working With Major Donors?

It's the rare donor who will write a truly impressive-sized check—in the range of $1,000 or more—in response to a mere letter. More typically, you'll need to make one-on-one contact for this level of response. No matter how wealthy a person is, it's natural to want to be fully informed (beyond what's written on a sheet of paper) and have a chance to talk or think over a decision, before parting with money that could have made an important difference elsewhere.

As a first step toward organizing and making these contacts, nonprofit consultant Sue Hall recommends, "Create a cultivation committee, onto which you invite people who have the connections to gain access to other high-powered people, and the confidence to take people to breakfast or lunch and ask them for something akin to a major gift. Don't launch right into asking people for money, however. Long-term cultivation is the key, where you find ways to develop relationships with your major donors, and bring them into your group's inner circle."

Is all this talk of big money and influence starting to make you squirm? Let's take a step back and remember what's really going on here. This isn't a shady finance deal, or a shameful situation where you need a bailout. A common misconception among new fundraising volunteers is that they're asking favors of people who'd really rather spend their money on personal pleasure, or will be horrified at the request. Experienced fundraisers, however, realize that sharing personal convictions and interests with other, like-minded people who can afford to help a cause can be a joy, not a source of mutual embarrassment. As a fundraising volunteer, you're a conduit to making change, and are serving a cause that's in everyone's interest. People who make gifts to charity tend to feel good afterwards, not bad—and the major donors can feel especially good, as you tell them about the great results that they personally had a measurable role in attaining.

This doesn't mean you'll get anywhere by asking random donors on your list for a big check, however. The best prospective supporters are, according to Melissa Irish, "People with a strong link to your group (which can include a personal connection to one of its leaders), the financial ability to give, an interest in your program areas, and philanthropic experience (meaning an understanding of the 'joy of giving'). The higher the prospect rates on all four, the better. If charity is new to someone, no matter how wealthy, the person's gifts will be tempered until he or she experiences how wonderful it is to make a difference."

CAUTION

"Get ready to make this a concentrated effort," adds Sue Hall. "Cultivating major donors should be seen as something that you'll incorporate into your fundraising plan for a long time. It won't work if it's just a one-off deal, where you try it briefly and forget it if it doesn't pan out."

What if you're just not ready for this type of a long-term effort? At many school PTAs, for example, where the membership changes year by year, major donor cultivation is more than the parent volunteers want to take on. In that case, at least try, within your existing fundraising activities, to track prospective major donors for special handling. For example, parent volunteer Debbie Essex describes, "At our SchoolCare foundation's annual phone-a-thon, we pull the names of prospective major donors off our list and make sure they're contacted by volunteers who can handle the call with diplomacy and experience." You may not get the same-sized checks as are possible with greater cultivation and personal interactions, but you'll get some larger-than-average ones.

Identifying and Getting to Know Your Group's Best Friends

If you're lucky, your membership list (as described above) includes notes on past gifts, allowing you to figure out who the most generous and most frequent donors are. Or perhaps this is already general knowledge within your group. If you don't have this information, or don't know anything about the people named on your current membership list, start with a little research.

TIP

Don't limit your expectations to people who've already made large gifts. Very few contributors start out as major donors—instead, they work their way up from smaller gifts. Signs that someone is ready to make a bigger commitment include repeated gifts of a good size, and progressively larger gifts. Another clue is that the person is making large gifts to other organizations. You can find this out by keeping an eye on other organizations' event programs, annual reports, and other publications.

Ask around within your group to find out who has had personal contact with any major donors, and to tell you what they know. Also check your lists of people who participated significantly in special events or projects—for example, to find out who bought an entire table's worth of tickets to a dinner, or was the highest bidder at your auction. Then put together a list of the hottest prospects.

Ideally, you want to learn much more about your major donors than their giving history. Learning about common interests and shared history between the prospective donor and members of your board or volunteer crew will in turn help build personal ties. This should determine exactly who in your organization should meet the donor to ask for continued support, because they'll enjoy each others' company and will be on the same page as they share ideas on how to help your group. Or, as Rhona Frazin more succinctly puts it, "People give to people, not to organizations." In addition, doing some background research will help you decide what size and type of gift to request.

We're not recommending that you do as some overzealous fundraisers reportedly have, and look up donors' homes on GoogleMaps in order to determine the make of their car or the size of their swimming pool (and thus adjudge their financial worth). However, Rhona Frazin advises, "As in anything, you've got to do your homework. If, for example, you're talking about a library, figure out: Does this person use the library, have they talked about formative experiences they may have had there as child or young parent? You can become uncomfortable if you don't know much about the person whom you're asking for the gift."

Identifying Possible Major Donors Outside Your Group

Finding potential major donors who aren't current supporters of your organization will require a little more research, and is an advanced fundraising topic that we won't cover here.

Deepening Your Friendships With Major Donors

Once you've identified the best prospects, take steps to confirm or cement their connection with your organization. For example, some organizations sponsor appreciation events, such as a complimentary "major donors only" dinner preceding a publicly open fundraising lecture or performance. At the Friends of the St. Paul Public Library, Sue Hall says, "We annually invite donors who've given major gifts in the past, or whom we believe have the capacity to do so in the future, to a donor society luncheon. We treat them to a nice meal and a program with an author, who signs a book for them. At that event, we don't ask them for anything. But it's a way to build connections, and even to get them thinking about how they might want to help the library."

You could also take donors to a reception with your actors, artists, researchers or others, or do something else that resonates with your group's mission or shows off its work. Gretchen Lightfoot, of Harmony Project, says, "Our Hip Hop Orchestra, led by Diane Louie, has become a real showpiece when we bring in major donor prospects. Visitors see from the beginning that the kids are getting great hands-on experience, and that Diane is an amazing role model, giving not just musical advice but life advice, like, 'Okay, I'm your employer now, and that means I don't care if you stayed up late last night, you're here to work with me.' She engages the adults as well as the kids, and we've gotten several major gifts from these donor site visits."

Assessing Major Donors' Financial Capacity

Before approaching a prospective major donor, you'll want to know how much the person is capable of giving—and use that information to decide how much and what to request. Open-ended requests make donors uncomfortable, and lead to lowball offers.

Your biggest clue to how much your existing donors can give is how much they've given in past years, so check your records. Also, notice whether the donor has typically made gifts of something other than cash, such as property or stock.

Consider the larger social context for the gift. If the donor has friends in your organization, how much do they give? Some donors, after discovering that they gave less than their friends or community peers, have been known to express annoyance that they weren't asked for a higher sum.

Try to choose an amount that challenges the person to give substantially more than past gifts, but isn't off their personal scale. For example, if a donor has given $1,000 for the last couple of years, you might ask for $1,500 or $2,000 more for a special project, perhaps divided into monthly payments.

One-on-One Meetings With Major Donors

The instructions in "What to Say in a Brief Personal Ask," above, apply here in principle. However, when working with major donors, you'll want to allow more time for the conversation, and not rush to the finish line.

Stopping your prospect in the hallway isn't usually the best strategy for a major donor ask. It undercuts the seriousness of your conversation, and wouldn't allow you to prepare the informational materials your donor might wish to see before making a decision. Better to schedule a formal meeting. (You might also send a letter in advance of your phone call.) Tell the person that you'd like to discuss the work of your group and how he or she might support it.

> **CAUTION**
>
> **Is the person part of a couple?** If you arrange to meet with someone who doesn't make decisions without his or her other half, then you won't get a decision on the day you meet—and may have to either schedule a second meeting or risk having the partner veto the gift without hearing your pitch.

Many (if not most) people you call will probably decline this meeting. But a surprising number will say yes. Be ready to suggest a location, such as the donor's home or office, your organization's office, or a restaurant (nothing too fancy). If the person doesn't want to meet one-on-one but is willing to talk more by phone, fine. In either case, plan on a minimum one-half-hour's meeting, and quickly send out a confirmation letter.

Who should represent your group at the meeting? A team of two people tends to work best. If the prospective donor has a friend in your organization, include that person, along with a group leader or another volunteer who can bring complementary knowledge or communication skills. Talk about your roles ahead of time—in particular, who's going to make the actual request for money.

You may want to assemble relevant written materials, such as your organization's brochure, budget, press clippings, annual report, a case statement outlining your request, and a list of how gifts of particular amounts will meet specified needs—for example, "It will cost $1,200,000 to build a study annex onto our school's library. To start our campaign, we're seeking 20 founders' gifts of $25,000." Written materials discussing recognition opportunities for particular major gift levels can be helpful, too. Assemble a packet that you can leave with the donor after the meeting is over.

> **TIP**
>
> **Bring your calculator.** Unless you're a math genius, you might need it when a donor says something like, "I want to give scholarships to ten children with cancer to attend your camp each year for the next ten years. How much will that be if I make a firm pledge now but write you a check on the first day of each year, allowing for 3% annual inflation?"

Now, all you have to do is meet! Some people wonder at first how they'll have enough to say to fill a whole meeting's worth of conversation. Remember, you've got two fascinating subjects to keep you busy: the prospective donor (practically everyone likes to talk about his or her background, interests, opinions, and current activities) and your organization.

Here's the usual play-by-play: You and your teammate meet a few minutes in advance to share any last-minute information and, if necessary, discuss what you'll talk about as an icebreaker. Once you're with the donor, start with any needed introductions. Remind the person that you're there to talk about a specific need or new program, the critical importance of financial support, and how long you expect to spend in this meeting.

The best fundraisers say that they like to spend the majority—say, around 75%—of any meeting just listening. This isn't idle or phony listening. Rhona Frazin, of the Chicago Public Library Foundation, emphasizes, "Good listening skills are essential—better than good talking skills." You'll not only be learning more about the donor's interests and passions, but also refining your understanding of how and why he or she might give.

At some point, bring the discussion back to the purpose of the meeting. Lay out what your organization is up to and why its work, or a particular project or program, is worth investing in. Be careful not to get too buried in your written materials. Always remember the things that get you personally excited about the organization. Draw on these and the inspiring conversations you've had with other staff and volunteers to build the supporter's interest.

Before long, it will make sense to start talking dollars. Candidly explain to the prospect exactly how much things will cost and how you arrived at that figure. Mention any in-kind donations that you've received, to show that you're trying to keep costs down, as well as any significant other donations that have come in.

Finally, once the preliminaries are over, and you've built—or reinvigorated—the potential donor's interest in your case, look him or her in the eye and say something like, "We'd like you to consider a gift of $10,000, to bring us within a realistic distance of our goal." Or if you're asking for a slightly raised renewal of a past donation, you might simply say, "Can I put you down for a renewal at the $2,500 level?" or something similarly optimistic.

Sit quietly and let the person have a chance to think. Try to look hopeful, while you resist the human urge to chatter or even apologize for a bold request.

If the person agrees, say thank you and be enthusiastic, but keep your wits about you. You'll need to discuss when and how the payment will be made, and discuss whether the donor is interested in any return gifts or recognition opportunities (as discussed above, under "Creating Donor Recognition Opportunities").

If the donor seems uncertain about whether to give, try to get to the heart of the ambivalence. Would he or she like more information, or time to consult with a family member? Is there a smaller gift amount the donor would be comfortable with? Make sure you ultimately get a yes or no answer. As one experienced fundraiser says, "I like to get to the point of hearing an actual 'yes' or 'no'—in fact, I'll follow up on a vague answer with a question like, 'Does that mean you can't make a donation at this time?' This makes it easier for the other person to respond directly, and allows us all to move on."

If the donor says no, say thank you for his or her time, and focus both your attentions on the positive—you perhaps had an enjoyable lunch or meeting, the other person learned more about your work, and you probably learned something about what ignites or dampens donors' interests. In the unlikely event that your meeting experience was truly horrible, at least it will make a great story at your next gathering of fellow volunteers.

As soon as you get back to your office, draft a thank-you letter—whether the answer was yes, no, or maybe. Promptly enter the pledge and other information into your records, and follow through on any other promises.

What to Do With Money You Receive

See Chapter 1 for details on money handling. Your most important follow-up tasks will include:

- photocopying and depositing all checks
- entering the donor information and gift amounts in your database, and
- sending thank-you letters that also serve as tax receipts.

Each of these should be done within 24 hours to two days of receiving the replies (the sooner the better). Some people don't balance their checkbooks, and will keep drawing out money until it's gone, unless you get there first.

> **TIP**
>
> **Thank-you letters can cement personal connections between your group and its donors.** For example, Rhona Frazin says, "Toward the conclusion of the summer reading program at the 76 branches of the Chicago Public Library—which is supported in good part by donor funds—the librarians ask the participating children to draw a picture or write a note about their favorite part of the program. The notes are wonderful, with messages like, 'I read Harry Potter and it was hard and took me a long time, but I was proud of it.' We send these out as thanks to the donors (with a cover letter, mentioning things like how many kids read how many books). I've had donors call me to say, 'I was having a crummy day until I opened this.'"

Event-Planning Strategies

Meet Your Adviser

Grace Boone, Events and Communications Manager at Girls Incorporated of Alameda County, a nonprofit in the East Bay region of California dedicated to inspiring all girls to be strong, smart, and bold. Girls Inc. provides academic enrichment and counseling services, including special outreach to young women in underserved communities.

What she does:
"I manage fundraising and donor-relations events. For example, I coordinate 'Women of Taste,' the East Bay's largest food- and wine-tasting event, which brings 1,200 guests to a terraced rooftop garden, and features 30 chefs, 30 beverage providers, a live band, and two auctions. I also work to inspire people to participate in the Girls Inc. community, for example by creating dialogue on Twitter and Facebook. The day-to-day work can involve a lot of details like calling vendors to make sure tables will be delivered on time, but that becomes secondary in my mind to focusing on the girls being helped and the people who will attend our events."

· ·

Earliest memory of taking part in a charitable activity:
A math-a-thon in kindergarten. I think it was to benefit St. Jude's Children's Hospital, and my parents paid a nickel for any questions I got right. But it wasn't until college that I realized that fundraising could be something that you do as a career, and not until I started working at Girls Inc., as a break from a high-pressure sales job, that I realized that it was, in fact, what I wanted to do with my life!"

· ·

Likes best about her work:
"I get to do something different every day. That sounds like something you'd say in a job interview, but it's true. And I get to work with our girls—for example, during our spring luncheon and at donor relations events—and they're the coolest people in the world."

· ·

Top tip for people new to nonprofit fundraising:
"You can never ask too many questions, and there are no dumb questions. Also, keep the mission in mind. It's easy to get bogged down and think, 'Am I really planning another party already?' But then I remember, I'm doing it for our girls."

f your group hasn't already put on at least one special event in the past, we're guessing that it will do so in the not-too-distant future. Sometimes it's just fun to get together with your members and supporters and have a party. Besides, as you'll see in subsequent chapters of this book, all manner of events are well-suited for fundraising by a small or volunteer-led group. You and many of your volunteers may already have more experience with event planning than you realize, perhaps dating back to a high school dance committee or a wedding.

Common types of nonprofit special events include dinners, auctions, fairs and festivals, lectures, benefit concerts, home and garden tours, tournaments, contests, sporting events, and walkathons. (You might also count things like garage sales, car washes, and bake sales, though we've chosen to cover them in a separate chapter on sales of goods and services.)

Unfortunately, you can have a great party but not manage to raise any money. Charity Navigator, a watchdog group, has found that special events are among the least efficient ways to raise money, bringing in an average of $1 for every $1.33 spent, and generating only 14% of the average nonprofit's total contributions from individual donors (as opposed to foundations or corporations). The exceptions are often large groups with well-connected boards and a compelling cause.

But before throwing up your hands in despair, realize that even events that don't bring in actual profits can be valuable, particularly if they bring visibility to your organization, mobilize and expand its donor base, or highlight a particular issue of importance to your members and/or clients. There are times when you might want to deliberately plan such an event.

Still, you picked up this book because you want to raise money, and that's what this chapter will try to help you do. In some cases, the reason that events fail to raise money is that the group hadn't done its homework. To make sure that isn't true of your group, this chapter will explain how to:

- choose an event that suits your organization
- go beyond ticket sales in finding ways to generate income from the event
- plan the event with respect for the natural environment
- create a realistic budget

- create a schedule of activities before and during the event
- get corporate sponsorships
- protect your organization from legal and financial liability
- make sure the event itself goes smoothly, and
- follow up after the event, to help get ready for next year.

TIP

Get attendees' names. No matter what type of special event you choose, you'll have an opportunity to put your organization's name and work in front of new eyes—which means you'll want to be organized about getting people's names and addresses (including email) for your mailing list. If you won't know in advance who will be attending—and you probably won't, because people bring friends—create a sign-in sheet. Then, to make sure people don't breeze right past it, try offering a door prize for people who provide their business card or contact information.

Choose the Right Event for Your Organization

The first step in deciding what type of event to hold is the same as the first step in planning your annual fundraising strategy—to examine your organization's assets. Chapter 3 describes the basics of how this is done. In this chapter, we'll give it some closer consideration in the context of special events.

If, for example, you've got a large physical facility, think about events that might attract a crowd. If you've got an unusually large volunteer corps, consider events that require large numbers of people to prepare or run, such as an auction, fair, festival, or home tour. If you've got access to celebrities or experts, consider lectures, benefit concerts, or major donor parties. If you've got Web-savvy people, ask them to help out with an online auction or other virtual event. Then, before finalizing a decision, consider the questions below.

> **TIP**
>
> **Fun is always good!** As Vivian Shnaidman, a member of the Jewish Center in Princeton, New Jersey, says, "I start feeling a little tapped out by how much I donate—but I don't mind giving a little more for something fun. A few years ago, for example, the Center brought in Henry Winkler as a speaker. He's a smart, thoughtful guy, who talked about his career as an actor, and made it funny. My husband still quotes things he said."

Will the Event Appeal to Paying Members of Your Audience?

Being able to contact or attract a pool of possible attendees who can pay the costs of admission or participation is your first priority. That means that having a broad membership base, including people who can afford, say, the ticket prices or to bid on auction items, is an important start. If you need to set entry prices low, however, it's not a deal killer—admission prices rarely cover the costs of dinner and similar events, and you'll be planning to make up and exceed the difference with corporate sponsorships and other forms of support.

Then there's the matter of members' tastes. A square-dancing festival may not attract people wanting to support your chess club, nor will a lecture on world affairs attract support of your hockey team. (We could be wrong, of course; it depends on knowing your members.)

Remember also that your event may be an opportunity to pick up new support, or at least increase the engagement of existing members. That means that you'll want to design events for people who fit your donor profile. A library patron who never thought about supporting the library before might not be able to resist buying a ticket to lunch with her favorite mystery author; at which time she'll hopefully hear more about how and why to increase her involvement.

Does Your Group Have the Person-Power to Pull Off This Event?

It's hard to exaggerate how much time and energy a good-sized special event can take to organize. Many experts suggest multiplying your initial time estimates by three. In any case, don't plan an event that's significantly larger or more complex than anyone in your group has handled before.

It will be particularly helpful if you've got volunteer leaders with events-planning experience, whether from past volunteering, or because their professional work involves project management, catering, or hospitality.

Try starting with scaled-down versions of a larger event—a house party at a volunteer's place rather than a dinner for 600 at a rented hall, for example. That will help you figure out things like who can be counted on to lead committees, who makes a good pitch for donations during the event, which food and drink items are most popular among your audience, and what to expect that you might not have otherwise expected! Once you've gotten the feel for staging an event, putting on a large one really isn't that much harder than a small one.

Choose an Attractive and Affordable Venue

Finding a location that's pleasant to spend time in, convenient to your guests, offers the services and amenities you need, and fits within your budget is key to the success of any event. Better yet is a location that offers environmentally friendly features, as discussed below under "Choose a Green Location."

If your group doesn't already own or have access to a facility, don't immediately rush to a downtown luxury hotel. Look first at facilities owned by the city or other nonprofits, where you might hold your event for free or at low rates. Talk to their managers, and if the space seems promising, visit in person. If a hotel ends up as your best option, try to bring down the costs by asking it to separately donate items for the menu, such as wine or chocolates.

When visiting a potential location, bring a checklist of your needs or interests, and ask questions such as:

- How many people comfortably fit in the space?
- Where can guests park cars, and what are the public transport options?
- Can we cook on-site or will we have to bring food in?
- Can we bring in our own (ideally, donated) alcohol—in fact, can alcohol

be served here at all, or do we need to get a special liquor license or pay a corkage fee?

- Is there space for other activities that we hope to include, such as a silent auction, art display, entertainment, or child care?

- What other equipment (table, chairs, stoves) are available for use, and is there an added cost for these?

- Do you have a high-quality sound system, that's suited for use with (a band, an auction, or your intended use)?

- Are we covered at all by your insurance, and do you require us to take out separate liability insurance for the event?

With any luck, you'll find a location that you can return to year after year. Adviser Peter Pearson (whom you'll meet in Chapter 8) says, "Sticking with one venue has helped us at the St. Paul Friends of the Library save money on our Opus & Olives event—the hotel blocks us into its calendar far ahead of time, at special low rates."

Now let's say you've found the perfect spot. Maybe the venue's owners have even offered to partially donate use of the space. Should your group risk dampening these warm feelings by formalizing your agreement on paper? Absolutely. A signed contract serves important purposes, such as:

- **Making sure both parties understand each other's intentions.** What if you thought a venue representative had said that canceling at the 11th hour due to low ticket sales would be okay, but in fact the venue policy is to collect payment no matter what? That's the kind of issue to work out in advance, in writing.

- **Reassuring both sides that you're making a formal commitment.** If either of you fails to live up to your end of the bargain, a written contract provides a basis to sue and demand money damages from the other—or, in some circumstances, compel the other to do things promised in the contract. That helps your group by, for example, assuring you that the venue can't just drop you off its calendar (or fail to provide a bartender as promised) without consequences.

- **Helping resolve any later disputes.** Let's say, for example, that at the close of the event, you and your volunteers go home, having been told by the hotel rep, "We can take care of the cleanup." But when you get the final bill, you find an extra cleanup charge. A well-drafted contract will cover issues such as which services are included in the venue agreement and at what price.

It's likely that the venue will already have its own standard form contract at the ready. But before signing, check to make sure it covers the following, and ask for amendments when appropriate:

- **Who's making the agreement.** The legally responsible parties (your organization and the venue provider) should be named, complete with addresses and other contact information.

- **Description of services, spaces, and products included.** The more detail the better, including date and time, which rooms you'll get to use, whether you'll have parking privileges, and what services the facility will provide, such as catering, audiovisual equipment and setup, tables and chairs, and a specified number of staff for setup, cleanup, and waiting tables.

- **Schedules and deadlines.** The venue may, for example, have a deadline by which you must supply your requested menu options and confirm how many people will attend.

- **Price.** This probably won't be a simple flat fee (beyond a set minimum). The fee is likely to depend on factors like the number of guests (which you'll probably need to confirm by a stated deadline), optional add-ons you request (such as linen, centerpieces, or bartending services), corkage, how long the venue's staff end up spending on tasks like cleanup, or how many guests park in the venue's lot. Expect a percentage service charge to be added based on the subtotal.

> **CAUTION**
>
> **Watch out for that corkage fee.** As nonprofit consultant Sue Hall explains, "Most hotels and venues charge an outrageous corkage fee—that is, a fee for opening and serving each bottle of wine or liquor you bring in from elsewhere. But it's in your interest to get wine donated, as we do for the Friends of the Saint Paul Public Library annual event that I'm involved with. Luckily, we've negotiated a very good corkage rate."

- **Payment schedule.** You'll likely be required to make a deposit (which you forfeit if you cancel past a certain date) and then one or more follow-up payments. Don't agree to pay the entire amount up front, which leaves the venue no incentive to provide excellent service.

- **Cancellation policy.** The agreement should be abundantly clear about what happens if you cancel—such as whether you lose your deposit, whether you can get some of it back if you cancel by a certain date, or whether you can get the full deposit back by simply rescheduling. Insist on language saying what happens if the venue cancels on you. If it has to cancel for reasons beyond its control (such as bad weather, a natural disaster, a strike, or internal damage) don't expect a refund. At least make sure it agrees to give you a 100% credit of the deposit against a rescheduled date.

- **Liability for damages.** Expect the venue to hold you legally responsible for any liability, loss, damage, or claims caused by negligence or misconduct by anyone associated with your group, and to simultaneously insist that you promise not to sue over anything arising out of the event. You can ask for similar return promises, along with proof that the venue carries adequate liability insurance. The venue is also likely to require you to take out insurance for any damage or injuries that arise from the event, and to provide proof of such insurance before holding the event.

- **ADA compliance statement.** Request written assurances from the venue that, as a provider of public accommodations, it's meeting its obligations under the Americans with Disabilities Act (ADA). This includes, for example, guaranteeing access to meeting rooms, speakers' platforms, and common areas such as rest rooms, and also providing auxiliary aids and services where necessary.

- **Dispute resolution.** Both sides can minimize potential expenses by requiring mediation, followed by arbitration, as the first steps in a dispute, instead of heading straight to court.

- **Signatures and dates.** It's not a binding contract until both parties sign. The signature section should ask for both parties' mailing addresses, names, and titles, as well as the date on which the contract is signed. Make sure that whoever signs on behalf of your nonprofit is authorized to do so, most likely as an officer or board member.

RESOURCE

For more information on entering into contracts, see *Starting & Building a Nonprofit: A Practical Guide,* by Peri H. Pakroo, J.D. (Nolo).

Choose Add-Ons to the Main Event

Remember what we said in Chapter 3 about adding mini-fundraisers to the main event? Now's your chance to find every possible way to attract attendees, or get them to open their wallets after they arrive. The silent auction combined with a dinner is the classic example. And as long as you're setting up auction tables, you might add a booth or two for a raffle, and sales of your group's T-shirts, calendar, or whatever else you've been trying to sell. Speaking of sales, selling food or drinks is a possibility at nearly every event.

Girls Inc., for example, holds two auctions at its Women of Taste event, as Grace Boone explains: "There's one large, traditional auction that features up to 200 packages of items and raises around $30,000; and a second auction called 'Art for Epicures,' featuring art from local artists as well as 'Power Platters' (signed celebrity platters), which raises up to $10,000. Most of the art is food-safe ceramic pieces that fit with the theme of the event. The Power Platters are a big hit; we send templates to 100 to 200 women who fit our mission—politicians, journalists, actresses, authors, and athletes. They sign the template, then local artists and volunteers transfer the signature and create a nice design on a ceramic plate. Additionally, we sell our branded merchandise (sweatshirts, mugs, aprons, stainless steel water bottles, oven mitts, and measuring spoons), for an extra $1,000 or so of revenue."

TIP

How about a signature drink? If you're planning an event with a no-host bar, you can ask the bartender to create a special mixed drink, which you name for something thematic to the group or season. Then you mark up the price a bit beyond the usual.

Giving Out Awards Adds to the Buzz—And the Guest List

Did you ever think about why so many groups give out things like "Community Achievement," "Outstanding Citizen," or "Good Neighbor" awards? It's a way to emphasize community values and honor others, sure. But—and we hate to sound too cynical about this—it's a great way to boost attendance at your fundraiser. The awardees will attend. Their families will attend—some of them with free tickets, but you can set a limit on these. (Normally tickets for a spouse or significant other and minor children should do it.) And some of their friends will also pay to attend. Your guest list gets a nice boost.

> CAUTION
>
> **Don't choose only celebrity awardees.** Grace Boone explains: "We honor three women every year with "Strong, Smart, and Bold" awards, but have found that BIG people come with BIG schedules and BIG requests. In 2009, for example, we honored Karen Bass, the speaker of the California State Assembly; Kamala Harris, a local District Attorney; and Kristi Yamaguchi, the skater. It was so hard just getting the three of them there! Now, we get just one big name/busy person, and then two people who are somewhat lower profile."

The awardees, feeling well disposed toward your organization, may additionally make a donation or perform other acts to benefit your group, depending on their level of means and influence. (Grace Boone notes, "Honoring Kristi Yamaguchi resulted in our receiving a $100,000 scholarship endowment from a donor to her foundation.") Frankly, when you look at the honoree lists for certain organizations, wealth and influence appear to have been prerequisites. Try not to be this mercenary, but do think of this as an opportunity to broaden your affiliations with interested community-minded people.

At the event, it's traditional to present a plaque or other form of recognition to your awardee. Ask that person to make a brief speech. Unfortunately, people's definitions of "brief" vary, so have your presenter stand close and, if all else fails, approach the person, get the applause going, give a warm thank you, and pick up the next person's certificate.

Make a Separate Pitch for Support

Too many groups go through all the trouble of getting people in the door to their gala dinner, performance, or other special event, and then forget to remind them of the cause they're supporting—and to give them an opportunity to provide further direct support. (The exception to making this pitch is if ticket prices themselves were very high, or if you'll be holding a live auction—Chapter 9 describes ways to work extra pitches for support into the auction itself.)

In some cases, we're not even talking about a reminder. Let's say your youth jazz band gives a performance, and some audience members bring friends. Those friends probably weren't told anything more than, "Pick you up at 7:30." They have no idea that your group is providing important music instruction to replace the lack of it in the public schools, giving students something constructive to do after school. Even your existing members may be a little vague on the details.

One way to counter this is to have your organization's most dynamic personality take the stage at intermission or some other obvious point during the event—preferably before the hour when people are looking at their watch, trying to remember what time they told the babysitter they'd return—and tell people about the great work you're doing and how they can help continue and expand it. The person should finish with a very direct pitch, as in, "My husband and I just made our largest donation ever, we feel great about it, and we hope you'll join us in doing the same. Our volunteers—there with the purple hats—are holding buckets, and this is your chance to drop in a check or fill out one of the pledge cards at your tables."

Keep It Green: Attend to Environmental Issues

With resource usage an increasing focus of world concern, your upcoming special event shouldn't present an example of waste and excess. Attention to environmental goals when planning and implementing an event can boost attendance, audience excitement and participation, and media attention.

But where do you begin? Greening every aspect of your event may not be realistic. However, with some prioritizing, budgeting, and consideration of your nonprofit's core values, you may be able to choose and use many of the tips below.

Choose a Green Location

A country inn or your board member's vacation home may be a beautiful setting for a gala event—but is it the best choice from an environmental standpoint? Your choice of venue will literally set the stage for whether you can achieve a number of other green goals.

First, think about how many people will be driving many miles, and therefore consuming gas and emitting pollutants, to get to your chosen venue. If public transport is an option, one way to ameliorate the distance issue is to provide alternate directions using public transport and bicycles (while ensuring the availability of safe bike racks or storage). Send this message loud and clear, or you'll find that most guests hop into their car without thinking twice. If public transport is not a realistic option, you might coordinate and encourage (or even sponsor) carpools or shuttle services. Or perhaps a more centrally located facility (such as a downtown museum, hotel, or gallery) will be your best bet.

Next, look into the venue's history of attention to and cooperation with environmental goals—and its willingness to sign a contract stating that it will comply with your agreement regarding environmental matters. For example, a venue that agrees to use compostable plateware, but whose staff hasn't been trained to separate the bags of garbage when throwing them out, won't help your goals at all. Along with this, consider whether the place has ready access to a waste management server providing recycling. Some indications that a venue is already committed to environmental protection include that it uses energy-efficient lighting, low-flow toilets, recycled paper materials, and places recycle bins next to the trash cans.

Many venues are taking the initiative and getting "LEED" certification (Leadership in Energy and Environmental Design) from the nonprofit U.S. Green Building Council, Inc. This certification means they've proven that their facility has been built, designed, and operated for improved environmental and human health performance. Also see the Green Venue Selection Guide published by the Building Council, which contains questions to ask venues that haven't yet obtained LEED certification (right down to the gallons per flush on their toilets). It's downloadable at www.usgbc.org.

Create Environmentally Friendly Invitations

Sending "Save the Date" notifications by email is now completely appropriate and will save a lot of paper. For the invitations themselves, you (and your donors) may prefer traditional paper—but you can talk to a printer about how to minimize the size of the invitation and amount of paper used. One possibility is to issue a small invitation, or even a postcard, and then direct people to a page on your website for detailed program information and registration.

Also look into using recycled paper and soy-based inks (made from a renewable resource and far less toxic than regular inks, plus easier to wash off during the recycling process). The costs are close to comparable.

Avoid Creating Mountains of Wasted Products

If you'll be serving food, consider what you'll buy or use in the way of cups, plates, and serving ware. "Real" or reusable china and forks and knives, as well as cloth napkins, are best. If these are impractical, a quick online search will bring up an array of environmentally conscious suppliers of serving products, so that you can comparison shop. But don't forget to prefer local vendors, so that the goods don't consume energy making one last trip across the country. Note that "compostable" is better than "biodegradable"—it refers to something that breaks down as easily as paper and is nontoxic.

You can both save money and make an important environmental impact by the simple step of not serving water in individual plastic bottles. Instead, put out pitchers, along with reusable cups or at least those made from recycled material.

> ! **CAUTION**
>
> **There's nothing worse than buying a "recyclable" product then learning that it's not recyclable in your community.** As Grace Boone explains, "It's worth partnering with your local trash/recycling company—the people who work on this every day and know what's recyclable, what's compostable, and what may be challenging. In our case, the local company has also given us great tips for making our event as green as possible—we're close to zero waste!"

If you'll be serving mainly appetizers or snacks, choosing bite-sized ones that can be eaten with one's fingers will save having to put out forks.

Don't Go Overboard on the Decorations

When planning flowers, decorations, and gifts, realize that less can be more. Now is not the time, for example, to plan a theme party with lots of newly purchased plastic leis, disposable hats, and so forth—unless you know you'll use them year after year (as Girls Inc. does with nylon Chinese lanterns). With a little creativity, you can save both money and the environment.

Start by asking around within your groups or others friendly to you—someone may already have a garage full of the very plastic leis you were hoping would fit your tropical theme.

Another pleasant way to decorate is to ask your volunteers if they have flowers or shrubs growing in their own gardens that they'd be willing to clip and bring to an event. You could still hire a professional to do the arranging, if need be. And while your volunteers are at it, ask them to check their houses for spare vases. Almost everyone has a cheap one—or five—taking up space from their last floral delivery. Another option for centerpieces is potted native plants, which can be reused or raffled off. Or, you can ask a local nursery to let you borrow plants. You just pick them up, treat them nicely, and return them after the event.

Serve Green Food

Your food choices for the event, and the way that food is served, make an important statement about your environmental commitment.

Organic, seasonal, locally grown, and sustainable food sources should be your first choice whenever economically possible. Many caterers and restaurant specialize in such menus—and some may be willing to offer you a discount. Try to offer vegetarian and vegan options.

Buffet service rather than individually boxed or served meals can reduce both food and packaging waste. It also lets people with special diets pick and choose. Even when it comes to snacks, avoid individually packaged items in favor of trays of fruit, crackers, or trail mix. The same goes for condiments, cream, and sugar (to go with your fair-trade coffee).

Develop a Realistic Budget

There's no great mystery to creating a special-events budget: You list all your anticipated expenses in one column, enumerate what you expect to bring in from various intended activities, and finally subtract your expected expenses from your anticipated revenues to give you a total.

The trick, of course, is accurately projecting your expenses and income. Part of this involves taking your analysis to a micro level, so that you don't forget to budget for items like paper napkins, ice buckets, and microphone rentals. (We'll point out your most likely big expenses in the chapters concerning particular types of events.)

Another critical factor in the eventual accuracy of your budget is how faithfully your volunteers follow through on certain activities. In other words, if you plan to keep expenses down by getting donated food and chairs, and to keep income high by getting corporate sponsorships, you've got to communicate this to those in charge of doing these things, and make sure the tasks get done.

Every fundraising event carries a bit of financial risk. You'll have to cover most of your expenses before you know how much the event will bring in— or whether an unexpected snowstorm or other disaster will soak your balance in red ink. One great way to minimize risk is to stick to events that don't cost a lot to stage. Then, if anticipated revenues don't materialize, you haven't dug yourself a huge financial hole.

Estimate Expenses

To help you launch into the expense budgeting process, we've provided the worksheet shown below. As you start to fill it out, you'll inevitably learn more about what you can afford, what key decisions need to be made (for example, how much you're willing to spend on advertising and promotion), and how many guests you'll need to attract. You'll also hopefully think up special items to add, based on unique features to your event. For example, Grace Boone says, "Because our event is held in the evening, outside, we need to rent outdoor heaters."

For every expense item, be sure to consider whether you can get it through donations, or cut costs in some other way. Renting as opposed to buying, for example, is one way to cut costs in the early years, when you're not sure whether you'll need to reuse the same item annually. (But at a certain point, it will make more financial sense to invest in purchasing items that you regularly use.)

If you're new at this, assume that your final figure for expenses will be on the low side—some suggest adding at least 20% for unanticipated costs or occurrences. And always remember that the value of people's time is a hidden cost. Although it doesn't show up in the budget, it's important to recognize the very real prospect that the whirl of activity leading up to a special event will pull paid staff or volunteers away from other separate but important responsibilities to your organization.

CAUTION

The wrong sound system can ruin your event. We've all been at events where the electronic feedback made our fillings ache, or the speaker equipment was diabolically positioned to blast the VIP table. This isn't random bad luck—it can be overcome by paying a little more for your sound system, and paying to have professionals operate it. For example, Fran Hildebrand, of the Community Music Center in San Francisco, says of an event she helped organize, "We got volunteer sound techs, and unfortunately they didn't do certain basic things, like switch microphones from the musicians to the speakers." Though paying more seems hard to justify at the abstract, budget-planning level, think of it as an investment against serious audience irritation or inattention.

Projected Event Expenses for _Annual Dinner & Silent Auction_

Your Group Name: _Centerville Soccer Team_   **Date:** _November 11, 2011_

Expense Category	Projected Cost	Description of Reasoning or Assumptions, Particularly for Discount or Donated Items
Physical Space		
Room, building, outdoor space	$ 300	Discount rate from Women's Club
Chairs, tables, performance platform	$ 500	Seating for 50
Site manager and other staff fees	$ 100	
Heating or air conditioning	$ 0	(included)
Sound system, projector, screen, other equipment	$ 4,000	
Traffic/parking permits	$ 0	(residential parking)
Subtotal:	$ 4,900	
Decorations		
Banners	$ 100	
Lighting	$ 0	(included in room fee)
Flowers	$ 0	Volunteers will donate
Candles	$ 0	
Balloons	$ 0	
Party favors, gifts, award plaques, and certificates	$ 25	
Other	$ 250	Tablecloths, ribbons, other silent auction decorations
Subtotal:	$ 375	
Food and Drink		
Snacks or appetizers	$ 50	
Main meal	$ 1,500	$30 a plate
Extra catering or corkage fees	$ 200	1 drink plus
Alcohol, other drinks, ice	$ 500	
Plates, cups, napkins, cutlery	$ 200	
Waiters and bar staff	$ 600	
Subtotal:	$ 3,050	

Estimate Income

Correctly anticipating income is a bit more difficult, particularly in the first few years of an event. Your crystal ball rarely reveals how many people will show up, how much they'll buy, or how high their auction bids will go. Using the Income Worksheet on the CD-ROM at the back of this book, make your best estimates, but protect yourself from risk by getting lots of advance support from major donors and corporate sponsors. If the event becomes a tradition for your organization, your projections will become more accurate, aided by your experience and by last year's records.

Whether to make the event tickets refundable is an important decision. Specifying that tickets are nonrefundable is a common method of assuring income regardless of whether it rains or some guests get sick or lose interest. On the other hand, you'll need to be clear about nonrefundability up front, and be ready to enforce it. Grace Boone says, "Our tickets are refundable—but this involves major risk, and means that I work hard to create an alternative plan if it rains. Refundability also has to be discussed with your accounting folks, especially if the event straddles fiscal years. If you enter ticket revenue as income in one fiscal year, hold the event some months later in the next fiscal year, and then end up refunding a lot of tickets, it will completely change your books for the year prior."

Compare Projected Expenses and Income

For a successful event, your income should exceed your expenses by a healthy margin (leaving space for things to go wrong). This is hard to quantify, but try aiming to earn at least five times your expenses.

Think about which of your expenses you can put off until you're sure of attendance figures. Hotels, for example, will generally ask for a deposit up front, then require that you confirm attendance and pay for a set number of meals by a certain date. Your ticket sales deadline will need to be set way before that date!

Fundraising Worksheet 7: Projected Special Event Income

Income Category	Projected Amount	Description of Reasoning or Assumptions
Tickets	$ __6,250__	__50__ guests at $ __125__ per ticket
Ad books or ad space in program	$ __800__	__20__ advertisers at $ __20__ per __inch__
Exhibitors' or vendors' rental fees	$ __0__	____ exhibitors/vendors at $____ per booth
Corporate sponsorships	$ __2,000__	
Sales of food or goods	$ __1,000__	(drinks)
Silent auction or raffle proceeds	$ __16,000__	
Total:	$ __26,000__	

CAUTION

Give ticket buyers the information they need for claiming a tax deduction. As explained in Chapter 1, they can't deduct amounts they spent in order to receive actual goods or services—only the extra amount that they paid or spent as a contribution.

Monitor Your Budget and Actual Costs as the Event Approaches

Don't just put the estimated cost and expense worksheets into a drawer. Refine, modify, and keep tabs on expenses and expected income in the days and weeks leading up to the event. Whenever possible, get written estimates or sign contracts with vendors. Grace Boone notes, "I get updated vendor quotes and update my budget three times before the event, so that I account for things like sponsorship amounts, changes in permit fees, and attendance estimates. I always walk into the day of the event knowing exactly what revenue needs to come in that day to really make the event worthwhile."

Also keep careful track of who requires advance payment and by when. Avoid the cash flow problems that can result when the bills start coming in before you've lined up corporate sponsorships.

Depending on the size and complexity of your event, there may be numerous bills rolling in, so don't rely on your memory to verify the amounts when paying them. Mistakes can happen! Double-check your written estimates and contracts to make sure that you're not being double-charged for something, or charged for something that you never asked for or used.

Plan and Pace Event Activities

The success of your event depends in large part on what goes on behind the scenes in the months or weeks leading up to it. First, you'll need to pick a date—ideally one that won't conflict with major holidays or even popular local events. Emily Shem-Tov, a volunteer fundraiser with the Morgan Hill Library Foundation, warns: "One year we held our Silicon Valley Puzzle Fest on the same afternoon as the Super Bowl. That was a mistake. We thought that crossword puzzle people and Super Bowl people would be mutually exclusive, but no, attendance was definitely down."

Allow plenty of lead time. The "classic" special event, such as an annual dinner, gala ball, or benefit concert, normally takes between six months to a year to prepare. Giving yourself a realistic amount of time will not only save your sanity, but also save your group money. For example, the design and printing costs will go down if you give your designers and printers ample time to work the tasks into their schedules—and will go up just as easily if you ask for a rush job.

It's also important to get a head start on corporate sponsorships. Most companies make their sponsorship decisions in either the last quarter of the preceding year or the first quarter of the year when the event will be held. This means that even for some fall events, you'll need to have gotten your sponsorship requests out in the previous year.

Besides, you'll drive your graphic designer crazy if you keep asking for changes to the publicity materials. One we know, who was volunteering her services to a wonderful group that takes underprivileged urban kids on camping trips, told us, "I may have to call it quits—this is the fifth time they've asked me to completely redo the materials to fit in corporate logos of newly added sponsors. I understand that they can't resist a last-minute sponsor, but they've just got to start the process sooner."

Your other publicity efforts may require a certain amount of lead time, as well. For example, Emily Shem-Tov says, "One of our first tasks in the months and weeks leading up to Puzzle Fest is to get our announcements into local publications, some of which have really early deadlines for their calendars and such. Also, we have to make sure we get our workshop presenters booked early on, so that we can mention their names in publicity materials, to attract people."

If you're mobilizing teams of volunteers, however, it's often better not to launch into full preparations until about six months before the event. If you give more lead time, people won't feel any time pressure—and some of them won't get over this feeling until a few weeks before the event.

Create Timelines and Checklists of Activities

The time-tested way to figure out what needs to be done by when is to work backward from the day of the event. What are the final steps—such as picking up rental chairs and flowers? By when do these need to be ordered? By when do decisions need to be made about how many chairs and what type of flowers? Who will be responsible for the decisions? When should this committee meet? Similarly, if you'll have a featured entertainer or musical group, when must you choose this person to make sure that the name will be announced in promotional materials? How much time before this should you allow to negotiate and sign a contract for the services? How many weeks in advance should be allotted for approaching different performers? When will the committee meet to select potential performers' names? You get the drift.

Once you've worked out what needs to be done and by when, create both a timeline and an actual calendar. We suggest creating poster-sized calendars for each month leading up to the event. Write in the dates on which you or one of your volunteers must start the various activities, not the dates by which they must be completed. For example, "Last day to choose menu" is not a helpful calendar entry unless it was preceded by one advising you to begin the selection process.

Working with the dates you've entered on the calendar, create checklists for yourself and your committees, itemizing every task that needs to be done. You or your committee leaders should review these checklists regularly, ticking off items as they're completed, and calling people to confirm that they've completed their assigned tasks by the required dates. Grace Boone notes, "If you're coordinating the event, then the fewer people who are asking you questions on event day, the better your life will be. Checklists can help with that. I've learned to be rather ruthless, when people ask me questions, about asking them in turn, 'Have you looked at the checklist?'"

For the actual day of the event, create especially granular schedules, perhaps right down to the minute. Below is a two-page excerpt of the timeline Grace Boone creates for Women of Taste, covering the time period from 4 p.m. to 10 p.m.

We'll suggest more specific entries for your timetable in the later chapters describing various types of special events.

Sample Event Flow, Overview

Women of Taste Event Flow

September 10, 2010

4:00 PM-10:00 PM: Task Overview

Chefs and Beverages

20 Volunteers Assigned

Staff Chef and Beverage Tables

Run Supplies

Art for Epicures

22 Volunteers Assigned

Staff Auction

Silent Auction

22 Volunteers Assigned

Staff Auction

Roving Clean-Up

5 Volunteers Assigned

Assist other teams in keeping garden tidy

Crowd Control

Run Supplies (as needed)

Welcome Area and Cashier Tables

10 Volunteers Assigned

Sell event tickets

Hand out board and VIP nametags

Give out will-call tickets

Assist guests

Collect tickets

Hand out gift bags

Sponsor Table Ushers

10-15 Volunteers Assigned

Escort table sponsors and guests to their tables

Inspire a Girl Tables

9 Volunteers Assigned

Move supplies to Inspire a Girl tables

Set up tables

Receive cash

Merchandise Table

4 Volunteers Assigned

Move supplies to Merchandise tables

Set up tables

Receive cash

Auction Cashier/Check Out

9 Volunteers assigned

Receive cash

Help guests collect items

Sample Event Flow, Task Details

Women of Taste Event Flow
September 10, 2010
4:00 PM-10:00 PM: Task Details

Silent Auction
Team Lead:
Team Supervisor: Krista and Debra
Staff Contact: Grace
Tasks: Staff Auction

Tasks	Instructions
Familiarize yourself with the list of packages	Look through all the items, ask questions, know where materials are, especially those that will be on the tables you are supervising.
Familiarize yourself with bidding procedures, the bid sheets, and auction rules	Team leads will conduct a training to introduce you to auction rules and procedures. See attached bid sheet and auction rules. Please ask a team lead if you have questions.
Leader should supervise all tables	2 volunteers at each table. Ensure that one volunteer is at each table at all times. Team leads will provide breaks to volunteers throughout the event
Field questions from guests/ bidders.	SELL! Talk up the items at your table. Encourage bidding wars.
Auction Closing Rules **Auction closing time is 9.**	Team Lead will help volunteers end the bidding and prepare for winner pickups. Also, please direct item winners as necessary. Auction closing procedure • At 9 pm, highlight winning bid and leave bid sheet in front of the placard. • When guests come to see if they won an item, check the bid sheet. If the guest won, give them the pink and yellow copies and instruct them to go to the cashiers behind the auction area to pay. • A cashier runner will come with the winner's name and item number. Please help runner collect items. • Or guest will return with a receipt and the pink copy of the bid sheet that will be marked "Paid" and have the cashier's initials on the bottom. • Every package has a white envelope that will have a label listing what should be included in the package. Envelopes will be under each table for the items on top. Physical items, that aren't on display, are under the table. Gift certificates for each package will be inside the envelope. • Give the item(s) to the guest. Mark the white copy of the bid sheet as paid. Check off each item on the envelope as you give it to the guest. • Place the white copy of the bid sheet into the envelope and put the envelope back in the box. • At the end of the night, put all envelopes together (paid and unpaid, claimed and unclaimed) in numerical order, and bring all items into restaurant

Define Committees and Assign Leaders

Every special event needs a central point-person to coordinate volunteers and keep things moving on schedule. But one person can't pull off an event alone. After looking at your budget and planning materials, identify all the activities that need attending to, then create subject committees to match them. For example, depending on the type of event, your committees might include some combination of the following:

- site planning
- meals or refreshments
- choosing exhibitors, performers, vendors, or home or garden tour destinations
- decorations
- transportation
- awards
- gathering auction or raffle donations
- obtaining corporate sponsorships
- event staffing and registration
- keeping it green
- promotion and publicity (including graphics and printing), and
- cleanup.

Some of these activities are discrete enough that they may require only a single person, or a committee of two or three. In fact, at times it's best not to assign too many people to a task, lest the abundance of people give committee members the idea that little is expected of them.

Assign a point person to be in regular contact with all committee leaders. Depending on the timeline and number of people involved, scheduling regular meetings or conference calls, where everyone will report on their progress and any difficulties they're facing, may be worthwhile.

In the name of good record keeping, the point person should ask for documentation of certain accomplishments, such as names of committed corporate sponsors, or copies of press releases. Unrealistic optimism has been known to result in situations where volunteers assert that everything is going great, when in fact little or nothing has actually been done.

> **TIP**
>
> **Get organized.** Your point person should create a notebook or a system of file folders, to track important pieces of information and ensure that nothing gets forgotten. Sections of the notebook should include your checklists, a month-by-month planning calendar, budgeting and finances, subject matter sections for each committee (containing important documents such as contracts or notes on decisions and accomplishments), a master contact list of all vendors, volunteers, and other participants, and anything else relevant to the particular event. The leader should also work with the committee heads to help them get similarly organized. Grace Boone adds, "My binder has a hot pink cover and my name all over it—when it's a big venue, making sure that your personal materials stand out is crucial."

Plan Promotion and Publicity

If you're hoping to attract members of the general public to your event, you'll need to pay particular attention to promotion and publicity. Promotion is advertising that you arrange or pay for yourself, such as posters and invitations; publicity is media reporting, usually in response to your press releases or other contacts.

What You Can Do to Promote Your Event

Step one in promoting your event is to tell your friends, members, and supporters about it. As big as the Women of Taste event is, for example, Grace Boone says that, "We discovered in a recent survey that the overwhelming majority of our attendees found out about it from friends and family—aided by the fact that we have a huge pool of volunteers. And this was despite our having spent a lot of energy getting media sponsorships!"

Your newsletter, website, and Facebook page should start generating excitement weeks or even months in advance, mentioning the date, location, and contact person for more information or volunteer opportunities. Even in phone conversations with friends, drop teasers like, "Guess who signed up to be our emcee?" or, "I'm so excited about Uptown Restaurant having donated dinner for two for our auction, I might bid on it myself."

Send a "Save the Date" email or postcard approximately three to five months before the event. Invitations, or opportunities to buy tickets, should be sent or announced six weeks before the event. Get ideas from invitations you've receive from other nonprofits regarding how to make these both enticing and informative.

In addition to putting your supporters on your invitation mailing list, give all your volunteers, board members, and any staff a piece of paper, and ask them to write the names, addresses, email addresses, and telephone numbers of any friends who they think might be interested in attending. Ask them early and often. And make sure you have a PDF of the invitation that people can email. Similarly, any featured speakers or honorees should be asked for the contact information of friends or relatives who might wish to attend, and sent invitations.

> **TIP**
>
> **Each one bring ten.** Sometimes the simplest and cheapest promotional methods work the best. You might charge each board member or other key leader with recruiting ten friends. Especially if you include a fun contest (the winning recruiter gets a weekend at a donated vacation home, for example), this can be an incredibly cost-effective way to spread the word.

Event posters should be created for any event to which the public at large will be invited. If pressed for cash, this is something you can do in black and white with your own photocopying machine, but don't try this if you plan to charge high ticket prices or attract high-income attendees. Usually the help of a graphic designer is required. An attractive poster can be a sought-after item, which coffee shops, stores, and other public places will be happy to display.

Paying for advertising is not usually cost-effective for a small group, so take a look at where you can get it for free. A fun site for all kinds of events is www.eventful.com, which provides a special page for charity and fundraising events. Also, if you sell tickets through an online company like Brown Paper Tickets or Eventbrite, it will add your event to its calendars as well.

Look also for media outlets or online sources that offer free community calendars. You can also get free publicity, and potentially reach a specialized audience, by arranging for announcements within the newsletters of local churches or other groups, such as a bicycling or chess club.

Even a printed invitation can seem impersonal—so try to counter that by having board members or other volunteers, particularly those who know the recipients, write short personal notes on the invitations saying something like, "Hope to see you and Bobby there, and hear about your trip!" Also follow up your invitations with personal phone calls.

Women of Taste makes it 100% guilt-free

Sample culinary creations by 30 of the Bay Area's best chefs. Savor wines, beers and ales from top wineries and breweries. Dance to the music of the Montclair Women's Big Band. Bid on fabulous items at the Art Auction and Silent Auction. All guilt-free pleasures, since every penny of your ticket goes to Girls Inc. of Alameda County. Girls Inc.'s programs give girls from underserved communities the skills needed to achieve academic success, a healthy lifestyle and strong self-confidence. So make sure you secure your ticket to this year's Women of Taste Fundraiser. You just might feel guilty missing it.

girls inc.
Girls Incorporated®
of Alameda County

Saturday, September 25, 6pm-10pm
The Kaiser Rooftop Garden, 300 Lakeside Drive, Oakland, California
Tickets can be purchased online at www.girlsinc-alameda.org or call (510) 357-5515

yelp EAST BAY EXPRESS diablo Tribune CLEARCHANNEL Oakland

Women of Taste Promotional Poster

How to Attract Media Attention to Your Event

A positive media write-up can be great advertising. And even if it doesn't directly bring people to your event, Grace Boone points out, "It helps raise public awareness of your organization." Think about how to attract both pre- and post-event coverage.

Your promotion and publicity committee should start by checking out which local newspapers, magazines, radio or television shows, or websites are most likely to be seen or heard by your potential ticket buyers. Get familiar with their coverage, to see whether the particular outlet, or more specifically one of its regular columnists or hosts, might be interested in a story about your event. Don't forget bloggers, if they've got a specific following in your community.

Note how certain shows, sections, or columns are dedicated to different types of information, including hard news (such as is found on the first page of a newspaper or a drive-time radio program), society features (gossip about personalities), in-depth feature stories (usually planned weeks or months in advance), or community interest stories. Style your publicity plans accordingly.

TIP

Society pages may be your best bet. As Grace Boone explains, "We plan to send post-event press releases to local society columnists. In fact, this year we specifically tasked one of our photographers with staying with our CEO and taking pictures of people on a certain list, which included our major donors, politicians, and other widely known people. There were other pictures from the event that I thought were lovely, with people having a fabulous time, but those aren't the ones we send to the media—they're far less likely to get picked up, though they're great for our Facebook page."

An event that your organization sponsors or participates in is, by its very nature, "news." Whether it's interesting news is another matter. Journalists typically look for a "hook" or unusual angle with which to entice the audience.

What's exciting about your event? The fact that you plan to hold it is not exciting at all. Imagine being a reporter and receiving a press release titled, "X Organization Plans to Hold Annual Dinner." Blah. But perhaps you could highlight one thing that will happen at the event, like (at the risk of sounding sensational), "One Year After Near-Fatal Crash, Student in Wheelchair to Receive 'Community Inspiration' Award." Now the journalist is thinking, "Hmm, human interest, good photo op." Also look for opportunities for humor, as in: "Pastor Will Hold Waterproof Bible While Enduring Carnival Dunk Tank."

Once you've found the hook, your next step is to send out press releases and get in touch with your favorite media professionals. Anyone can write and send a press release. You simply write up the story you want to convey, preferably in one page or less, in a style that the journalist can cut and paste

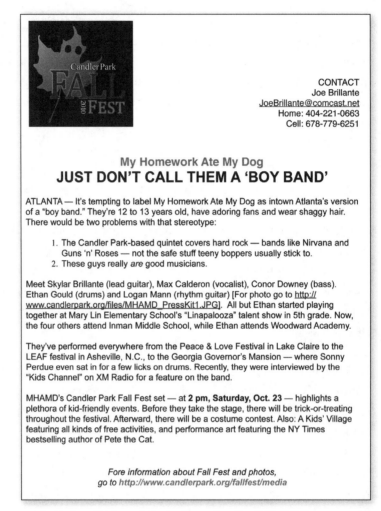

CONTACT
Joe Brillante
JoeBrillante@comcast.net
Home: 404-221-0663
Cell: 678-779-6251

My Homework Ate My Dog
JUST DON'T CALL THEM A 'BOY BAND'

ATLANTA — It's tempting to label My Homework Ate My Dog as intown Atlanta's version of a "boy band." They're 12 to 13 years old, have adoring fans and wear shaggy hair. There would be two problems with that stereotype:

1. The Candler Park-based quintet covers hard rock — bands like Nirvana and Guns 'n' Roses — not the safe stuff teeny boppers usually stick to.
2. These guys really *are* good musicians.

Meet Skylar Brillante (lead guitar), Max Calderon (vocalist), Conor Downey (bass), Ethan Gould (drums) and Logan Mann (rhythm guitar) [For photo go to http://www.candlerpark.org/files/MHAMD_PressKit1.JPG]. All but Ethan started playing together at Mary Lin Elementary School's "Linapalooza" talent show in 5th grade. Now, the four others attend Inman Middle School, while Ethan attends Woodward Academy.

They've performed everywhere from the Peace & Love Festival in Lake Claire to the LEAF festival in Asheville, N.C., to the Georgia Governor's Mansion — where Sonny Perdue even sat in for a few licks on drums. Recently, they were interviewed by the "Kids Channel" on XM Radio for a feature on the band.

MHAMD's Candler Park Fall Fest set — at **2 pm, Saturday, Oct. 23** — highlights a plethora of kid-friendly events. Before they take the stage, there will be trick-or-treating throughout the festival. Afterward, there will be a costume contest. Also: A Kids' Village featuring all kinds of free activities, and performance art featuring the NY Times bestselling author of Pete the Cat.

Fore information about Fall Fest and photos,
go to http://www.candlerpark.org/fallfest/media

Sample Press Release From Candler Park Fall Fest

from. There's a sample press release below, a fun one from the 2010 Candler Park Fall Fest (written by Ken Edelstein, Editor and Publisher of *Green Building Chronicle* (www.greenbuildingchronicle.com)). And you'll find a blank press release template on the CD-ROM at the back of this book.

It's best to send your press release by regular mail, rather than by fax or email (unless the media organization's website specifies otherwise). Follow up with a phone call reminding the journalist of why this is a great story for their show or publication.

Another great way to get journalists' attention focused on your event is to invite some to attend—for free, or in return for advance publicity from their organization. Don't just send press members a stack of tickets, or you won't know how many to expect. Instead, contact selected journalists (by press release, phone call, or email) and ask whether they'd like free tickets or a press pass. Offer two tickets to each journalist, so that he or she can bring a companion.

Will a journalist who attends your event necessarily do a story about it? No. Many consider freebie invites to be a perk of the job. But even so, this is a valuable way to build relationships. A journalist who doesn't think your current dinner, fair, or benefit concert is worth a story will still probably develop a warm feeling toward your group, and may look for a way to cover you later.

> **TIP**
>
> **Save photos of this year's event for next year's promotion.** Even if your event won't be highly photogenic, pictures of key speakers or people enjoying themselves are great for your website and promotional materials.

Create Corporate Sponsorship Opportunities

Despite the fact that many events charge admission fees, profitability often depends on garnering money from outside sources, such as corporate sponsors. Sometimes, getting sponsorship can be as simple as encouraging your board members to ask their employers to buy a table's worth of tickets for an annual dinner event, or asking local vendors and business owners (including sole proprietors such as financial planners or insurance agents) to buy space in your ad book (described below). Other times, you'll want to look for more major sponsorship—for example, by asking a company to be the lead name on your 10K run, with its logo prominently displayed on your banners and publicity materials, in return for underwriting the costs, or making in-kind donations of space, food, or other event necessities. Grace Boone says, "For Women of Taste, we pay all the vendors something (except those providing food and drink), but they give us, on average, a 25% to 30% discount." How and what to ask for is described in Chapter 4.

Advertisements in your event program or an ad book are other popular ways of getting corporate sponsorship. We know of one organization that earned $125,000 on its ad book alone, which was prepared in conjunction with an annual dinner.

An ad book is just what it sounds like—a brochure that displays either traditional advertisements or small testimonials to the organization on behalf of a business or person, such as "Bronze Medal Athletic Gear congratulates KidsClub for its 25 years of helping inner-city youth excel." Some ad buyers, such as solo professionals like lawyers, accountants, or music teachers, will simply want a copy of their business card in your ad book. A graphic designer or printer should be able to help you set guidelines for planning and selling ad space.

Deal With Risks and Liability Issues

Because making your event profitable will require keeping costs down, you must consider any minor or major disasters that might befall your event— such as a child getting injured on the site, a donor drinking too much and causing an accident driving home, or a thief taking your cash box or goods for sale. Important steps you can take to forestall mishaps and disasters include:

- making sure you've complied with all applicable laws and permit requirements
- putting your own sensible safety measures into place, and
- considering buying special insurance for the event.

For smaller events, accomplishing steps one and two would probably be enough, but for large-scale events attended by people you don't know, buying insurance also makes sense. Some event sites may require you to carry a specified type and amount of coverage as a condition of using their facilities.

Comply With Laws and Permit Requirements

Whether your event is on your organization's own site or elsewhere, unusual attendance or activities may bring up legal issues. Large numbers of people impeding traffic flow or parking in one area may require advance discussions with your local police department. If you'll be serving liquor, you may be required to obtain a license or permit, usually from your city. If you plan to have a volunteer serve the alcohol (which isn't ideal, as we'll discuss below), that person may be required to go through special training, covering issues like how to check IDs and when to cut someone off. Auctions (particularly of luxury items) and gambling activities may also require licenses or permits.

> ⓘ **CAUTION**
>
> **"I work a few hundred extra dollars into my budget for permit fees."**
> Grace Boone explains, "With the economy changing, cities and counties are trying to make extra money, or their staff have been laid off and the rules are being interpreted by new people, so I've had some unhappy surprises with significant permit-fee increases."

As appropriate, talk to other nonprofits, your police department, or to a city official before proceeding. And, if you still have legal questions, look for a volunteer lawyer to help you.

Implement Appropriate Safety Measures

The best way to minimize damage is to avoid it in the first place, then create backup measures. For starters, make sure that your event is well-staffed, and that every volunteer knows who to go to with a problem. The person in charge should carry a cell phone and give every volunteer the number. Or, Grace Boone says, "We've found headsets and walkie-talkies to be the most efficient way to communicate. They're rentable and quite possibly the best $400 you could spend when you have a large space."

Volunteers should wear something distinctive, so that members of the public know who to alert when the food has run out or they observe a burst pipe leaking in the direction of your sound system. The "volunteer uniform" also provides another opportunity to put your group's name in front of guests. At Women of Taste, Grace Boone says, "Our volunteers wear branded aprons that we spent just $2 on, but people love them."

Also consider whether there are any rules that you want members of the public to observe. For example, if it wouldn't be appropriate to allow children below a certain age to participate, make this clear in your publicity materials, and be prepared to enforce it at the door. Similarly, if people shouldn't bring certain materials like alcoholic beverages or firearms, warn them in advance and be prepared to check for violations. Depending on what your venue already provides, this may require hiring a security person who is trained in dealing with such matters.

We also suggest saying no to dogs, as well as to more exotic creatures—the cleanup problems are immense, and there's no upside unless it's an animal-centered event. (Working animals, such as seeing-eye dogs, are of course an exception.)

As discussed in Chapter 1, you should have carefully chosen who you're going to trust with sensitive tasks such as handling money, serving alcohol, or transporting people by car or van. But don't forget that these people will need to take breaks or spend some time enjoying the event themselves! Schedule additional people to spell them. Tell them who those people are, and remind them that they can't just hand their responsibilities over to someone else.

Ask to see the license of every driver, and if the person will be driving a large truck or bus, make sure he or she is specially licensed for this as well.

Serving alcohol creates its own set of issues. You don't want to serve drinks to minors, you don't want people who've had too much to create a scene or a medical emergency, and you certainly don't want a drunk guest driving home to injure someone—who may then sue your organization for the damages. Even if your area doesn't require alcohol servers to be specially trained, it's safest to hire one who is. (Bartenders aren't typically required by law to receive any sort of license.) If hiring professional bartenders isn't feasible, your servers should be ready to check IDs and tell patrons when they've had enough (or start mixing their drinks with nine parts soda). As the event winds down, someone should be stationed at the door to wish people farewell and to offer a cab or other ride to anyone who seems to be staggering toward his or her car. To be extra-cautious, you could arrange to have a couple of taxis waiting for this purpose, though they'd probably charge you for this service.

These are just a few of the safety measures you can put into place. You may need to develop others based on the type of event, the number of people and type of activities people will be engaging in, any special needs that your guests are likely to have, and your own common sense.

Purchase Insurance

Contact your group's insurance broker or company and ask to go over your policy, to make sure that all the activities planned for your event will be covered. In the best-case scenario, your group has a business liability policy that covers not only injuries on its premises resulting from your staff's negligent acts, but "off-premises" injuries, such as if a guest slips and falls while dancing at your downtown gala (and alleges that you didn't issue sufficient warning of the slick floor). Grace Boone says, "I double-check before every event that our insurance is still adequate for our plans."

Even a fairly comprehensive policy may contain some wicked exclusions. For example, you may find that coverage is excluded for injuries caused not by your group's staff members, but by volunteers—perhaps if your fundraising committee chairperson accidentally drops a case of wine on someone's foot. Another exclusion might apply if your event involves dangerous activities, such as a bungee-jumping competition. Insurance professional Mike Mansel, CIC, based in Pleasant Hill, California (www.publiability.com), adds, "One of my clients is a school, which has coverage for just about all special events, except that the insurer wants advance warning about any events involving liquor. In planning an off-campus talent show, for example, with wine and beer on the menu, the school needs to complete an alcohol supplement attesting that a qualified professional bartender will do the serving. The insurance company can charge them extra for this event if it wants to, but so far hasn't."

If your event is being hosted at a member's home, then coverage for injuries to guests should be found under the host's homeowner's policy. Again, it's wise to review the policy ahead of time, in case of exclusions.

If your group doesn't have insurance (perhaps because it hasn't formed a separate entity), and no one's homeowners' policy appears to apply, you should buy a special events policy. These can be obtained to cover mere hours' worth of activities. Nevertheless, such policies can be pricey, so call different agents for quotes and make sure you understand exactly what's covered.

Also realize that almost no insurance policy is a substitute for detailed planning, and won't cover harm caused by reckless or intentional acts (for example, if one of your volunteers drives a car filled with balloons at 90 m.p.h. and crashes, or if a staff member gets into a wrestling match with a guest).

Last-Minute Tasks and Tips

The days and hours leading up to the event are usually whirling-dervish time for even the most organized events planner or leader. Now you'll really want to put your checklists to work. Review them frequently and carefully, and double-check that all of your committee leaders are communicating with one another as needed. Although the precise tasks to be accomplished will depend on the type of event you're having, here are some things no event planner should forget:

Delegate shamelessly. If you're the event leader, make sure that your list of assignments for the actual day of the event is relatively open. As Jan Etre, who organizes a crafts fair for KPFA Radio in Berkeley, California, says, "You should be available for answering questions and putting out fires. Someone will tap you on the shoulder, and you never know what's coming next— perhaps a lost child, or a parking problem."

Also make sure that everyone's roles are very clear. Who is assigned to supervise the photographer? Who will play the role of timekeeper? See Grace Boone's task list, above, for further examples of how to assign roles, both supervisory and task-related.

Check and cross-check your lists. Take a last look through your notebook, to make sure no task got lost in the shuffle. Make confirmation calls to any important speakers or vendors to whom you haven't spoken in a while. Make sure that all money owed to you has been paid, and that you've paid all the appropriate vendors. You don't want to be signing checks and working out small disputes over financial matters during the event itself.

Create a seating chart. If you're having a sit-down lunch or dinner event, take your final list of ticket buyers and create a seating chart of who will sit with whom. Better yet, have it laminated. (Spills happen.) The topic of seating charts is discussed in Chapter 8.

> **TIP**
>
> **What every event planner packs ahead of time.** Apart from the items you've specifically planned to bring for the event, create a goodie bag of anything that could possibly be useful in a pinch, such as adhesive tape, duct tape, scissors, pens, glue, petty cash, a stapler, trash bags, paper towels, first aid supplies, and so forth. Grace Boone says, "Don't fall into the classic nonprofit syndrome of buying only just enough—buy extra! And while you're at it, buy a fanny pack. It sounds atrocious, but I tend to have thousands of dollars in checks on my person during the days leading into the event, and don't want to risk setting them down." Also consider whether any of your volunteers will be working long shifts, and bring snacks and water to keep them happy and energized.

Arrange for early entry by the preparation crew. If you've rented space, make sure you'll be allowed to get in with enough advance time to set up, decorate, arrange silent auction items, and more. These tasks always take longer than you think they will—three to four hours is usually considered the minimum.

Check that your registration tables will be adequately staffed and provided for. A whole book could be written about the event registration process. Your goal is to have people registered and into the event within a few minutes of arriving. Depending on how many attendees you anticipate, this may require a whole bank of registration tables, with easily visible letters of the alphabet if you wish to divide people by name. Make sure all your volunteers know your policies on issues such as check acceptance and dealing with lost tickets. Adviser Grace Boone remembers, "One of the more serious glitches we've had in recent years was when we'd changed venues for two of our events, and in both cases, ended up with long registration lines. Luckily, we had staff members in line who saw the problem, and we'd brought extra copies of the guest lists, so the staff were able to jump in and start taking tickets."

Create contact lists of key people, government permit providers, and vendors. Pass these out to your other lead staff or volunteers. This will help in case someone forgets to show up, or you need emergency help.

Create a final list of who needs to be publicly thanked. At some point during the event, a key staff member or volunteer may have an opportunity to address the crowd. If so, that person should start by effusively (yet briefly) thanking the people who did the most to bring about the event.

TIP

If something goes wrong, it's not the end of the world. In fact, counsels Grace Boone, "95% of the time, no one's going to notice. You'll know that something got delayed, or that something doesn't look like you thought it was going to, and it will rip you up inside. But the lesson tends to be that no one cares as much as you do. If you give people a fabulous experience overall, they'll be focused on that—and even the 5% who notice that something went awry won't say anything."

After the Event

A day or two after the event, you'll probably be dying to return to the other tasks you've been ignoring—the letters piling up in your in-box, the unreturned emails. However, if you don't tie up loose ends now, you may never get to them. This is the time to send out thank-you letters, assess the event's overall success (financial and otherwise), and assemble clear records for anyone who might handle the event in the future.

You already know the importance of thank-you letters when dealing with individual donors, but after a special event, you'll have whole new lists of people to thank—and each one is critical. If you haven't already done so, send personalized thank-yous to every committee head, volunteer, sponsor, individual donor (including donors who bought things at auctions, because part of their payment was a contribution—but not including people who purchased items from independent vendors at craft or art fairs), and business donors. Remember to note the amount of any financial contribution, minus the value of anything received in return, for IRS purposes.

If the story of what happened at your event is media-worthy, then you should immediately send out a press release—for example, describing and quoting the contents of your famous speaker's presentation, complete with his or her photo, or announcing the winners of your bicycle race. To speed this up, it helps to draft the release ahead of time, then fill in the details as appropriate when the event is over.

Even if your event was a roaring success, there are no doubt many lessons to be learned. And, if there's any possibility that you might repeat this or a similar event, you'll want to collect all relevant information about what worked and what didn't. Assemble your committee leaders, and potentially the entire committees, to collect impressions. Organizing participants' thoughts into "Do More? Do Less? Do Different?" can be a productive way to keep the focus positive and figure out how problems can be prevented in the future. As an alternative to a meeting, you can simply distribute paper or email surveys.

One of your most important tasks is to draw up a final event budget and compare it to the original budget, to see how well your projections ultimately matched up with reality. After you've collected all your information, write up all of your narrative and budgetary conclusions, and put them into your event folder for future reference.

Finally, imagine that this time next year, a bright-eyed newcomer is trying to recreate your smashingly successful event. Will your notebook and files be enough to tell the story of how the event was done, who helped out (or flaked out), who was invited, who did the graphic design, where to advertise, which media outlets were responsive, what other vendors to contract with, and the rest?

There will be a time when you've simply forgotten all the details that seem so deeply burned into your brain right now. Go through your notebook and add any documents that are floating around elsewhere, making sure every section is complete. Write memos to explain important issues that aren't otherwise covered.

Dinners and Other Food Events

Meet Your Adviser

Peter Pearson, President of The Friends of the St. Paul Public Library, a library foundation (www.thefriends.org) in Minnesota.

What he does:
"It changes every day. I've got a staff of 11, and oversee all that we do, including fundraising for the library, advocating for public funding, and creating cultural programming for the library system. A large amount of my time is spent on fundraising, including with major donors, corporations, and foundations. I also spend a fair amount of time in the community, putting a face on the The Friends of the Library, often doing speaking engagements. Then there are the management matters that come with running a nonprofit, such as developing and monitoring the budget. We have a 50-person board of directors, and I spend a lot of time nurturing those relationships and helping them to fundraise."

Earliest memory of taking part in a charitable activity:
"Church events. When I was in grade school, my mother was fairly involved in church bake sales, dinners, and so on. Like most kids, I thought these were a chore!"

Likes best about his work:
"Two things: One, it's extremely varied. I get to do a lot of different kinds of things, and rarely the same thing from day to day. Second, I'm so passionate about the mission of public libraries in our communities that I can't think of anything else I'd rather do."

Top tip for people new to nonprofit fundraising:
"Recruit the best, most influential board of directors to your organization. Fundraising success is all about your board. Even in small towns and rural areas, you've got the advantage that you know who the people of influence are, and can find them faster than is typically possible in a large town. Finding those individuals who can make a difference is key."

There's nothing like food to bring people together. Meals have been central to human socializing for all of recorded time—and somewhere down the centuries, people got used to digging into their pockets to pay for them. That's handy for your fundraising purposes, because your guests can feel good about spending what they already might have for dining and entertainment, while simultaneously supporting a good cause.

Nonprofit groups have come up with endless variations on the basic food-event theme, such as annual or celebratory dinners, pancake breakfasts, spaghetti feeds, summer barbecues, elegant luncheons, afternoon teas, wine, cheese, or dessert tastings, cocktail hour events, and so on. The ambience can range from formal, black-tie to laid-back and tie-dyed; whatever fits your group's culture and draws on its assets.

Most meal events try to incorporate some sort of entertainment or education, such as a speaker, auction, musical performance, video presentation, fashion show, or showcase of clients' talents or activities. See the appropriate chapters of this book concerning how to organize these added elements.

CAUTION

Serving homemade food? Check your local health department regulations, which may prohibit serving food from noncertified kitchens at ticketed events. Sometimes you can get around this with a "suggested donation."

Is a Dinner or Food Event Right for Your Organization?

If you've got people in your group who like to cook—or know others who do—and members who like to eat, you may be well on your way to planning a fun event. Just how profitable it will be, however, is another matter.

Let's take the classic spaghetti dinner as an example. Tickets for these are normally sold for $10 or less, so you'd have to feed 100 people at absolutely zero cost to clear so much as $1,000.

Tickets to a gala dinner, perhaps at a five-star hotel, might be sold for far more—$50 to $150 is typical. But after adding up the costs of renting a hotel ballroom and paying for catering (not to mention other add-on fees; get ready to spend sums like $5 per cup of coffee) you'll soon discover that ticket sales will hardly cover the costs. The Friends of the St. Paul Public Library provides an example, with its popular annual "Opus & Olives" event, held at the Crowne Plaza Hotel in St. Paul. The 800-guest evening includes a cocktail hour, three-course dinner, author presentations (including four well-known authors of varying genres, and one emerging talent), and book sales and signings. Tickets are $125, $250, or $350, depending on seating. Many of the higher-priced tickets are bought by corporate sponsors. Adviser Peter Pearson notes, "Given that the actual cost of the dinner is about $60, if we were to rely mostly on the $125 ticket sales to regular members of the public, we wouldn't make much of a profit."

So where's the "success" in all this? As with every special event, part of the point is community building. An inspiring food event puts a face on your organization and builds loyalty that may lead to later donations.

More directly, such an event creates a setting where you can raise revenue in other ways. These might include a silent auction (discussed in Chapter 9), a direct ask for donations (discussed in Chapter 6), and solicitation of businesses sponsorships, whether from a local car dealer who wants to hang a banner over your picnic area or an airline that wants to buy a table's worth of tickets and have its logo displayed in your gala dinner/auction program. (Getting such sponsorships is discussed in Chapter 4.)

Additionally, because the more formal, gala dinners traditionally give guests a printed program, there's a place you can sell ad space—or do so separately, in what's known as a "tribute book" or "ad book" (also discussed in Chapter 7).

Think of your event as a rallying point for a broader effort to collect individual and corporate donations, all the while keeping a sharp eye on the amount of time and money you put in compared with the amount you can earn back. Just don't think of food events as an instant moneymaker. Adviser Peter Pearson explains, "If someone from a small library or other group were to say to me, 'Our budget got cut, we're desperate for funds, should we hold a community dinner?' I'd say no, unless you already have a fairly large pool of people and corporate sponsors in place. If you're simply aiming to have an awareness raiser, sure, go ahead. But in a situation like you've described, direct asks to individual donors would be a better bet."

The resources you put into your meal event should, as always, draw on your group's existing assets. It's best if these include a number of the following:

- Access to free or low-cost event space (perhaps a space that your group or a member owns, or in a nearby public park where you can reserve an area).

- A group of volunteers (five to 15) willing to help with planning and preparation, including not only the basics (venue, menu, program, and publicity), but soliciting corporate sponsorships and other donations.

- Additional volunteers for the day of the event, some of whom will perhaps keep costs down by cooking, waitering, drink-mixing, entertaining, and so forth.

- A volunteer with events-planning experience, such as a caterer, chef, or even someone who has recently put on a family wedding.

- A volunteer with expertise in cooking an unusual cuisine (and the ability to teach others to cook it—lots of it).

- Connections with restaurants and other businesses that will donate or give discounts on premade or other food, wine and other beverages.

- Connections with high-profile people who will serve as emcee, speakers, or honored guests.

- Connections with musicians or other entertainers who will work for free or at low cost.

- A reason to celebrate or join together, such as the anniversary of your group's founding or the retirement of a longtime board member (such occasions tend to bring back alumni or long-lost members who want to share memories or honor a favorite person).

- An idea for an interesting theme that will resonate with your membership. For example, Peter Pearson says, "Our major Friends of the Library events, including Opus & Olives and the Minnesota Book Awards (with champagne and dessert), make great fundraisers because they're about publishers and authors. We most likely wouldn't do a golf tournament—it wouldn't resonate with the people who follow us."

TIP

A cooking pro can make all the difference. "When our fundraising committee suggested a pancake breakfast as a preschool fundraiser," says Mary Randolph, a parent-volunteer in Berkeley, California, "the teachers groaned. They thought it sounded like way too much work. But one of the moms was a professional chef, and she was willing to help out. She organized everything and everybody. We invited all the alumni families, and the event turned into a great reunion and successful fundraiser."

How Much Planning and Work Will Be Required?

As you might expect, the amount of planning and the number of people required will depend on the scale of your event. For a large-scale event, you'll need to begin your work—including identifying an event chairperson, other key leaders, and numerous committee members, and starting to solicit corporate sponsorships—up to a year in advance. For Opus & Olives, the St. Paul Friends group hires an outside coordinator, St. Paul-based nonprofit consultant Sue Hall. She says, "I start out at least nine months ahead of the event, and maybe spend a couple of hours a month. By the last week, I'm spending 50 hours a week."

Scaling down from a major event like this one, give yourself at least three months for anything but the most informal of events. Anything less than that and you'll end up placing rush orders, looking for space when most venues have already filled up, and otherwise racing the clock.

Deciding the Basic Food or Format

What will it be—a bratwurst festival or a five-course dinner? Let's zoom in on some of the variations on the meal-event theme, with tips and insights for each. Don't feel you have to choose one of the below. These are just to give you ideas.

In fact, "Going with the tried-and-true formats is often a waste of time," says consultant Sue Hall. "That may sound harsh, but we're all exposed to so much fundraising, we just want to do something that's fun. A library in a small town east of here does a wonderful event called Girls Night Out, with appetizers, wine, lots of chocolate, chair massages, an author speaker, and a really great silent and live auction, all for women. It's really clever, and all run by a volunteer committee. They're probably not making a lot of money, but they bring in people who wouldn't otherwise come into their organization, as friends or guests. That gives them an opportunity to turn those people into donors."

Even a little variation on the usual themes can help attract attention. For example, around the Fourth of July, charities have held a "Red, White, and Blue Pancake Breakfast" by adding strawberries, blueberries, and whipped cream.

Pancake Breakfast

It's a classic—but it's not entirely easy. Try feeding pancakes to your family next Saturday morning, and you'll remember why you don't do it every weekend. Pancakes occupy a lot of burner space and take a while to cook, often leaving someone waiting hungrily. To pull off a charity pancake breakfast, you'll need a good-sized kitchen space in which to work, such as at your local school, church, or fire house, or a restaurant willing to host. Make absolutely sure you've got a supervising cook who's accustomed to cooking pancakes, or you'll end up with burnt or squishy ones.

What's on the menu? To make it a full breakfast, most organizers include not just pancakes (with butter and syrup, of course), but bacon or sausages, coffee, orange juice, and fresh fruit.

Barbeque or Salmon Bake

Outdoor barbeques work well for summertime in the park, and are good for combining with other activities such as a carnival or games. What you serve may depend in part on what gets donated. For meats, make sure you've got someone in charge who can tell when the insides are no longer raw. The variety of available soy-based meat-substitutes means that you can advertise your event as vegetarian-appropriate, too.

Spaghetti and Other Easy-to-Cook Dinners

The virtues of a spaghetti dinner are that the ingredients are low-cost, and you can produce vast amount of noodles and sauce in single cooking pots. Don't try this carbo-loaded meal in an area where the Atkins diet is popular, however. Or if you do, serve a lot of salad on the side.

Other similarly simple food possibilities include baked potatoes (served with a variety of dressings), tacos or fajitas, hot dogs, and subs and other sandwiches.

Cooking Competitions

In this variation on the food theme, a group of chefs (professional or not) create dishes based on a certain theme. Diners pay to eat the results, and enjoy judging and voting on which is best.

For example, in Pennsylvania, a Japanese restaurant called Kome was the site of a "best sushi appetizers" fundraising challenge in October 2010, to benefit local schools. Chefs and teachers went head to head, and diners rated the results based on appearance, taste, and creativity. The winning teacher earned 15% of Kome's evening receipts for his or her school.

Community Potluck

There's no need to worry about who does the cooking if you invite all participants to do so! This type of event works well in churches and other organizations where members already know each other and would enjoy sampling each other's cooking. Ask everyone to bring a dish, then either charge admission, request donations, or find other ways to raise money once people get there. (You might want to specify that for families, it's one dish per adult, or per a certain number of people—otherwise the single people bear an unfair burden.)

Afternoon Tea

A chance to bring out one's hats, gloves, and best china, teas usually feature a menu of dainty sandwiches, cakes, tarts, scones, and pastries. Nothing needs to be kept hot except, of course, the tea. This is a good setting in which to auction or raffle off thematic items such as a quilt, antiques, homemade jewelry, or tea sets (not just English—think Chinese, or Japanese, too).

Some charities, instead of holding one big tea, encourage members to hold simultaneous tea parties for friends at their homes.

Food Tastings

A food-tasting event has two particular advantages: It appeals to people's curiosity and desire for variety, and it allows you to approach a number of businesses for small contributions, with the assurance that their products will be the focal point of your event. Alternatively, you can make it a potluck or challenge among your members, to produce their best chili, pie, or other fare.

What might your guests want to taste? Wines, cheese, champagne, chocolates, ice cream, or other desserts, microbrewed or other beer, whiskey, and signature dishes by local chefs or restaurants, are all possibilities.

Because part of the point of a tasting is to learn and compare, be sure to include detailed information on each offering (with the help of the donor).

Themed Meals

Holidays, regional specialties, and your group's own mission all offer opportunities to create interesting themed meals. For example, the mayor's office in Lansing, Michigan, holds an annual Ramadan Unity Dinner, commemorating the Muslim holy month and its tradition of fasting, while raising money for local food banks. Middle Eastern cuisine is on the menu.

Free Events With Food and Drinks for Sale

It's possible to have a food-related fundraiser where food isn't billed as the main draw. You entice people in the door with something that doesn't cost you much to put on, such as a movie, Easter egg hunt, or a reading by a local author, then sell popcorn, coffee, or other snacks.

For example, Edie Boatman, a volunteer board member at the German Immersion Foundation in Wisconsin (which supports two German-immersion public schools in Milwaukee) says, "We sometimes hold a 'Kinder Kino' in the school gym—Kino means movie in German. We show a popular movie, such as *Shrek*, only it's been dubbed into German. Whole families come. We sell mostly donated food, such as popcorn donated by movie theatres, drinks, and other snacks. It's an easy, effective way to raise money."

> **CAUTION**
>
> **Choose a viewing site with a license to show movies.** There's a common myth that if you don't charge admission, or you've bought the DVD, you don't have to worry about publicly showing the movie. Not so. The federal Copyright Act equires that, for any showings outside the home, either you or the owner of the viewing site have obtained a license. (There's an educational exemption for classroom use, but the audience must comprise only students.) With any luck, your school, library, or group has already bought an annual license. If it hasn't, get in touch with a service such as the Motion Picture Licensing Corporation (www.mplc.com), Swank Motion Pictures, Inc. (www.swank.com), or Movie Licensing USA (a division of Swank, for K-12 schools; www.movlic.com/k12/index.html.) The annual license is probably more cost-effective, but you can also buy a one-time license for a particular showing.

House Parties

A house party is an event where you don't charge admission, but invite between ten and 40 of your core supporters or friends to someone's home, often that of a board member. You serve beverages and food (hors d'oeuvres or dessert are fine, rather than a full meal). The object is to create a mostly social evening, in which supporters get to know one another and learn more about your group's latest efforts and activities.

The house party should feature remarks by a group leader or board officer about your current goals and why you need financial support. At the end of the talk, you ask people to take out their checkbooks or otherwise pledge their support to your organization. Given the intimacy of the evening, and the degree of efforts that the hosts have gone to in welcoming a select group of people, this is an appropriate setting in which to ask for large gifts.

CAUTION

The invitation should make the purpose of the event clear. Your guests will resent it if you play "bait and switch," pretending that the party is an ordinary social event when it's actually part fundraiser. Also, you want to make sure that your guests bring their checkbooks or credit cards.

Plan ahead of time exactly who will address the group and when the pitch for financial support will occur. Aim for a point after the party has gained momentum, but before anyone is thinking of leaving.

CAUTION

Make sure the host and other key speakers are prepared to ask for money! If not, you'll face a similar situation as did Gretchen Lightfoot, Development Director at the Harmony Project (a Los Angeles-based nonprofit providing music mentoring to at-risk youth): "The hostess stood up after the founder's pitch and said 'I'm not comfortable asking people for money.' It really took the wind out of everyone's sails, and no doubt reduced the level of donations. But it highlighted for us that if there's any discomfort about the fundraising part of such an event, you need to put it out there and work it through BEFORE the event."

Big Parties

If you're looking for an informal, festive atmosphere, without the need to provide a sit-down meal, any theme you can think up provides an excuse for a fundraising party. The St. Paul Friends of the Library's Oktoberfest, for example, features "books and beer, food and wine, German music and dancing, scavenging and tours, and games of brawn and skill. Oh, and librarians."

Search for "fundraising party" online and you'll find a slew of suggestions: tailgating parties, ice cream socials, chocolate lovers' brunches, an Oscar night party, eating contests, and themes such as Western, Renaissance, Moroccan, the roaring 20s, the kitschy Fifties, the grooving Sixties, disco, Mardi Gras, or a favorite movie or musical. (One group simply advertised "BIGGGGGG PARTY!")

You'll also encounter various companies that want to sell you accoutrements for events, such as a murder mystery game. Choose wisely, and don't forget that themes in keeping with your mission are most likely to attract your membership.

Gala Cocktail Hours or Dinners

Holding a gala event for a large group of people isn't something your group should do without prior events experience, because of the potential for cost overruns and overuse of people's time (and eventually goodwill). Sue Hall, a nonprofit consultant whom the Friends group hires to coordinate Opus & Olives says, "At first, I tried to refuse taking this on even as a paid consulting job! I hadn't coordinated events before, and knew that, as wonderful an event as Opus & Olives is, the Friends staff had been exhausting themselves putting it together. I didn't want to get overwhelmed by the details. Now I've been coordinating this event for long enough that it's a fairly seamless process, but I put in about 50 hours a week in the final weeks leading up to it."

Once you're ready, however, gala events are a great way to raise visibility in the community, attract major sponsorships and important guests, establish connections with people of influence, and hold silent auctions and other revenue-gaining events that bring in sizable donations.

Apart from following the advice in this book, there's no better way to learn the traditions and expectations of gala events than to sign up to attend or volunteer at a few yourself. Talk to friends or check your community calendar.

If you feel you've got the community and corporate support with which to make such an event a success, how do you begin? Sue Hall advises: "I'd probably try to get a really good team of volunteers together, who would give it their best shot; maybe five people who'd say, 'We're willing to try it for a year, to see if it's wise.' That will create some traction. Hiring an events coordinator can take some of the load off, but it probably won't be financially feasible in the early years. Wait until your event can be counted on to net a profit of at least $20,000—at an absolute minimum."

Key Preparatory Steps

Start with a core group of decision makers and volunteers (recruited using the principles outlined in Chapter 2). Then divide the following tasks below among them, perhaps in committees corresponding to the headings below.

Schedule Wisely

See the tips in Chapter 7 for scheduling. The good news is, there's almost no time of year when people aren't interested in food. In fact, building your event around the season can be fun, by having a harvest banquet or an "edible flowers" spring lunch. Or who could resist the event put on by the Plumas County Museum in Quincy, California, in autumn of 2010: "A Grave Occasion: Digging Up the Past." Held at the Quincy Cemetery, it featured a cemetery tour, dinner, silent auction, and more.

Plan a Budget and Ticket Price

Your main expenses, depending on your group's existing assets and what you're getting donated, may include food and beverages; rentals of a hall, tables, chairs, and electrical equipment; plates, cups, and utensils; printing invitations and programs; postage for invitations and thank-yous; insurance;

and decorations. If volunteers will be preparing the meal, you may need to rent special equipment, such as warming trays and coffee urns.

> **TIP**
>
> **"Sound, light, and electrical services are our single largest line item,"** says adviser Grace Boone regarding the Women of Taste food and wine tasting that she coordinates (described in Chapter 7). "Our vendor discounts his services by a good bit, but people are usually shocked to hear that I write him a check for around $16,000—and it's worth every penny. If he weren't there, people would notice. We take a space that has virtually no electricity (a rooftop garden) and transform it into a beautifully lit banquet area. The electricity allows the live bands to be heard, the chefs to provide hot food, the coffee shop to serve hot coffee, and more. Our chefs have told us horror stories about events where they didn't have enough electricity to power, for example, the freezer for the ice cream, and it all just melted."

How much should you charge for admission? Try to make the amount comparable to other fundraisers in your area, and to what people would pay for the same meal at a restaurant. For example, Kim Litland, Director of the Brookfield Public Library in Illinois and an organizer of their annual "Taste of Brookfield," explains: "We charge $35 a ticket, and it's all you can eat or drink. We're in a middle-class community, so this price matches our residents' spending habits. Almost all the food is donated by local restaurants and businesses, and we hold the event right in the library. It's very social; people come to see and be seen. We earned about $9,500 last year from a combination of ticket sales, a silent auction, and a raffle."

For community meals where the whole family will attend, it's customary to set a sliding scale based on age. For example, you might set a discount for kids under 18, and allow little ones, age two or less, to get in free.

Attend to Food Quality

Filling, tasty food served at the promised time will put people in a good mood and bring them back next year. But tiny portions, overcooked pasta, or having to wait until 3 p.m. to be served the "breakfast" pancakes will be remembered and complained about many years later. (There's a reason that fundraising dinners are sometimes referred to as the "rubber chicken circuit.")

As an example of how important food is, despite the fact that the Women of Taste event described in Chapter 7 includes not only wine and food tasting but live music, socializing, a silent auction, and more, coordinator Grace Boone says: "We did a survey of our guests this year, and discovered that 68% of them come for the food!"

If volunteers will be doing the cooking, they should consult with a professional about how best to prepare, cook for a crowd, and get hot food on the tables at the appropriate time. Cooking for five people is not the same as cooking for 50. Borrowing use of a restaurant kitchen and renting warming pans may be a good idea.

Select a Location

Choosing and securing a location is one of the earliest details you'll need to take care of. First off, you'll have to make sure the venue is available for booking. That allows you to announce it in any "Save the Date" notifications or on your website. If a certain space is clearly the cheapest or best, it's also important to know that, for purposes of decisions about how many guests the place will fit and other details. See the tips on choosing a great location and signing a contract with the venue owner in Chapter 7.

Choose and Plan Additional Income-Producing Activities

Adding mini-fundraisers to the main one will help maximize both fun and profits. Auctions are popular in this regard, particularly silent auctions. A full-scale live auction can overwhelm an event, so think twice if you want the food to be the focus—though you could have a very short auction, for example, where people bid on special desserts, or even on entrees. Other possibilities include a raffle, contest, or booths with items for sale.

Plan Emcee, Speakers, and Entertainment

For even the most basic event, it helps to have a group leader or other emcee to welcome people and direct the ceremonies. A high-profile or celebrity emcee can make people feel like this is an important event from the get-go. For formal events, it's also customary to have a few speakers or awardees, a video, music, or other entertainment.

Don't just leap at any celebrity or performer that one of your members has a connection with. Make sure that the person or group is actually interesting to your audience, and capable of speaking engagingly to a crowd. Your guests do not want to watch your emcee try out his or her amateur comedic routines. Sue Hall adds, "We had one author who sang for five minutes at the end of the program. Everyone sat with their mouths open."

This is also your opportunity to give people a feeling of personal connection with your organization. A few words from your board president and other leader (such as an executive director, school principal, coach, or library director) are practically de rigueur. No need for a 20-minute lecture, however. "We really try to keep the talking heads to a minimum at Opus & Olives," Sue Hall notes. "The library director makes a few remarks, but that's it, except for the author guests. People come because it's a literary event and a big party, and they don't want to hear a lot of yada yada. Reminding people what the event is about is important, but we do that within the collateral material sent out ahead of time, within the program for the evening, and via a really cool slide show that we have going on five screens around the room (including onstage) during dinner and dessert. It shows the activities of the library (with images of patrons, kids in the homework help centers, and so forth) and thanks corporate sponsors and individual table hosts."

Making sure your speakers stay within their allotted time is a perennial challenge. We asked adviser Peter Pearson how to deal with this. He says, "You'll inevitably run into the occasional emcee or speaker who oversteps the boundaries and speaks for too long. We brief each speaker in advance, explaining, 'We've got a full evening planned, and it really needs to go quickly, so you need to limit yourself to X number of minutes.' As reinforcement, we recently added a light to the Opus & Olives podium, which can be remote controlled from the back of the ballroom. After the author has spoken for 15 minutes, we flash the light. Only the author sees it. If the author nevertheless keeps talking, we flash the light again two to three minutes later. Almost no one will ignore the second flashing light."

Plan for Interesting Visuals

Before people sit down, they'll enjoy having something to look at and use for conversation starters. Helpful possibilities include photos, children's artwork, or other illustrations of your group's activities. After people have sat down, they might also enjoy a brief video presentation highlighting your organization's work. This should include some touches of fun and humor—no one likes to sit through a slick public service announcement.

Assemble a List of Invitees

To make your event a success, you'll need to have a robust mailing list—try to invite about four to five times the number of people whom you hope to attend.

Also brainstorm about anyone beyond your membership who might be interested in receiving an invitation—past business sponsors, members of nearby, kindred groups (such as affiliated religious organizations or parents of the middle school to which your elementary school students graduate), alumni, or simply friends of your members. Don't exclude people who live far away—inviting them adds to the buzz, and if they don't happen to be in town that day, they may send a contribution in any case.

Adviser Peter Pearson says, "One thing that has helped us tremendously is to invite representatives of the publishing industry to our events. They love attending, and this helps motivate them to the find the best authors for us as presenters."

Design, Print, and Send Out Invitations—Then Follow Up

Send "Save the Date" emails to your mailing list as soon as you've got the basic date, time, and place worked out—up to five months beforehand. Follow those with printed invitations, from 60 to 90 days before the event. Or, if it's appropriate to the informality of the event and your membership, use Evite (which saves resources and postage!).

The look of your invitations—or even your Evite page—should reflect the tone of the event, whether it's to be a black-tie ball downtown or an informal evening in your church meeting hall. For the black-tie events, it's best to not only send an elegant printed invitation, but include a return envelope with which people can buy tickets or make donations. For a less formal event, you can get away with directing people to buy tickets online, or asking them to call or contact a particular person.

Opus & Olives Invitation

It's the rare event where the needed number of guests sign up without a nudge, however. Get a phone or email tree going, and have friends call friends, to encourage them to sign up. For people who say yes, urge them to send a check in right away—and call back if you don't hear from them within a week or two.

Solicit Cash Sponsorships From Businesses

How to approach businesses for cash sponsorships is described in Chapter 4.

Arrange Publicity for the Event

Event promotion and publicity are covered in Chapter 7, so we won't repeat that material here—except to add Peter Pearson's advice that, "The profitability of your dinner event is directly linked to not only lining up an array of corporate sponsors, but ideally to getting a media sponsor that makes in-kind contributions of publicity. We've developed a long history of working with the daily newspaper here in St. Paul. It's a natural fit, since we both care about readers. The newspaper now provides us five half-page ads in advance of our events, complete with the names of our corporate sponsors and their logos (at certain sponsorship levels). Our biggest sponsor of Opus & Olives, at $30,000, is named as a 'presenting sponsor' in large font, with a huge logo. That's the kind of recognition corporate sponsors are really looking for."

Solicit Donations of Food or Supplies

Chapter 4 describes how to solicit donations from businesses. If you've got contacts in a restaurant or other business who are willing to supply most of the food, great. Sue Hall has made a remarkable success of this strategy: "I recruited a man who'd been on the Friends board and owns several wine and liquor stores to be one of my cochairs, and he now donates all the wine to Opus & Olives. That has saved us a lot of money."

If you can't get a major donation like this one, try bringing a combination of food from various places—like the "Taste of Brookfield" mentioned above.

Prepare Written Materials

For both internal purposes and for the public, you'll want to prepare an event program and possibly an ad book. The program should contain basic information like the timetable, the names of the emcee and speakers, and more. This is also a handy place to sell ad space and thank your sponsors again. Ad books are described in Chapter 7.

Sell Tickets Ahead of Time

Allowing people to buy tickets at the door makes it too easy for them to back out at the last minute. (It also adds to the amount of cash being handled by your registration people, which creates risk.) If you feel it's important to have some tickets available at the door, at least create an incentive to buying tickets early by raising the price for people who wait.

Don't just sit back passively and wait for people to buy tickets. Challenge each of your leaders and core volunteers to sell a certain number. Repeat this challenge if sales are slow—don't give in to the temptation to start giving out tickets for free just to fill the room.

Some businesses prefer to sponsor an event by buying a table's worth of tickets, which allows it to display its name on that table and have its employees mingle with community members—also known as potential customers.

Create Table Layout and Seating Charts

You'll find it helpful to measure your space, and the tables, and create a little map of how the tables will be arranged within the room (unless the venue does this for you). Visualize how people will move through the space, especially if great numbers of them will be heading in one direction at one time, such as to a buffet line. This can be dealt with by staggering the times at which you invite different tables to join the line.

Unless your dinner will be informal, a seating chart can help maximize people's enjoyment and make sure that top donors are strategically placed next to board members, leaders, or interesting honorees. Don't get too creative about mixing people up, however—if you know that some are friends, put them together. Sue Hall warns, "It takes us a lot of hours to create a seating chart for our 800 guests at Opus & Olives. The corporate sponsors (who've paid the most) always go up at the front, then we work toward the back depending mostly on ticket prices. In some cases, book clubs or groups of friends will buy tables together. If not, we try to figure out whether we know anything about the guests and who should sit together. We try to be accommodating, even allowing people to request whom they want to sit with."

For a large event, create an easy way for people to find their way to their table, such as a number on a flag in the centerpiece.

Plan "Day of Event" Assignments

Figure out every possible task that people might need to handle on event day, and then either assign volunteers or hire professionals to carry them out. For the more complex roles, you'll want to hold trainings, following the principles laid out in Chapter 7. The job assignments might include, for example:

- Leaders, emcee, and speakers. Make sure each understands exactly what role to play on event day and at what time to be ready to get on stage or otherwise take charge.

- Coordinator with the venue (someone to pick up the keys or otherwise interact with whoever's in charge of the facility)

- Pickup and delivery crew (for gathering any donations of food, drink, decorations, or other items from off site)
- Setup and decorations crew
- Cooks and bartenders (if you haven't hired a caterer)
- Check-in crew, greeters, ushers, and ticket takers (using entry tickets is particularly important if people will be mingling with the public in between checking in and entering the event hall)
- Food servers and waiters (if you won't be hiring the venue's staff)
- Child care, if children are allowed at your event but who may need to be kept occupied during quiet or serious portions
- Photographers, to take pictures for future publicity and for your website or newsletter
- People to pass the hat or otherwise collect donations, if you'll be making a pitch
- A few miscellaneous crew members, to call upon for backup or special assignments
- Cleanup crew
- Two financially responsible people to count up and deposit any earnings, either from late ticket purchases or other on-site sales. (See the suggested financial controls described in Chapter 1.)

Some training can be appropriate for certain volunteer positions—or, at a minimum, lots of communication to make sure everyone understands the basic goals and timing of the event. Young or inexperienced volunteers might, for example, think that they're being friendly by telling people, "Oh, don't worry about that donation jar," or by chatting up customers when you need them to be getting food on the tables, quick.

Call or email your volunteers a day or two before the event, asking for them to confirm their attendance.

Create a Day-of-Event Timeline

See Chapter 7 for a sample.

Plan What to Do With the Leftovers

It has become traditional to donate leftovers to a food bank, homeless shelter, or battered women's shelter. And it's a fine idea—although not required. If you've got a number of volunteers who are not wealthy themselves, and would appreciate having some food for the coming week's meals, you might instead plan to divide the leftovers among them. Bring lots of containers or foil!

Holding Your Dinner Event

Even if your event is in the evening, your core organizers will need to start the day early, double-checking that all preparatory tasks have been done and supplies have been picked up, checking the phone and email for last minute cancellations, reservations, or questions, readying supplies (such as the cashbox), and monitoring the arrival of any out-of-town speakers or performers.

Depending on the complexity and size of the event, you'll want to get to the venue a few hours ahead of time for setup, to check on the sound equipment, and to verify that all your requests have been met.

Once the event begins, getting people in the door efficiently is your first important task. We've already recommended having well-staffed registration tables, but someone in charge should keep an eye on the lines. If they're getting long, either assign helpers or create distractions, by serving snacks and saying hello to the people waiting.

A leader should also keep an eye on the clock and timeline throughout the event, and prompt anyone who seems not to realize that it's time to give the welcome speech, close down any auxiliary fundraisers such as an auction, or serve dessert.

At some point during the evening, when spirits are high, consider having a leader of your organization deliver a brief fundraising pitch, as described in Chapter 7.

Event Follow-Up

Apart from evaluating the event and assembling a written file for future event organizers as described in Chapter 7, your most important task after the event is to send out thank-yous to everyone involved.

As soon as possible, send letters to guests, speakers, the emcee, your volunteers, and business sponsors. There's a sample thank-you letter in Chapter 1. You might want to add some interesting tidbits, such as how much the event raised overall, or a reminder of where to get the chocolate dessert that was voted everyone's favorite.

Personalize the letter for anyone who put in extraordinary efforts. If, for example, a person or a company filled a whole table with guests, mention that. ●

Auctions: Live, Silent, and Online

Meet Your Adviser

George Hofbauer, Principal, St. Joseph School (kindergarten through 8th grade) in Seattle, Washington, and board member of the Fulcrum Foundation, which provides financial assistance to promote and support Catholic schools in the Archdiocese of Seattle.

What he does: "I teach one class in American History, and I'm the outward face of St. Joseph. That means acting as liaison to the parish and church staff and dealing with the governance structures, including the school board, finance committee, development committee, buildings and grounds committee, parent association, and endowment board. I'm always very involved in our annual fundraising auction, which goes for two days and includes both silent and live bidding. In fact, for 15 years I served as the auctioneer!"

Earliest memory of taking part in a charitable activity: "That was about two weeks after I'd accepted the job here at St. Joseph, when I was in my early twenties. I realized that the school had absolutely no money—in fact, it was in debt. This happened to be during the oil embargo, when people could get a tax write-off for donating big cars, so we started soliciting vehicle donations and selling cars straight out of the parking lot. We also tried a few other dubious schemes, like a worm farm. We raised the worms on the third floor of the school—until the cow manure required for the worms to live in made the whole place stink. Eventually we figured out smarter ways to raise money."

Likes best about his work: "Meeting the many different types of people who are interested in providing quality education. The high point of my day, however, remains the teaching. The energy of the kids, and the interplay back and forth with them, gives me life. Those 8th graders are a ball of fire."

Top tip for people new to nonprofit fundraising: "My first one is, don't let the task intimidate you. If the tasks were easy, they wouldn't be worth the effort. The second one is, don't let the 'No' answers stop you from asking people to help or donate. It's a statistical thing—if you keep on asking, sooner or later you'll get 'Yes' answers, so you've got to keep going until you get what you need."

Some of your members may shy away from making outright donations—but will eagerly sign up to attend an auction. This type of fundraising event is fun, it lets people shop for things they'd never find at the local mall, and it offers the prospect of snagging a major prize or bargain. Bargain hunters shouldn't, of course, be your only participants if you hope to get high bids, but they're a large and necessary part of the bidding community. This chapter will tell you how to organize auctions and how to make them work for your fundraising purposes—and how to motivate guests to get past the bargain-hunting mentality.

Is an Auction Right for Your Organization?

The first question on your mind is probably, "How much can we earn?" Established, well-organized auctions often bring in major returns, from $150,000 to $400,000. Starting out, however, figures of between $2,000 and $10,000 are more common—but could go higher, depending on the resources and energy your group puts into the event, and the size of your likely audience.

As you developed your chart of organizational assets, you might have noticed some that would serve you well in holding an auction. These might include:

- a good-sized group of volunteers (an absolute minimum of 20 or 30, and more as the event gets larger)
- access to an appropriate venue
- enough interested members to show up and bid at reasonably high levels
- contacts with merchants, professionals, or skilled members who will donate potential items for bidding or provide sponsorships and other assistance, and perhaps even
- a professional auctioneer.

Take a closer look at the size of your membership list. If you've only got 100 active members to begin with, an auction may not be ideal for your organization—unless all your board members and other volunteers can commit to bringing a certain number of their friends to the event. (The exception might be an online auction, discussed below, where every one of your members can participate, plus their friends, contacts, and others.)

> **TIP**
>
> **There's a reason auctions work as school fundraisers.** George Hofbauer explains, "Parents have a personal interest in supporting their kids, so they'll show up and bid. I've auctioneered for smaller groups, such as Girl Scout troops, where there wasn't that built-in audience. You have to put in a lot more work to get people to attend. When that work hasn't been done, it's sad to watch, with top-quality stuff being sold for, say, a mere $100."

How Much Planning and Work Will Be Required?

There's good news and bad news here. We'll start with the bad: Procuring items for bidding can take huge amounts of time. You'll already be dealing with the planning and publicity that comes with putting on any special event, and on top of that you'll have to approach merchants or other donors, pick up items, create certificates for intangibles such as dinner at a board member's house, assemble gift baskets or packages, display the items attractively, and send out thank-you letters to every gift-giver (and buyer).

This is more than one or two people can pull off alone—you'll need a good-sized group of dedicated volunteers. On the positive side, it's easy work to divvy up. Reasonably motivated volunteers will enjoy using their creativity to arrange unusual or desirable gifts and prizes.

Unless you're planning a small-scale, casual event, start your planning for a live or silent auction at least five to eight months ahead of time. George Hofbauer says, "We start planning next year's auction the minute one ends." For an online auction, two or three months is doable.

Key Preparatory Steps: Auctions

Here are the basics to setting up an auction, whether live, silent, or online. Many of the categories below might be appropriate for a small committee to work on.

As you can see from the number of steps, this presents an organizing challenge. Keep good records at every step, covering whom you've contacted for gifts, who gave or promised what, when and whether donated items have been picked up, where they're being stored, the items' retail values, who bid what amount at the auction, whether winning bidders have paid for and picked up their items, and so forth. (With an online auction, a certain amount of this information will be captured for you.)

> **RESOURCE**
> **Auction software can help with the record keeping.** Some well-regarded choices include Proven Benefit (www.provenbenefit.org) and MaestroSoft, by Northwest Benefit Solutions (www.maestrosoft.com).

Decide Whether to Hold a Live, Silent, or Online Auction

Let's first examine the distinctions among the three main types of auctions:

- A **live auction** is one where an auctioneer (preferably a professional) is at the helm, and people call out or otherwise indicate their bids. The highest bidder wins.

- A **silent auction** is one where people write bids on sheets of paper, placed next to displays of the items up for auction. There's little time pressure; people can go back to see whether they've been outbid, then write in higher bids. At an appointed time, you close the bidding, and later announce winners or let people check for their names on the bid sheets. (One interesting variation is to make the bidding secret, with bidders slipping sheets of paper into a box. The theory is that someone who really wants the item will bid extra high, to outpace the competition.)

- An **online auction** is one in which items are displayed, with photographs, on an auction site such as MissionFish (a 501(c)(3) nonprofit that has an exclusive relationship with eBay), IDonateToCharity.org (which offers a flat-fee payment structure rather than taking a commission on items sold), or BiddingForGood (formerly known as cMarket). Participants register, enter credit card information (which means guaranteed payment for you from the winning bidders), and place their bids within a set period of time, ideally one to three weeks.

Which type of auction should you choose? There's nothing quite like the excitement of a live auction, with audience members locked in competition and a skilled auctioneer whipping them into a frenzy. If you know of or can afford a good auctioneer, and would like the auction to be the focal point of your event, it's worth going this route. Live auctions usually bring in bids close to or in excess of the items' market value, while silent auctions bring in only about half their market value. Even the people who start out looking for a bargain may, at a live auction, get caught up in the action and spend a lot of money, having to remind themselves that, "At least it was for a good cause."

But perhaps your group is looking for something lower key, for example, to be held in a side room during your annual dinner. A silent auction can be conducted quietly, without disturbing speakers or cocktail hour conversation. And silent auctions reportedly attract greater participation by women, some of whom may draw back from the highly charged bidding environment of live auctions. One drawback, from a profit-making perspective, is that many attendees at silent auctions place only one bid, and then move on. Perhaps caught up in talking to friends, they forget to go back and see whether they've been outbid, until the last few minutes when they hear an announcement that the silent auction is about to end. That's why some experts recommend not placing anything on the silent auction table that you'd hope to sell for more than $500.

An online auction is quieter still! It might be your best choice if you aren't ready to fill a room with people, your members are spread out geographically, or you want to be able to open the bidding up to the whole world (which you can do if your service links up to a portal such as BiddingForGood.com). In fact, no matter where your members live, some will appreciate being able to participate in a fundraising event at any time of the day or night, without having to leave their home. Demographically, women between the ages of 40 and 49, with household incomes between $50,000 and $99,000, are the most frequent participants in online auctions. If that group is well represented in your organization, you may do very well. Don't forget that up to 100% of your members and even the world at large will have access to an online auction. And they won't have to pay admission or line up a babysitter.

Another advantage to online auctions is that you won't need the army of volunteers that are required to set up an auction space and create attractive displays. A few volunteers who are eBay savvy, and perhaps have time to spare at odd hours, can handle the setup end of the process. Then you'll need a few more volunteers to take care of shipping or delivering items once they're sold. (If you don't want to ship overseas, be sure to put that into the "special instructions" of your online auction site.)

"Another advantage to auctioning items online is that it's lower risk, particularly for fragile items," says Hilary Cooper, a parent volunteer and co-chair of Spring Fling 2011 (a Piedmont, California, Tri-School Fundraiser). "Fancy bottles of wine, for example, can be an issue—by the time you've stored them at the school and transported them to the hotel, their value has dropped in the eyes of the people most likely to buy them—the aficionados who know exactly what temperature wine is supposed to be kept at."

The online auction method isn't free; you'll have to pay the hosting website or auction service provider. Someone will also need to pay for shipping, but you can specify ahead of time whether it's the buyer or the organization.

TIP

You can combine types of auctions. For example, some nonprofits hold a live and silent auction during the same event (which helps sell more, while limiting the time spent on the live auction). Some hold an online auction before a silent auction, in order to reduce the number of goods they'll have to display. It's also possible to integrate an online auction with a live auction. People begin bidding online before the live auction, with the highest online bid serving as the live auction starting bid. Online bidders may also be able to enter a maximum dollar amount for an item ahead of time, which is kept private from other bidders but told to a volunteer proxy who bids on that person's behalf. Another option is to hold an online auction after your live or silent auction, to deal with items you didn't have room for, or that didn't sell.

As for which method is most profitable, that depends. Different items may sell better at the different types of events. For example, an expensive vacation for six will probably receive higher bids at a live or online auction than a silent one; while an item that needs to be examined up close or tried on will probably do better at a silent auction than an online or live one.

To amp up participants' willingness to bid high, find ways to remind them of the auction's purpose to raise money toward a specific and important goal. In a live auction, the auctioneer will play a role in doing that. In silent or online auctions, you'll want to make sure that visual or written reminders are featured prominently on your display tables or website, and that roving members of your group talk up the items on the tables and steer people toward them.

Decide Whether the Auction Will Be the Main Event

The degree to which the auction is the main event will help you make decisions about its scale and budget. Just remember that you can't do it all: A full, live auction is most commonly a central focus, and shouldn't be stuffed into an event that also features dinner, dancing, performances, videos, and speeches. But a silent or online auction can make a fun addition to another event. Or you can have an event serve as an advertising teaser for your online auction, by displaying the auction items during the event such as a gala dinner, but not open the bidding until afterward.

In cases where the auction will be the main event, consider heightening the fun by serving food (whether appetizers, a meal, or dessert) and drink, and choosing a theme. George Hofbauer says, "Themes can be fun to play off of. One year we chose 'It's a Wonderful Life,' and created a video highlighting the story of St. Joe's as it would have been without the auction, broke and struggling."

You'll find suggestions on creating a successful meal event in Chapter 8. Avoid all-you-can-eat dinner buffets, which will mean your guests are either standing in line, distracted, or stuffed when you want their attention on bidding. Better to go with waiter service or finger foods.

Set Your Participation, Procurement, and Earning Goals

To make sure your auction will earn money, it helps to identify workable goals for the number of people who will attend, how many items will be available for bidding, and how much these items will earn upon sale.

Optimally, you'll want 200 or more people in your auction-bidding audience (whether the auction is live, silent, or online, and not counting children). The lower the number drops below 200, the higher the odds become that items you're selling won't happen to suit the needs or tastes of this limited group. There's no point in even considering an auction if you expect to attract fewer than 25 people. Also try to have at least two people per item to be auctioned, so that there's decent competition for each item.

Children tend to be a distraction at auctions, so some groups prohibit them entirely. If this feels too harsh, consider creating a separate area for entertaining or babysitting the young ones.

> **CAUTION**
> **With too few silent auction bidders, some get stuck buying more than they'd expected.** "At our annual dinner," explains Helen, from a nonprofit in Berkeley, California, "one attendee—who happened to be a major donor—ended up as the top bidder on nearly a dozen items. She wasn't happy. We reviewed the bid sheets with her and got some second-place bidders to agree to buy the items after all, until she felt comfortable with her total outlay. This isn't something I'd want to do often."

Once you've decided what size audience your event can attract and accommodate, estimate how much each person—or, given typical spending patterns, each couple—will be willing to spend. It's usually not more than $1,000 per person or couple per evening, though this of course depends on local culture and demographics. Let's imagine that you're aiming for an audience of 100 people, 70 of whom are in couples (so you'll count them as 35 people), and 15 of whom are unlikely to bid (perhaps because they're honorees or on comp tickets). This leaves you with 60 active bidders. You figure they're willing and able to make average bids of $300 apiece. That would make it possible for your auction to raise 60 x $300, or $18,000. Not bad, at least for starters.

Now you need enough goods for them to eagerly spend that money on. To reach a goal of $18,000, you'd need to procure donated items whose worth is at least double that amount, or $36,000. That rule recognizes the fact that, while some bids will go over the items' market value (and the live auctioneer will be doing everything possible to make sure they do), many others will go for lower.

For a live auction, it's also best to have enough individual items to fill between 30 minutes and two hours of bidding, which typically means around ten to 40 items. For an online auction, you're not limited by time or display space, and can bring in as many items as you think you can feasibly deal with handling, storing, and shipping.

Plan a Budget

Your major expenses, depending on your existing assets and what you're getting donated, may include a hall rental, food and beverages, decorations (unless you can borrow them from another group), an excellent sound system for a live auction (don't blast people with the typical sound system that's loud in front and quiet at the back of the room, or you'll lose bids), printing of catalogs and programs, clipboards and pens, and the auctioneer or Web host's fee.

Got a truck? Ask around to see if a member will provide one for ferrying auction items to the hall—if not, you might need to rent one.

Many fundraisers suggest working at least one free drink per person into the budget, to loosen guests up before the bidding begins. George Hofbauer adds, "Of course, we have to be responsible, and have designated drivers ready. But if you were to hold the same auction with and without drinks available, it's practically guaranteed you'd earn more at the one with drinks."

Hilary Cooper, a parent volunteer in Piedmont, California, echoes, "One year I was involved with a school auction where we ended up with not enough food, but plenty of alcohol. People were whooping it up, spending at all-time highs. The last item was a cruise to Alaska, and at the last minute a friend of mine raised her paddle at $3,000—I thought her husband was going to have a heart attack. The following year, we found a fancier place, with caterers who made the yummiest food. Everyone ate like crazy, but didn't drink as much. The live auction was a dud."

On the income side of the ledger, you can plan to charge admission (discussed below), sell ad space in your catalog (discussed in Chapter 7), solicit business sponsorships along with donations of goods (discussed in Chapter 4), hold raffles or balloon pops (discussed in Chapter 5), sell a signature drink (described in Chapter 7), and of course, bring in profits from the items auctioned off.

Set an Admission Charge

Will you charge admission? If you won't be serving food, and it's your first year, a charge might deter people who don't yet trust you to pull off a quality auction. In all other situations, however, asking people to buy tickets—in advance, no less—not only brings in guaranteed profits, but emphasizes that this is an important event for which you'd like committed participation. If key people might not be able to afford the tickets, you can set aside comps for them and other honored guests.

See whether you can reasonably charge an amount that covers your costs, so that all of your auction proceeds are gravy. Anywhere from $15 to $150 is considered an appropriate auction ticket price, though for the higher figures, be prepared to deliver a swanky event. Ask around, too, to see whether there's a typical auction ticket price in your geographic area. Hilary Cooper notes, "To make our Spring Fling auction less exclusive, we recently hit on a strategy of giving people a choice: pay $175 to attend the whole event, with sit-down dinner and live auction, or $75 to attend the cocktails and pre-dinner silent auction only."

> **TIP**
>
> **Have the guests bid on dessert!** You can both save on food costs and create a separate profit center by getting donations of as many unique cakes, pies, or sets of cupcakes as you have tables, and then asking each table to place a bid. The highest-bidding table chooses the first dessert, and so on.

Schedule Wisely

See the tips in Chapter 7 for scheduling. Many nonprofits choose to hold auctions in the fall, for people beginning to buy holiday gifts but not yet in a state of shopping fatigue. Research has found that over two thirds of bidders in online auctions are shopping for gifts.

For silent or live auctions, weekend evenings are generally best, so that guests won't mind staying late. If there's a reason to choose a weekday, consider starting early, such as at 5:30, so that people can get home in time for a good night's sleep. Plan to feed them dinner, too.

Choose a Location

If you've already got a location in mind, perhaps your school's auditorium or board member's extra-large living room, great, If not, this is one of the earliest details you'll need to take care of, both to make sure the venue is available, and so you can announce it in any "Save the Date" notifications or on your website. Choose wisely: Adviser George Hofbauer says, "Location is the number one factor in the success of your event (followed by a good sound system and the technological ability to process everything properly)." Look for a venue that's:

- indoors, particularly in the case of a live auction; you don't want people's attention to wander

- large enough to seat your intended audience and let them socialize, as well as display items you plan to sell (figure on one foot of space per item, and nearly six feet between rows of tables), but not so large that guests feel lost or warehoused

- well-lit enough that people can see what they're bidding on, ideally with lighting controls for dimming during meals and spotlights on the live auctioneer

- convenient for your likely attendees, ideally with public transport options and plenty of parking

- able to accommodate your needs, such as to set up displays the day before, and allow people to pick up their items the day after, and

- if you're holding a live auction, has a high-quality sound system or acoustics—though this is rare, so you may need to plan to bring in your own system regardless.

Of course, if you'll be combining the auction with another event, such as a wine-tasting or dinner, you'll need to factor in your other needs for the space. Also see the general tips on choosing a location in Chapter 7.

Choose an Auctioneer (Live Auction Only)

The services of a professional auctioneer—who may, in fact, come with a staff of helpers—will probably cost several thousand dollars (sometimes depending on your earnings level). Of course, a true professional will earn back the salary and then some, through the art of pacing the bidding appropriately, inspiring audience enthusiasm, and knowing how to deal with issues like a lull in the bidding. Jackie T., who coordinated her children's school auction in Portland, Oregon, noted, "Hiring a professional auctioneer was one of our bigger expenses, but it more than doubled what we've gotten out of people in years when we've used volunteer auctioneers. You just don't get that frantic energy going otherwise. The auctioneer knows clever ways to ham it up, for example by putting his arm around a bidder and saying, 'C'mon, Grandpa, don't you want your baby's kindergarten quilt?' then rushing across the room and saying something similar to another grandfather in the bidding."

There's a reason that the auctioneers prefer to bring their own staff. These folks have crucial roles—including "pointers," who alert the auctioneer to bids from audience members who might be hard to see; "recorders" on stage who write down the winning bidder's number on prepared bid sheets for each item; and "runners," who pick up the bid sheets from the recorders, run them to the person who made the winning bid to have them sign saying, "Yes I did," then leave one copy with that person and take the other copy to the checkout room.

That doesn't mean you can't incorporate your own people into the process. In fact, says Jackie T., "Our hired auctioneer suggested clever ways to us to have the kids help out—like having a little girl carry the quilt onstage that all the kindergarteners had helped make, with cutout patterns of their hands— it sold for several thousand dollars, our top revenue-producer for the live auction—or having the Cub Scouts get on stage in their uniforms to model the leaf raking that they'd do for the highest bidder."

Of course, the auctioneer is the face of the process, so you'll want to choose one you're comfortable with. Some audience members may have trouble getting used to a traditional commercial auctioneer's rapid-fire patter or sing-song chant—and as a result, become too confused or fearful to enter the bidding. And they'll probably be turned off by one whose demeanor comes across as slick. A Berkeley parent, for example, complained about an auctioneer trying to goad people into bidding higher with remarks like, "Oh, so the little lady holds the pursestrings, does she?" or "Well, I know what neighborhood he lives in, and he can certainly afford more than that bid. Give it up!"

So if you decide to hire a professional, find one who has actual experience with charity auctions, who inspires trust rather than contempt, and who will agree to talk in plain English. The National Auctioneers Association website at www.auctioneers.org has a "Find an Auctioneer" function, where you can choose "Benefit & Charity" as a specialty. Watch the auctioneer in action and check references before making the hire. We recommend signing a written agreement covering the auctioneer's fee and scope of services. He or she may already have a standard contract, but you can ask for changes or amendments.

As an alternative, it's possible to find a volunteer willing and able to take on the role of auctioneer (as George Hofbauer did for many years). The person should already be accustomed to being in front of an audience, and capable of quick pacing. Hofbauer recalls, "I found it similar to teaching;

you have to know how to multitask, and get into a flow. In fact, it's a rush—one year, I had a terrible pain in two teeth that needed root canals, and the pain was excruciating. My dentist came with a whole packet of needles, and every ten minutes I'd go backstage for another novocaine shot—it wore off almost instantly, due to the adrenalin. I was drooling. But I got a lot of pity bidding!"

If the volunteer auctioneer knows the audience members, that can be good for building rapport (so long as he or she refrains from pointed personal observations). The volunteer should then study up on auctioneering techniques and styles, either by attending auctions or going to YouTube and searching for "benefit auctioneer." The volunteer auctioneer will also need to do some homework on the items being sold (so as to explain them to the audience convincingly) as well as the bidding rules.

> **CAUTION**
>
> **Remind your auctioneer not to say "tax-deductible."** In trying to drive up bids, more than a few auctioneers have been known to call out things like, "C'mon folks, you'll help a cause and get a tax deduction!" The trouble is, this perpetuates the common—and false—perception that donors can deduct their entire bid. As discussed in Chapter 1, they can deduct only amounts over the fair market value of an auction item—possibly zero.

Send Out Invitations to Attend or Participate

Charity auctions tend to attract members of your group more than the world at large, so to make it a success, send members Save the Date emails as soon as you've got the basic date, time, and place worked out—up to five months beforehand. Follow those with printed invitations, from 60 to 90 days before the event.

The look of your invitations should reflect the tone of the event, whether it's to be a fancy gala downtown or an informal evening in your church meeting hall. Some school auctions have kids create the artwork.

Ask people to RSVP by buying tickets ahead of time. Why not just sell tickets at the door? It makes it too easy for people to change their minds at the last minute, and it adds to the amount of cash handled by your registration people. If you want to have some tickets available at the door, at least create an incentive to buy early by raising the price for people who don't do so. With any luck, you'll have a sellout event.

For an upscale event, your invitation package should include an RSVP form and return envelope. For a less formal event, you can get away with directing people to buy tickets online, or asking them to contact a particular person.

For an online auction, email is the customary way to invite participation, since your most likely bidders are already glued to their computer screen. Of course, you'll want to email more than once, before the event and then while the auction is underway, to encourage people to place bids.

Sample RSVP

Solicit Donations of Goods and Services

The key to making your silent or live auction profitable is to auction off mostly or entirely donated goods. Even items that attract low bids are pure profit for you—and will bring back the bargain hunters in subsequent years. Get this process started as soon as you know the date of your event. Having a committee of volunteers begin soliciting items three to six months before the event is optimal.

> **TIP**
>
> **You'll need photos of every item for an online auction.** In fact, multiple photos are best, as you know from your own online shopping experience.

Collecting a Wide Range of Auction Items

Your auction should have something for every type of audience member. For starters, gather items that suit different interests, such as tickets for travel, recreation, and sports; celebrity and sports memorabilia; gift certificates for dining, culture, and entertainment; health and beauty products and services (spa gift certificates are popular); arts and crafts and home décor; electronics; professional services; internships for young people; gifts for children (a hit with grandparents); and packages or unique experiences combining any of the above.

Prepare at least one or two big-ticket items, like the trip to Ireland in a private jet that was once featured at St. Joseph's live auction. If you can't get outright donations of such items, you may need to pay—hopefully at a discount—for parts of them. For example, George Hofbauer says, "We once received a donation of the use of a condo in Hawaii, but wanted to include airfare in the package. We accomplished this by soliciting cash donations."

Of course, the top items need to be within the financial reach of a reasonable number of your audience members. If your group has done a live or silent auction in past years, check the records to find out what the highest-yielding items were. (You might even go back to the same source for something similar.) As an example of how audience-driven the top-yielding items can be, the Suitcase Clinic, a student-run nonprofit at the University of California, Berkeley (which provides medical and hygiene services to the local homeless population), usually finds that review courses for the MCAT (Medical College Admissions Test) are big hits among its annual silent auction audience—who are mostly pre-med undergrads.

Avoid creating items that require a lot of conferring with friends or advance planning. For example, "A boat tour down the Nile for ten, next month" would require figuring out which friends are available and whether they've got passports. That might be more than bidders want to coordinate.

> **TIP**
>
> **Can you get two of the same high-value item?** A donor who, for example, is willing to part with one week's stay at a vacation cabin may be willing to give you a second one. If you can arrange duplicates, and you're holding a live auction, don't publicize this fact in advance. Instead, when the bidding seems ready to peak, have the auctioneer announce that the donor has consented to providing another of the same item, with both offered at the second-highest price. You'll probably make both bidders happy, with an instant boost to your proceeds.

Balance big-ticket items out with others at more affordable prices, as appropriate to your group's demographics. A silent auction traditionally offers items in a wide range of prices. It's worth having a few lower-value items in a live auction as well, because they can be bid on relatively quickly, to keep up the momentum.

Doing both a live and a silent auction? Definitely set aside some of the most interesting and valuable items, with mass appeal, for the live auction. But mix it up a bit, too. You want enough high-quality items in your silent auction to keep people interested and to avoid insulting those donors whose gifts were "relegated" to the silent auction table.

Some items, however, should always be saved for the silent auction. That includes ones that will embarrass the donor in attendance if they're not sold (you don't want a whole room of people sitting in pained silence as the auctioneer tries to hawk the donor's watercolor self-portrait); ones that need to be tried on personally, such as sports gear or handknit sweaters; ones that come with complex specifications, like computer equipment; or ones that can't be seen from far away.

When to Say No to Auction Donations

There are limits on the types of items you can or should accept. Your auction chairperson is the ultimate decision maker, but all procurement volunteers should be prepared to gently refuse donors' gifts of the following:

- **Used goods.** (Other than genuine, interesting antiques, or just-opened but unwanted birthday or holiday presents.) This is not a garage sale.
- **Yesterday's computer equipment and technology.** "Even if it's still in the box," says George Hofbauer, "no one will bid on outdated technology."
- **Amateur or tacky art.** Hilary Cooper warns, "When you get a call saying, 'I've got a piece of art,' groan internally. Our school auction once got a giant photo of Peggy Fleming with her 60s' beehive hair and skating outfit. Luckily, that one turned into an inside joke; it kept coming back, year after year." George Hofbauer adds, "Some people think they're phenomenal artists, and will give you a piece they're sure is worth $500—but no one wants it."
- **Supposed services that are really meant to drum up business.** Watch out in particular for "consultations" that would have been free anyway, such as to meet with a financial adviser, insurance consultant, or real estate agent.

CAUTION

Wrap up solicitations well before the event. Particularly in the case of a live auction, you need to give your copywriters, catalog preparers, and printers time to do their job—at least four weeks. Make the deadlines clear to your procurement volunteers. (But you can accommodate a few last-minute items by preparing a catalog addendum, as described below.)

Start picking up items earlier rather than later, to reduce the risks associated with last minute flurries. For organizing purposes, it's best to find a clean, dry, single space to store everything (except items requiring special handling). Have it all in your storage area by two to three weeks before the event.

Getting Donations From Businesses

Chapter 4 describes how to solicit donations from businesses. Be sure to ask for estimates of each donated item's fair market value, which you'll need to tell bidders. Also encourage business owners to buy tickets to attend.

When thinking "businesses," don't limit your outreach to storefronts. Local sports franchises, for example, are great for donations of signed sports equipment. Adviser Gail Drulis also recalls, "I asked a local fire department to donate dinner at the firehouse to a service club auction. Someone I know had done the same in a nearby city, and explained to me that cooking is part of the culture of fire departments. The firefighters are there all the time, doing long shifts, so many of them become great cooks. The firefighter's association donated a four-course dinner for eight at the firehouse plus a ride on a fire truck, which brought in more than $1,000 at the auction."

While many businesses want to give gift certificates, you must solicit a good number of tangible items too, such as decorations (holiday included), bottles of wine, and toys. Otherwise, your display tables will look barren.

If you're holding an online auction, ask businesses such as theaters and sporting venues whether they ever have last-minute extra tickets to donate. Because your turnaround time is fast, it's usually easier to incorporate such gifts into an online auction than other auction types.

Getting Donations From Members

Your own membership is a good source of auction items, particularly services or unique experiences. You can solicit these both through a mass mailing (or emailing, including through your online-auction service provider) and by approaching people individually. For example, a board member might offer brunch for six at a nearby weekend cottage; school classrooms might create artwork; a member from another country might give an ethnic cooking class or a jar of homemade chutney; and anyone with a pickup truck can offer its use for a few hours.

At schools, gifts by teachers are a big draw. For example, Kaleo Waxman, with the Parents' Club of the Belmont Oaks Academy in California, says, "Our preschool teacher threw a rock-and-roll beach party for eight kids in a parent's back yard, complete with music, tubs of water, dancing, and a picnic; another teacher dresses as the tooth fairy and comes and reads books to kids."

To keep the mood festive, include humorous gifts, or ones that put authority figures into silly situations. George Hofbauer notes, "I and other school staff members have been drafted into doing singing telegrams, dressing up as Superman or a bunny to deliver cupcakes on someone's birthday, and so forth. These are always a hit. Kaleo Waxman adds, "Our kids beg their parents to bid on the chance to be 'Principal for a Day,' where they're allowed to issue decrees about things like bringing a toy to school or having a free dress day instead of wearing uniforms."

You can also challenge your members to create something thematic. For example, at the annual City of Piedmont Harvest Festival (in California), parents and kids create scarecrows, which are silently auctioned off to benefit the Piedmont Elementary Schools. Hilary Cooper, who has organized the scarecrow silent auction, says, "This year we had 45 scarecrows. Most were the traditional hay-stuffed kind on a wooden stake, but many parents got creative. The two that sold for the most were, in fact, a giant crow, and a papier-mâché Day of the Dead-style skeleton. We also had sports scarecrows, a pirate, a Michael Jackson, and one from old computer parts. The minimum bid was $40, and most came in at around $100. We

Scarecrows at the City of Piedmont Harvest Festival

made about $3,600, plus another $400 from our optional delivery, the fee for which was $25. (We may need to set a higher delivery fee next year for bigger items, like that crow!)"

> **TIP**
>
> **How about creating gifts to welcome attendees?** This isn't required—but it's a lovely way to welcome people to your auction (and make them feel right away like their ticket money was well spent). The idea is to create little bags of donated items to hand out upon registration. You'll be approaching businesses anyway, so see whether you can get multiple donations of things like product samples, individually wrapped cookies, pretty pens and pencils, and so forth. A pen serves the double purpose of coming in handy for silent auction bids.

Set Starting Bids, Minimum Raises, and "Buy-Now" Bid Amounts

You'll need to set starting bids for your silent or online auction, and may want to suggest amounts to your live auctioneer, as well. Successful auctions set starting bids of at least 25% and up to 50% of each item's market value. That helps avoid creating the impression that your event is a mere feast for bargain hunters. It also helps avoid insulting the goods' donors, who may ask or find out the selling prices later. Start higher (75% or so) on items that are essentially cash equivalents, such as gift certificates for grocery stores or restaurants.

For the silent auction, you'll also want to set minimum raises, to avoid people upping the bids by a penny or two. Choose simple amounts like $2, $5, $10, or $20. Base the increments on the items' value, with the goal of reaching its market value or your realistically hoped-for amount within three bids.

For a live auction, you can also suggest increments to the auctioneer in advance. But give the auctioneer freedom to judge the crowd's mood and adjust the increments as appropriate.

For either online or silent auctions, you may also set a top-end amount (called a "guaranteed" or "buy-now" bid) that lets the person forestall other bids and declare themselves the winner. At a silent auction, this allows people who need to leave early to walk away happy. It also lets your group reap the financial reward if someone really, really wants an item. Of course, you'd set a high figure—typically 150% of the market value.

What Sells for the Most Online?

According to BiddingForGood's statistics regarding its online auctions, the top ten item categories (by dollars raised) in 2009 were in the categories of:

1. Travel

2. Unique experiences and products

3. Tickets and entertainment

4. Antiques, collectibles, and art

5. Home, garden, and automotive items

6. Tickets to sporting and other events

7. Food, wine, and gourmet items

8. Restaurant gift certificates

9. Health and fitness

10. Services

Their three top-grossing items in 2009 were: (1) a pair of NFL Pro Fade Gloves worn by Santonio Holmes, auctioned off by the Reebok Foundation for $70,200; (2) an around-the-world trip by private jet, auctioned by United Way of St. Louis for $60,000; and (3) a full year's tuition at the Gary Gilchrist golf academy, auctioned by AJGA for $35,200.

Prepare Written Materials

For both internal purposes and for the public, prepare some or all of the following:

- master list of items available for bidding
- auction catalog
- event program
- bidding instructions
- bid sheets (for a silent auction only)
- recorder sheets (for a live auction only), and
- pickup receipt forms.

Master List of Items

Start getting organized by creating a grand master list of all your auction items, with a description of each and notes on who made the donation (including contact information, for next year). Assign each item a number, to be used for organizing your displays and preparing your auction catalog (described below).

Auction Catalog or Item Descriptions

For a live auction, it's customary to prepare a catalog; an attractive, multi-page document welcoming people (often with a short greeting from your president or executive director), presenting a numbered list of the items for sale along with their descriptions, thanking the auction committee members and donors, and covering rules for participation (writing up these rules is described below).

Descriptions of the items will also be important for an online auction, where buyers won't be able to touch and see your actual goods. For a silent auction, a catalog isn't necessary—bidders can circle the room, looking at items and bidding as they see fit. Nevertheless, some groups prepare catalogs for their silent auctions as well, particularly if combining it with a live auction.

Descriptions of items should always include informative titles (such as "B&B Stay on Chincoteague Island"), intriguing and informative descriptions, and photographs, if possible. Don't get too cutesy or clever: Calling the B&B stay mentioned above "Pillows, Pancakes, and Ponies Getaway" would lead to furrowed brows—and in the case of an online auction, to fewer hits by people who search for, say, "B&B" on a portal like Bidding for Good.

Descriptions need to be brief, accurate (don't say "diamonds" if they're fake sparkles), create some excitement, and help people decide whether the item fits their needs (for example, by listing sizes or measurements). Always have two people look at descriptions, to save you from mistakes. This might have helped a group that recently advertised a birdbath for online auction, with the item description "This birdbath will look lovely in your garden!" Too bad for bidders who wanted to know basics like what the birdbath was made of (it looked like breakable ceramic) or how tall it was.

Printing live-auction catalogs can be a major expense. One way around this is to prepare a PDF version and advise people to access it online before the event and print it out if they wish; and then create a short, summary version to be distributed at the auction itself. If you pick up last-minute donations, you'll also need to create an addendum to the catalog.

Event Program

If your auction will be part of a larger event, it's a good idea to create a program containing the timetable, names of the emcee and speakers, and more. This is also a handy place to sell ad space and thank your sponsors again. (See Chapter 7 for more discussion of selling advertising space in event materials.)

S38	**Miss Larsen's Class Project** **Beautiful!**
	Inspired by the works of Wayne Thiebaud, 5C has whipped up a tempting collage of individual oil pastel depictions of their favorite desserts mounted on a 24 x 36-inch canvas. The artist, April Richardson, worked with 5C to create this unique and delicious piece of art.
	Thank You, *Beth Silverberg*
S39	**Graduation Night Seating** **100% Tax Deductible!**
	Up close and personal! Reserved parking and a row for ten people in the best "parent seats," located in the first row behind the graduates. The 8th grade graduation is June 2, 2011; you will be able to see, hear, and take pictures of your special graduate.
	Thank You, *St. Joseph School*
S40	**Walk Down Memory Lane with 2011 Grad DVD $25 each**
	Raise your paddle for this! If you have ever had the pleasure of seeing the slideshow that highlights all the graduates at the 8th grade graduation in June, then you know this is a priceless memento you should have in your DVD library.
	Thank You, *St. Joseph School, Kathy Marion*
S41	**Night on the Town** **Fun for Four!**
	Celebrate a great performance with family or friends with this Night on the Town. Make your holiday memories shine as you and three others see any Friday or Saturday night performance of "A Christmas Story", the musical at the 5th Avenue Theatre (November 26 - December 30). Travel in style by limousine and add a fabulous dinner at the Capital Grille with a $200 gift card. It will be a night to remember!
	Thank You, *Bonney-Watson, Robert Branson and Judith Raab*
S42	**Seven Nights in Poipu** **$2,400**
	Enjoy seven nights in sunny Kauai in a luxurious two-bedroom, two-and-a-half bath, 1600-square-foot condo. Located 200 steps to the world-famous Poipu Beach, sixty seconds to the pool and tennis courts and walking distance to almost a dozen restaurants. Spectacular views of the ocean from two floors. Subject to availability. Check out homeaway.com #181085 for more information.
	Thank You, *James Ross and Shelly Chinn*
S43	**Mrs. McDonald's Class Project** **Game On!**
	The amazing artists of 6A, along with Pilchuck-trained glass artist Connie Walsworth, have created a beautiful glass chess set that features sea creatures vs. land creatures.
	Thank You, *Janice Savidge, Connie Walsworth*

Excerpt From St. Joseph Live Auction Catalog, 2010

TIP

Will your auction benefit a school or kids? Jackie T., a parent and volunteer auction coordinator recommends: "Have the children write handwritten notes to put on the tables. For example, our elementary school students would draw a super-cute picture and say something like, 'Thank you for helping our school, now we can get new pencils.' People have fun reading these, and sharing them around—and it's supposed to soften them up before the bidding starts."

Rules and Bidding Instructions

For a silent or live auction, decide on the rules for participation and bidding, and write these up in a clear and friendly manner, either within your catalog or as a separate document. Some of your participants may have never bid at auction before—and may be nervous that they'll inadvertently buy something they never meant to. This is your chance to put them at ease and maximize participation. (In addition, make sure you'll have volunteers ready to answer questions.) It's also a good time to remind them that all purchases are final—no returns or refunds will be accepted!

For a live auction, people will be especially interested in how to place bids. It's easiest and clearest to go with a system where you register each bidder upon entry, and give each a big card or paddle with a number. Bidders will raise this and hold it in the air for as long as they want to stay in the bidding. Explain that the auctioneer will decide the increments by which bids must be raised.

Also advise people that flash photography is prohibited during a live auction. You don't want to blind the auctioneer, who's trying to see the audience.

For a silent auction, your rules should cover when the bidding starts and ends, how to bid (most likely by using the bid sheets described below), and what guidelines bidders will need to abide by (such as starting at the minimum bid and raising bids in the increments stated on the bid sheets).

If you'll be using guaranteed or buy-now bids (described above), you'd state at the bottom of the bid sheet: "A bid of $[an amount that your group fills in] will make you the guaranteed winner! To bid this amount, bring your form to the checkout table now." The reason to require people to pay for and remove the guaranteed-bid items immediately is to avoid confusion—other bidders often fail to notice when a guaranteed bidder enters a name at the bottom of the page, and they keep bidding, creating frustration when they assumed they'd won.

For either a silent or live auction, describe your expectation that the winning bidders will try to pick up and pay for items that very day, and your acceptable payment methods. A choice of cash, check, or credit card is optimal. Explain that there will be a 15-minute wait between the end of the live-auction bidding or the closing of the silent auction and the opening of the checkout tables for payment and pickup. (That gives your volunteers time to get organized.) You will, however, need to make arrangements for people who leave early, so describe these or give the contact person's information here.

Bid Sheets

Create "bid sheets" for each item at a silent auction. You'll place these next to the items themselves, allowing people to read each item's description and record a bid. The bid sheets should contain the following, as shown on the sample below (a blank version of which is on the CD-ROM):

- At the top, your group's name and logo (to make it look official, and as a reminder of what cause they're supporting).

- The name of the event.

- The item number (which you should also put on the item itself, for example on a sticker).

- A brief but complete description of the item, with date, location, and any restrictions or important instructions, such as "dry clean only."

- The name of the person or company who donated the item (both an enticement and a way to say thank you).

- The estimated market value, when possible. Don't overestimate this to drive up the bids, or you'll anger bidders. Besides, they'll have to subtract this amount from their tax deduction (as discussed in Chapter 1).

- The required minimum bid.

- Required bidding raises (as described above, under "Set Starting Bids, Minimum Raises, and Buy-Now Amounts").

- Space for bidders' names; either phone numbers and email addresses or, if they've preregistered to participate, registration numbers (we chose the latter in the sample below); and bid amounts. For most items, one page's worth of bidding entries will be enough, but add a second, just in case.

- The "buy-now" bid amount, if any (described above).

Sample Silent Auction Bid Sheet

Bethesda Preparatory Academy

2011 Silent Auction Bid Sheet

Item #42

A Night at the Opera

This package includes dinner for two at the award-winning restaurant "Parisa" in Georgetown, two Dress Circle tickets to Puccini's "Turandot" performed by the Washington National Opera between July 10th and August 1st (advance reservations required), and a pair of opera glasses (donated by Lew's Fine Gifts).

Estimated retail value: $360

Minimum bid: $140

Bid increment: $10

	Bidder Name/Registration Number	Bid Amount
1	Joe Caballero	$140
2	Kathy Alto	$150
3	Serge Fan	$160
4		

Be a Guaranteed Winner

A bid of $750 will make you the guaranteed winner! To bid this amount, bring your form to the checkout table now.

Don't plan to just lay the bid sheets on silent auction tables by the items—they'll get moved or lost. Find clipboards or bring tape to hold them down.

While you're preparing bid sheets (which you should do well before event-day), take time to consider whether any advance work needs to be done to make sure items will be displayed attractively. For example, if someone gave a verbal promise to "provide one hour's handyperson services," you'll want to have a volunteer with graphic skills create a handsome certificate for this. If you notice that an item such as a painting would best be displayed on the wall or on an easel, plan ahead for that. If a member promised a weekend's stay at a time-share, get photos of the location, inside and out.

> **TIP**
>
> **Bring a few blank bid sheets with you to the event.** Some last-minute donations may be too good to leave out.

Recorder Sheets

For a live auction, you'll need to create recorder sheets. You'll use one for each item, describing it and containing space for notations as to who made the winning bid. They'll be kept onstage, to be filled in as soon as the auctioneer says, for example, "Sold, to Number 78 for $600." A so-called "recorder" will enter this information on the sheet and then a "runner" will take the sheet to the person who placed the bid for acknowledgment and signature. A sample is below and a blank copy is on the CD-ROM at the back of this book. If you hire an auction company, it may provide you with these forms.

Sample Live Auction Recorder Sheet

West Houndville

Canine Training Club

Silent Auction Recorder Sheet

Item #12

Handpainted Pet Portrait

A custom, framed painting, up to 2' by 3', of your favorite pet.

Donated by artist Sally Painter.

Estimated retail value: $250

Top Bidder's Number: _____

Bid Amount: $_____

Bidder's Name and Signature: s/_____

Print name: _____

Pickup Receipts

You'll need to prepare one last slip of paper for a live or silent auction: a receipt that the checkout people will give to winning bidders after they've paid, allowing them to collect their items at the pickup table, with a duplicate copy for their tax records. You'll find a blank Pickup Receipt form on the CD-ROM. Fill in as much as you can ahead of time.

Sample Auction Pickup Receipt

Southstar Ski School

Auction Pickup Receipt

Midwinter Gala & Auction   August 23, 2011

Item number: 34

Item description: Pie-making kit

Estimated fair market value: $38

Bidder's name: Bradford Bidder   Bidder's number: 102

Amount paid: $45

Southstar Ski School is a nonprofit, 501(c)(3) organization.

Promote and Publicize the Event

If you're lucky, your invitations alone will be enough to lure people to your event—but additional promotion may be necessary. How to effectively promote and publicize events is covered in Chapter 7. When publicizing an auction, generate excitement by describing some of the major items up for bidding. Also challenge each of your leaders and core volunteers to sell a certain number.

Create a Seating Chart

Unless your auction will be very informal, perhaps with people lined up in chairs, a seating chart can help maximize people's enjoyment and make sure that potential top bidders are well placed in the room. If people will be seated at tables and having dinner, it's especially important to make sure they enjoy their tablemates. Also, this is your chance to strategically seat board members or other leaders with potential high donors.

Set Up Displays of Auction Items—Early!

Dealing with both the creative and the organizational aspects of the auction display (including attaching item numbers and, in the case of a silent auction, bid sheets) will take more time than you think. Ideally, you stored all your auction donations in one place, and have arranged for a truck to deliver them to your event venue. Better yet is if the venue will let you deliver the goods and start setting up at least one day before the event.

For a silent auction, set up an area that serves to both display the items and allow people to write down their bids. With live auctions, it's customary to display items separately, at the opening of the event, before they're moved to the stage for the actual auction. If you're having both silent and live auctions, you might want to initially display the live-auction items within the same space used for the silent auction.

Your goal is to create visually appealing displays, plus make it easy for people to move through the space and, in the case of a silent auction, place their bids. Choose rectangular rather than round tables, arranged in long parallel lines.

If your silent auction items fall into thematic groups, arrange them accordingly, with a big sign overhead. That way someone who, for instance, is mostly interested in jewelry can go straight to the jewelry table. (You definitely don't need to group things by their tracking number—those are just for tracking.)

For high-value or easily lifted items, protect against theft by either putting them in a display case (a local vendor might lend you one), having a volunteer guard the table, or simply keeping them in storage and putting up photos or a storyboard. The latter is useful for gift certificates—people don't need to see the actual certificate, which may actually be less enticing than a visual display of what it includes. You can also get creative, perhaps by having a volunteer walk around modeling an expensive necklace.

Think up other clever ways to display the intangible items. For a dinner at someone's house, for example, you might set out a china plate, wineglass, and silverware, with a menu on top. Storyboards are always a possibility. To make one, take poster-sized cardboard sheets and cover them with photos, explanations, and other decoration, then prop them up on the table (flat or in a tri-fold).

Place a clipboard with the appropriate bid sheet, and a pen, in front of every item. The final touch should be a large poster or banner with your organization's name and logo placed on the front of or over the podium where the auctioneer will stand, to remind the audience, in the thick of bidding, that this is all for a good cause.

Set Up a Checkout System

One of the biggest challenges in holding an auction comes at the end, when you need to collect payment and unite the bidders with their goods. George Hofbauer cautions, "If this process is slow, your money will literally walk out the door. Some people may even take what they've supposedly bought, without paying for it—especially in cases where they've had a few drinks."

The larger nonprofits commonly hire someone to handle checkout, either the company providing the auctioneer, or a service such as Greater Giving/Auctionpay. The latter lets people swipe their credit card at check-in (using electronic terminals the service provides—no hand entry required) and sign a receipt. Their credit card data is linked to their bidder number. Upon departure people show their bidder number, confirm what they owe after being given an electronically calculated total, pick up their items, and leave. (Note: When this book went to print, Auctionpay cost $395 to set up, plus a minimum $495 service fee and percentage fees for credit card processing.)

A lower-tech way of achieving speedy results is to have someone fill out a blank credit card slip or check—but some customers may feel nervous about this.

If you don't have such a prepayment method, you'll need to equip your checkout cashiers—lots of them—to handle cash, check, or credit cards. For cash, put up signs encouraging people to produce exact change.

Then there's the matter of figuring out who bought what, and handling all the goods. One of the simplest systems is to create files for each bidder number. Once the silent auction bidding has ended, your volunteers quickly put the bid sheets in the appropriate files. At the same time, they'll record both the item number and the winning bidder's number on a separate tracking document. Any paper or gift certificate items can be put into the appropriate bidders' files as soon as the silent auction tables close. (For security reasons, these should be kept behind the scenes throughout, rather than being put on display.) For the live auction, the runners will bring the bid sheets to the checkout room for filing.

At the end of the auction(s), when bidders reach the checkout tables, they show their bidding number. The checkout volunteers will then check the appropriate file, confirm with the person what the filed records show them as having bought, tally up any sales tax, and tell them the total amount owed. After the buyers have paid, the checkout staff give them a pickup receipt (sample shown above), with a copy for their records, and a more traditional receipt (such as a credit card slip).

Buyers next move to the pickup area, where volunteers have been madly arranging everything in order of item numbers. Buyers simply present their pickup receipts, volunteers hand over the items, and everyone is happy.

Plan "Day of Event" Assignments

Figure out every possible task that people might need to handle on auction day, and then either assign volunteers or hire professionals to carry them out. For the more complex roles, you'll want to hold trainings, following the principles laid out in Chapter 2. The job assignments might include, for example:

- Setup crew. Some artistically skilled people will be helpful, to arrange the auction items in a visually pleasing way.
- Registration table crew. Six to eight people is best.
- For silent auctions: Judges—one per table—to monitor the bidding, answer questions, make sure the bid sheets haven't migrated elsewhere,

and at the appointed time, close down the bidding and gather the bid sheets. The judge may even have to act as an on-the-spot live auctioneer if two bidders are jockeying for position, wanting to be the last one in before the final closing. Have judges wear something to indicate their status.

- For live auctions: An auctioneer (if you haven't already hired a pro), and several assistants, including someone onstage to hold items up for audience viewing; so-called "pointers" arranged around the audience to alert the auctioneer to bids; "recorders"' on stage to write down the winning bidder's number on the recorder sheets; and "runners" who, after a winning bid, pick up the recorder sheets, take them to the winning bidder for confirmation and signature, and leave one copy with the bidder and run the other to the checkout room where it's recorded and filed in the winner's file.

- Child care, if children are allowed at your event.

- A few miscellaneous crew members, to call upon for backup, answering questions, or special assignments.

- Photographers. Photos are great for future publicity.

- Checkout staff who, at the end of the event, will either collect money or take charge of the pickup area. At least eight people will be needed for this to run smoothly, depending again on the size of the event and how many items you're selling.

- Cleanup crew.

- Two financially responsible people to count up and deposit the earnings afterward. (See the suggested financial controls described in Chapter 1.)

- Someone to take home and deal with items whose bidders left before the end of the evening.

Call or email or your volunteers asking for them to confirm their attendance a day or two before the event.

RESOURCE

For more details on planning and holding auctions, see *Benefit Auctions: A Fresh Formula for Grassroots Fundraising,* by Sandy Bradley (Pineapple Press). The author has herself been an auctioneer, and fills the book with nuts-and-bolts tips.

Holding Your Auction

At last, it's auction day! Getting guests in the door efficiently is your first important task—that's why we recommended more than the usual number of volunteers, to not only collect tickets and greet people, but register attendees for bidding.

As the event proceeds, find ways to make clear what phase it's in, by, for example, by stopping the music, having the musicians play a quick "Ta Da!" sound, or bringing up or lowering the lights.

TIP

When making everyone feel welcome, don't forget the volunteers. As always with special events, try to give each volunteer a chance to enjoy the evening, get some food, and say hello to friends. Also be sure to give volunteers information on how to place bids.

The Silent Auction, Step by Step

Silent auction tables are traditionally opened at or near the beginning of the event, with drinks and appetizers available. If people are shy about placing the first bid, encourage them, or set an example by placing bids yourself. If you've got other sources of entertainment, such as music, make sure that during at least some period of time, people don't face too many distractions, and can get down to bidding.

> **TIP**
>
> **Remind your group leaders to not get carried away with socializing!**
> They should be helping the event to succeed. For example, ask them to observe
> when guests are having such a fine time that they're ignoring the auction tables—
> and then gently say something along the lines of, "You know, there's something over
> here at the auction tables I just know you'd love!"

Silent auctions are traditionally closed within two hours after they open, and before dinner or a live auction begins. Your judges should warn people that the silent auction bidding is soon to close, with announcements at 15, ten, and then five minutes beforehand. (Synchronize those watches!) Large auctions set different closing times for different sections, to minimize lines at the checkout tables. If you have around 30 items or less, however, you can close the silent auction bidding all at once.

Expect a last-minute rush of bidding. The judges must quickly empty the room at closing time (unless it's in the main event space) and gather the bid sheets. They'll need to retreat to a quiet spot and review each sheet to make sure the winner complied with the minimum bids or bid increases. If the final winner didn't meet the rules, he or she is disqualified, and the judges must either award the item to the next qualifying bidder or, if no one met the minimum bid, cancel the sale of that item.

The Live Auction, Step by Step

If you'll be serving dinner, it's traditional to start your live auction while people are still enjoying their meal, or at the start of dessert. Waiting until afterwards risks them getting restless. So even if you're not serving dinner, be sure not to bog down the event with long-winded speeches and videos before the auction begins.

To open the auction, have a group leader give a brief (two to three minute) inspirational speech about what you're raising money for and how audience members who place quick, high bids will be helping achieve those goals. Then introduce the auctioneer and assistants.

Try to limit the time spent on the live auction to an hour and a half.

Again, it's the auctioneer's job to keep things moving along—while keeping it fun. You and other leaders or volunteers can support this process by clapping, cheering, admiring, and throwing yourself into the bidding process.

The most advantageous order in which to place live auction items for sale is:

- First, present reasonably affordable crowd-pleasers, like gourmet food, to get a broad spectrum of people used to bidding.

- Next, move to high-value items that people can actually see and get excited about (such as antiques or signed sports gear).

- Then, turn to high-value intangible items (such as gift certificates or recreation packages).

- Finally, present a mix of lower-value items and higher-value, "life necessity" items, such as gift certificates for groceries, which people will buy even after they've spent as much as they'd intended to.

Although your natural instincts might suggest saving the best items for last, experience has shown this approach to be counterproductive. It leads to people "saving up" for that last big bidding push. By getting the expensive items out of the way, you'll leave some people with the realization that they still have money in their pockets for a bit more fun.

Another way to capture any last good feelings—and unspent cash—is through what's called a Last Person Standing contest. Kaleo Waxman, with the Parents' Club of the Belmont Oaks Academy in Belmont, California, explains how this works: "The auctioneer says to the audience, 'How many of you would be willing to donate just $25 to support the school? Stand up now! How about $50?' The idea is that people sit down when they're not willing to give a higher amount—but a runner quickly goes and gets confirmation of their donation. Meanwhile, the auctioneer keeps upping the amount until there's a 'last person standing.' Last year that person, who donated $800, received a surprise bonus gift of a two-night stay at a Ritz Carlton resort near Lake Tahoe. Many people said afterward, 'If we'd known that was coming, we would have stayed standing longer!' But this year, they know there'll be a nice surprise in store."

After the live auction is over, if you've planned your event efficiently, you can still work in a speech or two. That gives your checkout table volunteers some time to prepare for the onslaught of paying customers.

Dealing With Unsold Goods: St. Joseph's Pot of Gold
At St. Joseph, items that don't sell at the live or silent auction are put into a "Pot of Gold." Literally, this is a large pot that volunteers started passing out at the beginning of the evening, into which people throw whatever they want—money, something interesting or funny, or a last-minute donation (or a description of a donation). George Hofbauer explains, "It's the last item we auction off, and people know there's lots in there, including straight cash. It always brings in big bids."

The Online Auction, Step by Step

You've hopefully notified people ahead of time that the online auction was coming—now it's time to tell them it's really happening. For the first 48 hours after the auction has opened, you'll see your highest volume of bidding. So it will be important to remind people several times over the next one or two weeks to keep visiting and bidding. Email is often the best way to do this. You might also hold back some items and feed them into the auction over time, to continue generating excitement and give you an excuse to send out another mass email. Don't worry about over-emailing—the "game" aspect of auctions means that most people regard these emails as less intrusive than the average email missive.

The online auction service itself may also send out some email notifications, for example "bid alerts" telling people when they've been outbid on or won an item. (Not all services offer this, however, so if it's something you want, double-check that it's included.) The longer a person stays in the bidding, the more attached they become to the item, and the more likely to bid higher than they originally intended.

Payment and Pickup of Auction Items

At the end of your silent or live auction, direct people to the checkout tables (ideally in another room), where they can pay for their items and pick them up (using the system described under "Set Up a Checkout System," above).

At the end of the evening, implement the financial precautions described Chapter 1. One person shouldn't be left alone to count the money—nor should that person have to walk out alone to a dark parking lot.

Event Follow-Up

Apart from evaluating the event and assembling a written file for future event organizers as described in Chapter 7, your most important task after the event is to send out thank-you notes to all involved—participants, volunteers, business sponsors, and individual bidders.

The next important task is to analyze your sales results. Take a look at:

- **What sold for the highest prices?** Make sure to have more of the same at your next year's auction.

- **What didn't sell?** Drop it next time.

- **Who bought what?** Figure out who your top spenders were, and keep an eye on their interests and availability for future events. If you had people bidding in groups (perhaps for vacation packages), seat them together at your next auction. ●

Fairs and Festivals

Meet Your Adviser

Cherie King, Volunteer cochair of the 2010 Candler Park Fall Fest (annual festival put on by and for the Candler Park Neighborhood Organization in Atlanta, Georgia, www.candlerpark.org); chairperson of the Mary Lin Education Foundation; and board member at Clifton Sanctuary Ministries.

What she does:	"This involves identifying individuals to take lead and support roles for the various festival committee activities, attending lots of meetings, making conference calls, negotiating, and establishing and managing the festival budget. It's all part of coordinating this two-day event, which attracts close to 10,000 people, with 16 live bands, 100-plus artist booths, ten food booths, a kids' area, a 5K run, and a local tour of homes."
Earliest memory of taking part in a charitable activity:	"When my daughter started preschool, I had the opportunity to organize a bake sale for its annual festival. (I love to bake, as does my mom.)"
Likes best about her work:	"It's very rewarding. I've met a lot of people, and by now have worked on enough different types of fundraising activities that I can spot ways to maximize the return on our efforts (and avoid activities with a low return)."
Top tip for people new to nonprofit fundraising:	"Know your limits, and understand your strengths and weaknesses. For instance, if you're not a social, sales-y person, don't force yourself into cold-calling businesses for in-kind donations. You won't do yourself any favors if you're agonizing over every phone call and taking it personally when they say no. Similarly, don't take on a leadership role if you're a follower or a doer. But if you can multitask and manage other people, then your skills are definitely needed in a leadership role."

I f your group is looking for a fundraiser that brings out the crowds and builds community, a fair or festival might work. This category encompasses events like crafts fairs, carnivals, harvest festivals, Renaissance fairs, music festivals, and other occasions that showcase a variety of vendors or talents, with lots of opportunities for audience involvement.

Is a Fair or Festival Right for Your Organization?

Whether or not they're trying to make money, many schools, churches, and ethnic groups enjoy the social and community aspects of putting on a fair or festival. For example, adviser Edie Boatman (from Chapter 5) says, "The Secret Santa shop held annually in our school gym started out simply as a way for the kids to buy presents for their loved ones. For instance, the second graders come in with $20 or so to buy all their holiday gifts, and they're connected up with fifth graders who help them shop. The vendors are mostly people who make jewelry, candles, knitted wear, and other craftsy things on the side. They do pay a booth fee, however, so this event has turned into a nice way of making money for the school."

The nonprofit groups best suited to turning a fair or festival into a successful fundraiser are those that already have:

- Access to free or low-cost event space (perhaps in your school or church auditorium or parking lot, or in a nearby public park where you can reserve an area—preferably at a time of year when the weather can be counted on).

- Inside knowledge of, or an idea for, an interesting theme that will resonate with your membership. For example, the German American Society of Tulsa, Oklahoma does an annual "Christkindlmarkt," with arts and crafts, imported German food and crafts, puppet shows and storytelling, and visits from St. Nikolaus, to parallel the Christmas markets taking place in cities and towns across Germany. (There's nothing like having a local source for Wurst and Kartoffelpuffer!) Admission is free, but they charge for booth space, and have volunteers prepare and sell some of the food items.

- A sizable group of volunteers willing to help with both planning and preparation, and day-of-event activities such as running the show, staffing the booths, or appearing in costume. For example, Matt Lovett, past PTA President at Pleasant Hill Elementary School, says, "Our school has been putting on a Halloween event for over 50 years, called 'Carnoween,' with a haunted house, food, contest booths, and other entertainment—but even though we've got it down to a science, the real reason it's successful is that the school has a culture of volunteering, with wonderful committed parents who give of their time—up to 200 of them on the day itself."

- Connections with restaurants and other businesses that will either donate or give discounts on premade or other food, wine and other beverages, or set up booths where they sell their own goods or services.

- Connections with musicians or other entertainers who will work for free or at low cost.

As an example of a successful combination of these features, Debbie Essex, who volunteers with her children's schools in Albany California, says, "One

Carnoween poster

of our more effective fundraisers was 'Chalk-It-Up,' which supported buying art supplies for the classroom. Families paid $25 for the chance to color in, with chalk, an allotted 2' x 2' square right on the school grounds. Parent volunteers played music in the background. People willingly spend money on this because it's exciting, fun, and personal—your friends and many teachers are there, all mingling. Plus, the kids love to come to school the next day and walk around enjoying the drawings."

It's best to not to try undertaking a large-scale fair or festival until you've had experience with other or smaller special events, such as the school-based ones described above. There is a difference! For example, if you hold a carnival at your school, you won't have to worry about issues like obtaining municipal permits and insurance.

> **TIP**
>
> **Treat your artists well and they'll come back next year.** Jan Etre, who has been coordinating the annual KPFA community radio Crafts Fair in San Francisco since 1988, says, "The best advice I have for someone starting a crafts fair is to start small, and put the artists first. If you try to put on a huge event and it fails, word will get out—and if you've made 200 artists unhappy, they'll tell their friends, and you'll have fewer quality artists to choose from next year. On the other hand, if you start with a small number of artists and focus on making sure they turn a profit and feel happy about your event (even if it means keeping your booth fees artificially low at first), they'll return. What's more, they'll bring other high-quality artists with them, and your event will grow naturally."

As the scale of your event gets larger, you can make additional money by charging booth fees of anywhere from $15 to $650 to the exhibitors and charging admission to the people who attend. Also, because a fair or festival is already a variety program, it offers you a great opportunity to mix in other fundraising methods, such as raffles, bake sales, T-shirt sales, and more. And, although your costs start to go up as you look at larger venues and more equipment, you'll also be providing a greater community benefit. That's something you can point to as you ask for help from sources such as your city government (for example, with waived parking fees) or local businesses (for example, with loans of equipment).

> **TIP**
>
> **Ordering T-shirts?** Don't just order equal amounts of small, medium, and large without considering your audience age and demographics. As a musical festival organizer once described, "I discovered that, for a jazz festival, I needed lots of the XXX large-sized shirts—while, for a bluegrass festival, I needed lots of XX smalls, for the teenage girls who wanted their belly buttons to show."

How Much Planning and Work Will Be Required?

The amount of planning and the number of people required for your fair or festival will depend on its scale and the degree to which you rely on outside vendors. For a large-scale event, such as one you open up to an entire community or city, with perhaps thousands of people attending, you'll need to begin your work—including identifying an event chairperson, other key leaders, and numerous committee members, and starting to solicit corporate sponsorships—up to a year in advance. A core group of about ten people can handle the advance planning, but you'll probably need at least 250 volunteers available on event day. At the Candler Park Fall Fest, for example, they've called in the local Girl Scouts to help pass out guidebooks (with schedules and other information) on the day of the event.

> **TIP**
>
> **"I helped plan our Fall Fest in a mere four months.** We were able to pull it off, but it came with a cost—little time for family or friends for the entire time," says Cherie King. "I've volunteered to cochair the event again in 2011, and I'm excited to do so, but this time, we're starting the planning process ten months in advance, with a focus on the bottom line and building a sustainable event in terms of identifying future cochairs and key committee members to shadow the event in 2011 (so they can hit the ground running in 2012). And we're lining up enough volunteers so that we're not killing ourselves trying to manage everything at once."

For a smaller event, such as one that will mostly draw members of your school or church, the intensive planning doesn't need to begin until three months or so ahead of time. Nevertheless, try to set a date and identify your chairperson as far in advance as you can, up to a year ahead of the event. And expect some seriously busy days just before the event.

Deciding the Basic Theme

The great thing about fairs and festivals is that you can mix a lot of good ideas together in one space. Nevertheless, it's good to have a unifying

concept, even if it's just celebrating a particular season, school, or neighborhood. At Carnoween, for example, autumn and Halloween provide the
unifying theme, with the haunted house and decorated Halloween cookies
and cakes setting the tone—after which, no one really thinks twice about
elements that aren't a perfect match, such as the much-beloved annual banjo
club performance. The Candler Park Fall Fest also used Halloween as its
2010 theme, with trick-or-treating at each booth, a costume contest, and
Halloween-focused craft activities.

> **TIP**
>
> **Plan activities that appeal to your attendees' ages.** Teens might not
> care about a puppet show, and toddlers won't understand most science exhibits.
> At the Candler Park Fall Fest, Cherie King says, "We found that providing free crafts
> activities for kids of various skills levels was an excellent way to keep everyone
> happy."

Festivals around the United States show an amazing variety of themes:
There's the "Good Energy Festival" in Manhattan Beach, California,
celebrating socially conscious goods and services; the "Lafayette Quaker
Oatmeal Festival" in Colorado, featuring an oatmeal breakfast, health
screenings, and an oatmeal baking contest (sponsored by guess-which
company); and the Polar Bear Jumpoff Festival in Seward, Alaska, featuring
a jump into the bay in wacky costumes to raise money for the fight against
cancer, as well as a parade, chili cook-off, quilt show, ice bowling, cross-
country ski race, snow machine rides, and a hair cutoff to help children with
cancer.

Other festivals have been built around themes like dogs, airplanes, Elvis
Presley, model trains, gingerbread houses, wine, beer, chocolate, oysters, and
other foods—explore some of the possibilities yourself at www.festivals.com
or in the Ronay Guide to events in the South, at www.events2000.com. (By
the way, if you're thinking about holding a so-called "book fair," which is
more like a straightforward sale with a single vendor, turn to Chapter 5.)

Once you've got the basic theme figured out, below are some elements to
consider including.

Vendor or Artist Booths

Merchants, artists, craftspeople, and others selling goods or services (such as massage or face-painting) can help provide both the person-power and the variety needed to pull off a successful fair or festival. The vendors may be looking for additional exposure, particularly if they don't have their own retail space (as is increasingly common for individual artists). Many are regulars on the fair "circuit," and will have an attractive booth ready to go, and perhaps more knowledge of how to make the event run successfully than you do. (Listen to any suggestions they might offer!)

Don't forget to invite other nonprofit groups, both for your sake and theirs. Your local animal shelter may be delighted to set up an adoption booth; a community health clinic may provide screenings and information; and a museum or community arts center might provide hands-on activities as well as information on its programs.

Contests and Races

Not everyone likes to shop, so you'll need some other attractions. Your festival will benefit from opportunities for participants to run, bike, or walk (in everything from a three-legged race to a 12K), navigate obstacle courses or mazes, join in a dog trot (costumed or not), compete in bean-bag throwing or other contests, attempt to send their school principal or other known leader into a dunk tank, play games, take dance lessons, and so on.

One of the most popular events at Carnoween is the "Fishing for Fun" booth. It always draws long lines of kids, according to Matt Lovett, who further explains, "People donate little toys, and the kids can pay a ticket and dangle fishing poles behind a nautically painted board. Someone in the back attaches a toy to the hook, and the child pulls it out. It requires donations of numerous bins' worth of toys. I suspect many are donated back from previous years." (Digging in a sandbox for prizes is a similar, also popular activity for kids.)

Another popular Carnoween contest is the rubber duck races, which involves setting up two lengths of roof gutters, filling both with two inches of water, and placing a rubber duck at one end of each. Then, Matt Lovett explains, "Two kids get to compete with squirt guns, each squirting at their respective duck's butt to try to get it to the other end. The child whose duck reaches the end first wins a little prize."

Hands-On Crafts and Activities

Continuing on with the alternatives to shopping, it's nice to include some nonathletic interactive activities. These might include hayrides, horse and carriage rides, and booths or areas for blowing bubbles, playing instruments, creating arts and crafts, carving pumpkins, going on scavenger hunts, and so forth.

Live Entertainment

Whether roving or on stage, live entertainment adds vitality to your event. Possibilities include stories for kids, live music (from bagpipes to rock bands to barbershop quartets), jugglers, magic shows, characters in costume, and more. At Christkindlmarkt, for example, Christy Fell explains, "Volunteers, dressed as St. Nicholas and the the ChristKindl (meant to be the Christ child, but it's usually played by a blond woman), circulate the audience. Everyone wants to have their picture taken with them, even the adults."

Matt Lovett says, "At Carnoween, we've found that the homegrown entertainment can be the best, like where students get up and perform, perhaps doing a lip sync or karaoke. Their friends get to watch, and everyone loves it."

Key Preparatory Steps

Start with a core group of decisionmakers and volunteers (recruited using the principles outlined in Chapter 2). In fact, Cherie King says, "I highly recommend having event cochairs, both to balance out the workload and because you don't want that much knowledge in only one person's head." Then divide the following tasks below among your volunteers, perhaps in committees corresponding to the headings below.

> **TIP**
>
> **Can you divide up responsibilities by booths?** That's how the Pleasant Hill Elementary PTA makes Carnoween manageable. Each classroom is assigned a booth, such as for food sales, the bake sale, duck races, and "fishing for fun." As Matt Lovett describes, "The PTA asks each room parent to line up parents from that classroom to fill the schedule for the assigned booth. So instead of the volunteer coordinator trying to call 100 people, he or she just has to stay in touch with the 30 room parents. That makes the process a lot easier."

Plan a Budget and Ticket Price

Your main expenses, depending on your group's existing assets and what you'll have donated, may include renting space; renting pickup trucks or golf carts (if needed for setup or moving goods); hiring police and security personnel (particularly for large, outdoor events); food and beverages (for hospitality and for resale); tables and chairs; electrical and sound equipment and people to set it up and run it; plates, cups, and utensils; printing of posters and publicity materials; insurance; and banners and other decorations.

In addition, Cherie King suggests, "Getting radios for key volunteers is a must—we got the use of 14 radios donated, and they were constantly in use, for the entire weekend. Make sure to have an accountability plan for the radios, too. After the first day of the Fall Fest, we realized that someone needed to keep watch over the radios and make sure that they were properly signed out—the volunteers were not doing this on their own."

On the income side, you must first decide whether to charge for admission. In the first year, it's probably better to entice people in for free, then find ways to have them pay for things once they're there. After your event has gotten popular, however, an admission charge can help cover costs. You can make sure people realize they're getting something for their money by providing free entertainment such as live music.

Whether or not you charge admission, it's fine to put out a donation jar at the entry booth. Also post signs or literature reminding people that your group is sponsoring the event, and providing interesting information on what your group does and how to get further involved.

Your other main source of income is likely to be food and beverage sales. "Our number one moneymaker is alcohol sales," says Cherie King. "We bring in an outside vendor, which gives us a cut of its proceeds."

If you plan to rent out booth space to vendors, it's customary to either charge them a flat fee (based on the size of the space to be occupied) or a percentage of the profits.

Select a Location and Map Out Its Use

Choosing and securing a location is one of the earliest details to take care of, whether it's a hall, a park, or a city street that you'll arrange to seal off for a day. First, you'll have to make sure the space will be available, and get any permits taken care of. You may also want to start announcing the event to your membership and on your website, and submit it to any community calendars.

As soon as possible after selecting the location, analyze it to see how the space can best be used and divided up among booths or activities. Then, if you'll be renting space to vendors, set a price for each space. Think first about size and location when setting the fee. Some vendors may want more space than others, and prime territories likely to attract the greatest foot traffic should also command a premium.

Also think about advantages and disadvantages to the various spaces that might be unique to your site. For example, Cherie King explains, "We had some booth spaces available on grass and others on concrete. The concrete spaces allow vendors to drive straight in for setup and breakdown—which is a major advantage when traffic gets very tight in the parking area. For the 2011 festival, we're looking at ways to make the grass area a little more desirable and shopper-friendly, by adding more signage to promote the area and making changes to the layout."

Figure out what other resources or facilities will be required to support your planned use of the space. If your event is indoors, are there sufficient electrical outlets for lighting and otherwise supporting the various activities (such as small refrigerators and hot plates)? Even a haunted house needs lighting in some places! If your event is outdoors, providing sufficient electricity for food vendors and others who might need it will also be a major issue. "Even with sufficient electricity," Cherie King notes, "we found that many of the vendors had issues with their wiring. Thank goodness we had an electrician on-scene."

Also, you'll need to figure out whether enough public restrooms are on site, and whether they can handle the crowds you anticipate. You may need to rent portapotties. Cherie King notes, "One of the main complaints at festivals is the lack of bathrooms. We rented 42 portapotties—which was more than the city permit required, but avoided having long lines."

Select Booth Vendors and Plan Your Own Booths

If you'll be creating a venue in which artists or other exhibitors set up booths and sell things, your first task is to find those artists and exhibitors. For a small event, where you're happy to have any group member or parent set up a table to sell handmade candles and potholders, this can be a fairly informal process. However, if you're aiming for a fair or festival with broader community appeal, you'll need to get more organized about recruiting and choosing your exhibitors.

This means creating criteria for entry and an application process. See the sample exhibitor application below, which is tailored for an event where you'll be seeking artists or craftspeople. (The parts that your group would need to fill in are shown in italics.) A copy is included on the CD-ROM at the back of this book.

> **TIP**
>
> **Be proactive about finding high-quality artists.** Cherie King says, "Although many artists return to our festival year after year, we also visited festivals taking place before ours, looked around, and hand-selected artists we thought would do well at our festival. We particularly looked for juried festivals where certain artists had won awards."

We've included some of the key information for exhibitors in the sample application form, but you'll probably also want to create a document or Web page providing further explanation of your event, including its rules, information on booth size, location, and fee, what types of products or artworks you're looking for or will accept, what you'll supply in the way of tables, electricity, other supplies, and physical help, vendors' responsibilities (such as booth setup, paying their own sales taxes if required in your state, and buying their own insurance or assuming the liability for theft or damage, as discussed below), how many visitors you expect, and any other amenities or restrictions that an exhibitor would want to know about.

With regard to artistic criteria, many groups prefer original work as opposed to resold imports or prints made from the artists' original paintings. Jan Etre, for example, says, "Sometimes our philosophy of putting the artists first means we have to make some counterintuitive decisions. For example, there's been some pressure to allow imported goods into the KPFA Crafts Fair. However, this would undermine our basic tenet of providing a viable marketplace for our U.S.-based exhibitors, who are trying to make a living wage with their original work. We do, however, carve out a limited exception for imported 'fair trade' goods, which meet international sustainable-trading standards based on principles of economic justice."

Set a firm schedule, so that exhibitors know by when they'll hear back from you with either yes or no answers. They need to plan their calendars, too.

Sample Application for Exhibit Booth Space

Asiatown New Year's Fair
Application for Exhibit Booth Space

Thank you for your interest in exhibiting your work at ___The Asiatown New Year's Fair___ ,
to be held on ___February 22, 20xx___ from ___10 a.m. to 5 p.m.___ .
This event is sponsored by ___Asiatown Community Center___ , a nonprofit whose mission is to
___promote inter-ethnic dialogue and community spirit in the Asiatown neighborhood and___
___beyond___ . Space is limited to ___48___ exhibitors.

In order to provide a wide selection of high-quality products, we review all applications for
quality and originality. In addition to providing the information below, please include at least
four photos or reproductions of your work, as well as one photo of your booth display.

Full name: _____

Business name: _____

Email: _____

Website: _____

Phone number(s): _____

Street address: _____

_____

Insurance carrier, liability limits* : _____

Artistic medium: _____

Description of your work, including typical dimensions and materials used: _____

_____

Past awards or other recognition: _____

Notes on or descriptions of your attached photos: _____

_____

The deadline for submitting this application is midnight ___November 13, 20xx___ .
Please return this application and its attachments to ___Tom Zhang___ at ___tzhang@email.com___
We will email you our decision by ___December 20, 20xx___ .

* Vendors who are selected will be asked to add ___Asiatown Community Center___ to their liability
policy as an additional insured, and will be asked to provide ___Asiatown Community Center___ with
an ACORD 25 proof of insurance form, which is readily available from your carrier.

Reviewing artists' or exhibitors applications can be fun—assuming you've got some basic agreement among your committee members on aesthetics, themes, and what's likely to be popular with your audience. Cherie King notes, "Identifying the jury committee is one of the key volunteer positions for an artists' market. The jury committee should have some artistic background and understand the artistic goal of the festival. For example, our festival looks for artists who have handcrafted their items. We don't allow vendors who resell items they've purchased."

How about setting up some booths of your own? Your group might raise added money with a bake sale, raffle, face painting, or another activity coordinated by your volunteers. To stock up the raffle or silent auction, it's common to ask any and all participating artists and vendors to donate an item. (If you ask whether they're willing to do this on the initial application, they'll be especially likely to say yes!)

TIP
Consider awarding prizes to the best exhibitors. For example, you might have awards for Best of Show, Artists' Choice, and Honorable Mentions. Cash prizes will delight the artists (or at least a reimbursement of part of their booth fee), but you can keep costs down by getting donated gift certificates, for example. Such prizes add to the fun, and if you attach a big ribbon or other indicator to the particular booth, will further ignite visitor interest.

Plan Live Entertainment

See "Live Entertainment," above, for suggestions as to other ways to add color and interest to your event using your own volunteers. You might also bring in paid or volunteer entertainers. At the Candler Park Festival, for example, they usually pay their headliner bands, and then rely on donated services by other bands. Cherie King says, "We've been happy to find that a lot of bands will play for free, and love the exposure—enough of them that we can be somewhat choosy, and go for ones that have a reasonably sized following."

Arrange for Safety and Security

If valuable goods are being sold, or artists and other vendors are leaving their goods on your site overnight, you'll need to think about how to protect the goods from theft, vandalism, and so forth. Cherie King notes, "You can't issue an outright guarantee of the safety of all the vendors and their possessions—in fact, at the Candler Park Fest, we make this clear in our written materials—but we do our best to head off trouble by hiring police and other security, including two uniformed police officers and one or two security guards during the day, plus overnight security guards."

For a smaller event, such as at a school, you may be able to borrow its existing security personnel, or designate parent volunteers to keep an eye on the action.

First-aid is also an issue. A large event may require an ambulance standing by, while for a smaller one, a first-aid booth or kit may be sufficient.

Purchase Insurance—And Check Vendors' Coverage

Chapter 7 discusses the wisdom of buying insurance to cover your special event, or at least checking with your insurance carrier to make sure that your existing policy covers the event adequately. You may have no choice but to increase your coverage if you'll be renting a venue that requires it.

The greatest risks with a fair or festival tend to come from bringing together large numbers of people, and potentially dogs and automobiles, in one place. For example, says insurance expert Mike Mansel, "I know of one case where someone brought a supposedly docile dog to an event, and it bit a child—then bit the same child a second time when the mother came over to the dog's owner to inquire about the first bite. And with a lot of cars trying to park in a limited space, there's always the risk that one will hit a pedestrian, or that a passenger will open the door of a parked car and injure someone. A shockingly small percentage of people carry adequate auto insurance these days, which means that the injured person might sue your nonprofit, instead of or in addition to the car's owner."

Ideally, your vendors will have their own liability insurance (our sample application form asks for the carrier and the policy limits). The application advises applicants that those selected will need to add you to their policy as an additional insured. When you select vendors for your event, be sure to follow-through and obtain an ACORD 25 form from their carrier, which will be proof that the vendor has done as you asked.

Protecting the booth vendors' goods from theft or vandalism is also an issue to consider, though it's not up to you to provide insurance. Any vendors who have formally established their own businesses should have their own insurance. Even the hobbyists should be able to get an inexpensive endorsement or rider on their homeowners' or tenants' policy for covering their goods at your fair. If that seems like too much to ask, make sure your written agreement or correspondence makes clear that you accept no responsibility for the security of their goods while at your fair.

Promote and Attract Media Attention

You have a dual motive for promoting your event well—bringing in crowds from which you'll collect any admission, ticket, or raffle fees; and bringing in customers for the booth vendors. The more the vendors earn, the happier they'll be, and thus the more likely to return next year. See the tips in Chapter 7 for event promotion.

Candler Park Fall Fest 2011 Poster

Emphasize to your vendors that you're anticipating they'll do their own promotion to their customer base. Supply them with Web links and photos that they can email to their mailing list, post on their Facebook pages, and so forth. Cherie King says, "When selecting artists, we look at their submitted photos (one of which must be a booth shot), look at their website, and check out their Facebook following. We want them to draw folks to our festival. This makes it a win-win for everyone."

If you're trying to reach a broad audience, get creative in your marketing efforts. For example, Cherie King says, "A neighborhood Halloween parade took place a week before the 2010 Fall Fest, so we entered a float—a truck that we'd decorated with Halloween decorations, with a guy walking in front dressed up as our leaf logo—and we handed out candy and postcards for the festival. We also contacted local restaurants, and asked them to hand out postcards with their tabs. Then we created yard signs, like the ones politicians use. They were really pretty—the 100 that we printed got snapped up so fast, we'll have to do more next year. And we even found a billboard vendor that gave us an attractive price on two electronic boards advertising the Fall Fest, one on a major interstate. One of the things we realized halfway through the planning was that we needed to increase our PR budget. The additional advertising that we did was worth the extra expense."

Solicit Cash Sponsorships From Businesses

"Having sponsors was key to the Fall Fest's success," says adviser Cherie King. "Without them, we would not have been profitable."

How to approach businesses for sponsorships is described in Chapter 4. Some sponsors may also want to set up their own booths for further public interaction and promotion. If your event will be outdoors, or on a blocked-off city street, then you'll naturally want to think of ways to partner up with the businesses nearby. Perhaps they'll want to set up booths, or offer coupons or incentives for your customers to visit them.

Solicit Donations of Food or Supplies

Chapter 4 describes how to solicit in-kind donations from businesses. At the Candler Park Fall Fest, Cherie King adds, "We found some great ways to partner with local businesses in our children's area. Some businesses paid us to set up a booth, where they could not only promote themselves, but also offer free crafts activities for the kids. Lowe's, for example, did an amazing building workshop, which drew around 800 kids. And the hair salon Great Clips sprayed kids' hair different colors (temporary and washable, of course), for free."

Prepare Written Materials for Participants

Upon entering, your participants will expect a flyer or even a sheet of paper containing a map of the various booths with names and brief descriptions of the vendors, a schedule of activities, and basic safety, lost-and-found, and other relevant information. This is also an important place to thank your sponsors and display their logos.

Cherie King notes, "We learned the hard way the importance of mapping out which artists' booths were where. Our booklet listed the kids' activities, and the schedule of bands, but not the artists. The result was that I got a lot of radio calls asking, 'Where's this artist's booth?'"

Plan Hospitality for Vendors and Entertainers

If you've got artists, musicians, or others who are perhaps spending all day at your event, or donating their services, it's in your interest to keep them happy. For example, providing a hospitality area, or goodie bags containing bottles of water, snacks, and tickets for free drinks at the event will be appreciated (and cost very little to create).

Plan "Day of Event" Assignments

Figure out every possible task that people might need to handle on event day, and then either assign volunteers or hire professionals to carry them out. Be sure that your volunteers are clearly identifiable, such as with T-shirts or aprons. This is particularly important for large events, where the information booth or event coordinator may be far away from the person needing help.

Although you'll give your volunteers individual assignments, let them know that anyone in a volunteer T-shirt or apron can expect to be approached by random members of the public asking questions ranging from, "Where's the bathroom?" to "Help, my dog got away and was last seen heading toward the barbeque." And all volunteers should be made aware of basic information, your safety plan in case of emergency, where lost-and-found items will be kept, and who to call or find when trouble has arisen.

For the more complex roles, you'll want to hold trainings, following the principles laid out in Chapter 2. The job assignments might include, for example:

- Coordinator with the venue (someone to pick up the keys or otherwise interact with whoever's in charge of the park or other space)
- Pickup and delivery crew (for gathering any donations of food, drink, decorations, or other items from off-site)
- Setup and decorations crew
- Traffic crew (to guide artists and others to likely spaces, particularly if parking is tight)
- Cooks and bartenders (if you're creating your own food)
- Check-in or ticket-selling crew for vendors and the public
- Staff for any booths that you'll be running, including information and hospitality areas, lost-and-found, and raffle ticket sales
- Live entertainers, perhaps appearing in costume or playing music
- Photographers, to take pictures for future publicity and for your website or newsletter

TIP

Take individual photos of all your volunteers, if possible. Adviser Gail Drulis explains: "At the Albany YMCA's Halloween carnival, we take pictures of every volunteer (they're usually in costume, looking great), with the kids. We then have an artist create cards, saying 'We couldn't have done it without you.' We want to thank them all anyway, and these cards provide nice reminders of all the fun they had at the event."

- A few roving crew members, to spot issues while they're still small, and upon whom you can call for backup or special assignments
- Cleanup crew
- Two financially responsible people to count up and deposit your group's earnings. (See the suggested financial controls described in Chapter 1.)

Call or email your volunteers a day or two before the event, to confirm their attendance.

Create a Day-of-Event Timeline

See Chapter 7 for a sample timeline. For example, when to meet the person who will open the building or restrooms, when and where to pick up any last-minute food or other items, and when to expect the security people you've hired, might all be important items to include.

Holding the Event

After your careful planning and assigning of volunteers, the event should, to some degree, roll out by itself. But given how many moving parts are involved in a fair or festival, emphasize to your volunteers that proactively walking around and spotting issues will prevent a host of problems.

For example, Cherie King says, "We got feedback from a lot of artists saying that they appreciated that we walked around asking them, 'Are you okay, do you need a bathroom break, would you like me to watch your booth in the meantime?' and so forth. They knew we were trying to help."

After a long day full of activities, breakdown is when many such events start to fall apart. Particularly if it's starting to get dark, and your event is outdoors, you'll want enough volunteers on hand to help with traffic control, booth breakdown, and final cleanup. Cherie King recalls, "We had a huge backup of artists trying to get their cars packed up and out of the parking lot. Next year, we plan to monitor this process more carefully, and not let any vendor's car into the parking area until we've confirmed that the booth is all packed up and ready to go."

Follow-Up to the Event

Follow the advice in Chapter 7 about, for example, having a postmortem meeting with committee chairs and members to capture things that were done well and figure out what needs improving next time.

And, as always, get those thank-you letters out, to your volunteers, sponsors, vendors, and exhibitors. Better yet, have a party a few weeks after the event where your volunteers and sponsors can get together, reminisce, and celebrate. ●

Benefit Concerts and Lectures

Meet Your Adviser

C.J. Hirschfield, Executive Director of Children's Fairyland, a ten-acre park on the shores of Lake Merritt in Oakland, California, where children's literature comes to life and kids can be kids.

What she does:
"As E.D. of Children's Fairyland, I'm in charge of everything from the care of our 21 animals to oversight of our renowned puppet theater. Currently, I'm helping establish a concert series in our recently built children's performing arts theater, for both children and their parents to enjoy. Outside of work, my activities include serving on the board of the Oakland Parents' Literacy Project, which sponsors family reading nights at low-performing Oakland elementary schools."

Earliest memory of taking part in a charitable activity:
"I volunteered as a hospital Candy Striper when I was about 15 years old—it was an eye-opening experience, especially since I'd never been in a hospital before. But I enjoyed the feeling of being useful."

Likes best about her work:
"Seeing some of the results—for example, stemming from our children's theater program (for eight- to ten-year olds), which has been going on for about 55 years. When I first got here, I had no idea of the impact that such a program could have. But I've since seen the participating kids come in to their own, show up and learn, and become ambassadors for helping the smaller kids to learn. One of our alums was recently elected to the Oakland City Council—she played Raggedy Ann back in the 1970s."

Top tip for people new to nonprofit fundraising:
"Enthusiasm is an astounding, powerful force. If you believe in what you're doing, it helps you to be fearless, and you'll be surprised at what you can make happen. Another piece of advice: Ignore local politics at your own risk. I don't care what type of organization you're involved with—you must be proactive in getting to know your elected officials, because there will be a time when there's some vote going on, and you don't want to be introducing yourself to them in the midst of a crisis."

You've probably been to a benefit concert or lecture at some point, whether because you wanted to support a cause, or you simply wanted to see a terrific musician, comedian, theater piece, dance or choral group, or speaker. The concept of these events is fairly simple: A performer agrees to appear on your behalf, either for free, at a reduced cost, or even at full price; and you sell tickets, bring in sponsorships, and sell refreshments and more on the day of the event.

So the question is, should your group put on its own benefit concert or lecture? The answer may not be entirely clear cut. Such events can be great crowd-pleasers, but also financial disasters—sometimes at the same time.

Is a Benefit Concert or Lecture Right for Your Organization?

The groups best suited to putting on a benefit concert or lecture are those that already have:

- Access to free or low-cost event space (perhaps at your school or church auditorium; in a nearby public park where you can reserve an area; or, for smaller gatherings, in the living room of a board member's house)

- A fair-sized group of volunteers willing to help with both planning and preparation, and day-of-event activities such as picking up the performers at the airport and getting them ensconced in their hotel; greeting, taking or selling tickets; selling refreshments or CDs; cooking for the performers; ushering; security; and more

- Connections with restaurants and other businesses that will donate or give discounts on food, wine, and other beverages for you to either sell to the audience or give to the performers

- Connections with musicians, authors, comedians, storytellers, monologists, jugglers, trapeze artists, or other performers who will work for free or (more likely) at reduced cost

- A mutual interest among your members in arts, music, culture, books, or other topics that can be brought to a stage

- A solid social media network, as a way to get the word out. "For example," says C.J. Hirschfield, "We've got a 'Fans of Fairyland' page on Facebook, and our followers love knowing what we're doing. Plus, we've got over 1,000 followers on Twitter, many of whom retweet our postings, which gets our message to a whole new audience. In addition, we can notify the 5,000-plus people on our ConstantContact e-newsletter list."

It's best not to attempt a large-scale benefit event until you've succeeded with similar ones on a smaller scale. Instead of renting out the Paramount Theatre and booking Lady Gaga or a Nobel Prize winner, for example, start by arranging with your synagogue to host your local high school jazz band or favorite local author. Of course, a smaller-scale event has lower profit potential—though you're likely to bring in the performers' friends and family! But the potential for major losses is also reduced.

How Much Planning and Work Will Be Required?

The amount of planning and number of people required for your benefit event will depend largely on its scale. If you're trying to fill a rented auditorium with a major act that draws hundreds (or even thousands) of people, you'll need to begin your work—including identifying an event chairperson, other key leaders, and numerous committee members, and starting to solicit corporate sponsorships—up to a year in advance. A core group of about five people can handle the advance planning, but you'll probably need at least 30 volunteers on event day for an average-sized venue.

For a smaller event, such as one that will mostly draw members of your school or church, the intensive planning doesn't need to begin until three months or so ahead of time. For example, Simon Wang, an undergraduate student at the University of California, Berkeley, who volunteers with the student-run Suitcase Clinic (providing free health and social services to homeless people), says, "We start planning our annual benefit concert at the beginning of the school year, with about 15 student volunteers actively involved. The concert, with about five bands and 200+ attendees, happens in early December. But we do have help from additional volunteers with selling tickets (all 60 of our officers pitch in on that) and with planning the silent auction that happens at the same time."

In any case, try to set a date and identify your chairperson as far in advance as you can. And it's never too early to start working on sponsorships, which will be key to the event's success.

What Are Some Easier Variations on the Benefit Concert or Lecture Theme?

If you've got a membership that might be interested in seeing various types of performances, but you don't have the means or the time to line up venues and all the rest, some fine alternatives exist. For example, your group might:

- work with other organizations that regularly hold events on behalf of nonprofits, or
- create an event around an existing performance—for example, by buying tickets and reselling these to your members along with a dinner or a chance to meet one of the performers.

Partnering With Other Groups or Venues (For-Profit or Nonprofit)

Check around—there may be for-profit groups that already make space on their calendars and at their venues to partner with nonprofits. For example, some performance spaces, partly in an effort to increase their own attendance, will designate a certain evening as a benefit, and give your group a percentage of the proceeds.

City Arts & Lectures, in San Francisco, provides an interesting example. This group not only puts on its own calendar of lectures, onstage conversations, and other performances, but also partners with nonprofits to create speaking events—or sometimes series of events—with themes that resonate with its members. Participating nonprofits typically (but not always) pay a share of the costs or turn over a percentage of the eventual ticket proceeds, and they enjoy the advantages of a ready-made venue, equipment, and staffing, plus promotion through City Arts & Lectures' website and other marketing media.

Nonprofit groups, particularly performance groups, also have a potential incentive to partner with you. For example, C.J. Hirschfield explains,

"Children's Fairyland has established a partnership with Bay Area Children's Theatre, in which they put on summer performances using our theater space, and our two groups split the proceeds. This gives us a way to expand our membership within a closely matched demographic, and it's a revenue producer. At every show, we ask how many people have never been to Children's Fairyland, and it's consistently around 25%—a huge marketing benefit, since all the audience members are encouraged to enjoy the rest of Fairyland that day (as part of their price of admission). Also, on the day of the performance, we put up posters encouraging Fairyland visitors to check out the theatre performance, thus expanding the number of people who've heard of Bay Area Children's Theatre."

Bay Area Children's Theatre
Actors: Reggie White, Slater Penney, Tamara Miller, Charlie Cromer

Creating an Event Around an Existing Performance

Check the events calendars and listings for your favorite local theatres, music halls, and other performance spaces. You may be able to reserve a block of tickets (perhaps at a discount), and resell these to your members at a markup. Of course, people might not be eager to buy tickets from you that they could get cheaper at the door—which is why it's wise to combine the performance with some extra activities. These might include drinks or dinner beforehand, a discussion group afterward at a member's beautiful home, or something similar.

The biggest potential draw is to create an experience that your participants can't get anywhere else, or that makes them feel like part of an inner circle. For example, for a large enough group, the venue may be willing to arrange a meet-and-greet with one of the performers or directors. If the performers themselves aren't available, think creatively. The costume designer for an opera or theatre work, for example, will have lots of stories to tell about finding the right fabrics, researching historical fashion trends, and more.

We probably don't have to tell you the importance of publicizing and promoting such an occasion, and getting commitments from your members, well before buying a block of tickets. (Put out feelers to gauge interest levels first.)

Key Preparatory Steps

Start with a core group of decision makers and volunteers (recruited using the principles outlined in Chapter 2). Then delegate the steps below, perhaps to a series of committees.

> **TIP**
>
> **"I believe in giving the audience more than it expects."** So says Sydney Goldstein, founder and Executive Director of City Arts & Lectures in San Francisco. "For example, we held an event featuring the actor Michael J. Fox, who'd recently written a memoir, in conversation with author Michael Pollan, who happens to be Fox's brother-in-law. As if that double bill weren't enough, we showed a rich array of film clips about Fox's career. It's always good to give more."

Choose the Performer or Speaker

Got connections? It's time to ask every one of your board members or other volunteers whether they've got a friend, cousin, or other contact who is a speaker or performer—better yet, one whom people would actually pay to see. And better still is if the performer's style or subject area fits in with your group's mission.

> **CAUTION**
>
> **Lots of performers = lots of expenses.** Before you get too excited about bringing in an entire band or orchestra, realize that each member may require a separate hotel room, extra electronic equipment, rental of instruments that they

don't travel with, and more. A monologist or solo acoustic performer starts to look pretty good!

"Choosing the attraction is key, and you've got to know your audience," says Sydney Goldstein of City Arts & Lectures in San Francisco. "For example, one of the less successful benefits we've hosted in recent years was for an education nonprofit, which chose speakers whose focus was too narrow and academic to attract a wide audience. Then again, the City Arts & Lectures audience tends not to show up for the bestselling, mass-appeal authors. But when we brought in Slavoj Zizek, a Slovenian who's sometimes referred to as the world's hippest philosopher, he sold out the house."

It's best to start working on lining up your performer at least six months ahead of time, which is the time frame in which booking agencies start their scheduling.

> ⚡ **TIP**
>
> **Look for unfilled time in performers' tour schedules.** As Robyn Lydick, former concert, production assistant at Swallow Hill Music Association in Denver, Colorado, and former Concert Director at the Colorado European Festival explains, "If an artist has a break between gigs that's not long enough to go home and relax, or is perhaps stopping over on the way to someplace else, the artist may not want to spend time doing nothing, all the while having to pay for hotels—and may willingly do your benefit for a reduced fee."

Depending on how many seats you need to fill, realize that you may not have to look for someone of national interest. If a local band, for example, has a devoted following—even if it's mostly family and friends—this may be enough to pack a coffee shop that donates its space for the evening.

At the Suitcase Clinic's annual Benefit Concert at UC Berkeley, nearly all the performances are by student groups—except, Simon Wang notes, "In 2010, one of our homeless clients, who happens to be a really talented pianist, also played." Simon also describes the benefits of putting on a variety of performances rather than a single show: "Our concert takes place at the end of the semester, during the one-week gap between classes and finals, when our performers are putting on performances of their own. So we have to offer something different, and that's why we invite several performers instead of just one. The audience enjoys the variety—they're not going to see this lineup anywhere else."

You can also approach performers with whom you have no connection, although it's harder without a personal introduction. Most celebrities and groups have publicists who handle their bookings, and are expert at diplomatically saying "no" to the many charitable organizations requesting low-cost or free services (though some musicians commit to playing a certain number of benefits per year, or favor certain causes close to their heart). Your job is to convince the publicist that your event will be good publicity for the performers, who will also be well taken care of.

CAUTION

Avoid any performer famous for trashing hotel rooms. That's the extreme and rare case, but as Robyn Lydick observes, "You never know what an artist is going to do. I've had to sit in the office rocking a musician who'd just freaked out and walked offstage, while his musician friends in the audience took over. (Thank goodness they'd seen this coming, or we would have had to refund a lot more tickets than we did)."

If you don't have any personal contacts, the celebrities most likely to be interested in participating in a benefit are those with something to sell—such as authors. By watching local bookstores' speaker schedules, you may be able to figure out who's coming to town to promote a new book.

But also realize that, as Sydney Goldstein of City Arts & Lectures describes, "The fact that people can attend bookstore events for free may reduce your audience. When I started doing this work, bookstores didn't often do readings, but now there's a lot more competition. The result is that many lecture benefits don't benefit anyone except the union stagehands."

With the right thematic tie-in, a local author—perhaps one who isn't even touring, as publishers' budgets have been cut to the bone—might be your best bet. To arrange this, contact a publishing company whose works would be appreciated by your audience, and ask for suggestions from one of its publicists. The author may be delighted at a chance at some publicity.

Or not. One more caution about authors is in order: Despite the common perception that writers just sit around dreaming, and occasionally putting pen to paper, their lives are as busy as anyone's, and their profits often low. For some, giving public presentations—for example, entertaining kids at a school assembly—is part of how they make a living. Don't be taken aback if they ask for compensation.

> **TIP**
>
> **Avoid canned and rehashed speeches.** "I try to create an event that otherwise wouldn't have happened, and preferably won't ever happen again," says Bob Baldock, Events Coordinator at KPFA radio in Berkeley, California. "For example, I ask authors to not simply read from their books, but to talk about how they're apprehending the world at this time. Or, I'll try to put together an interesting pair— or even a small group—of people."

Schedule Wisely

See the tips in Chapter 7 for scheduling. Benefit performances and lectures offer year-round possibilities, perhaps drawing on seasonal themes. But you'll want to check which performers are booked at the major concert halls or theaters on the same dates as you've got in mind. If a big star will be drawing the very audience you were counting on, choose another night.

Set the Performers' Fee

The first issue in booking performers is, of course, the basic fee. Robyn Lydick advises, "You're better off asking them to play a benefit for cheap, rather than for free. For one thing, do you really want to be taking advantage of an artist who is, say, living in a bus? When I was helping organize the Colorado European Festival, if a group had a required honorarium of $500, we might be able to talk it down to $200. It helped that they were gaining exposure to an affluent community, in Highlands Ranch, Colorado. Another scenario was, if the group was willing to play for free but hesitant to sign up because they'd have to drive 1½ hours to get to the event, we'd try to at least pitch in on their gas."

The performance fee itself can be structured in one of four ways:

- a flat fee
- a percentage of the proceeds (called "percentage of the door" or "percentage of the gate")—in which case the performer will want reassurance that you're only giving away a certain number of free or comp tickets
- a guaranteed flat fee or percentage of the door, whichever is higher, or
- a combination, with a flat fee plus a percentage of the door.

If you use a booking agent, he or she will also expect to be paid, normally as a percentage of the fee.

Sign a Contract With the Performer

Although arrangements for this type of event can be handled through letters back and forth, your safest bet is to protect your organization's interests by signing a contract. This is particularly true if you'll be covering a number of costs, such as transportation, hotel, room service, and so on. Unless the contract clearly specifies and limits such costs, you may face unpleasant surprises, such as a bill for your performer's personal assistant's three-hour massage at the hotel spa.

The performer may already have a standard contract prepared—or at least an attachment, called a "rider," specifying its requirements. These typically include things like what food and drinks you provide backstage, what level of lighting and sound the group will be counting on, its rights to sell merchandise, and the level of insurance coverage you'll take responsibility for providing in case someone gets injured (so that the performers themselves won't have to pay damages in a lawsuit).You probably won't have too much bargaining power over terms like these. But look at the contract and rider carefully, to make sure they're reasonable and protect your nonprofit group's interests as well. Besides the fee and costs, other issues to make sure that the contract covers include:

- **Who you're hiring.** Sounds obvious, but if it's a band or troupe, you want the name of every member whom you're anticipating will show up and whose costs you may be covering.

- **Number of comp tickets for the performers' family and friends.** They may expect or want some. If you've got the space, one or two per person, up to 20 for the group, is plenty. (Remind them again that this is a benefit. And plan to have lots of extra ways to extract money from the guests!)

- **Exact times, dates, and places at which you expect the performers to be present.** This may include not only the schedule for the performance itself (including how long each set will last), but for any meet-and-greet for your VIP ticket holders (as described below) and for the "sound check" (prior to the event, when the technicians figure out how they'll need to set and calibrate the audio equipment).

- **Merchandising rights.** If the performer intends to sell CDs and other paraphernalia, or you will sell these on their behalf with a percentage cut, spell these terms out in the contract.

- **What happens if the event gets canceled.** If you cancel the event (perhaps due to low ticket sales), it's possible the performers will want to be paid a cancellation fee—after all, they may have given up some other money-making opportunity or were counting on merchandise sales. But what if a performer cancels on you? You can try negotiating what's called a "liquidated damages" fee, to help cover what you've spent on promoting the show, printing and preselling tickets, and perhaps paying for nonrefundable hotel rooms. But expect serious resistance from the performers on this, especially if they're playing for cheap. You're better off staying in close touch with the performers to make sure they don't forget your plans. For "acts of God," like cancellations due to bad weather, neither of you should owe the other anything.

- **Method and time of payment.** The industry standard (particularly among union musicians) is that you pay at least half the guaranteed portion of the fee in advance. After the performance is over, some bands expect you to reach into the cash box that very evening, and hand over the remainder of their fee or their percentage. If that's more than you can handle, negotiate that issue in advance.

Plan a Budget and Ticket Price

Your main expenses, depending on your group's existing assets and what you're getting donated, may include airfare and hotel for out-of-town performers; renting space; hiring security personnel (particularly for outdoor performances); food and beverages for resale, along with plates, cups, and utensils; tables and chairs; electrical, lighting, and sound equipment and personnel (don't skimp on these); printing of posters and other publicity materials, tickets, and programs; insurance; and any other requirements based on the space, such as the need to hire a shuttle bus if people will be parking far from the venue.

> **TIP**
>
> **Can you put artists up for the night instead of paying for hotel rooms?** Robyn Lydick advises, "Yes, you could put them up at a board member's home, for example, if it's nice enough. But for a big enough act, the homeowner might not want to deal with the performers' security detail. Also understand that the artists usually want some space to themselves—maybe the board member could go stay in the hotel for the night!"

On the income side, you'll of course be selling tickets, and will need to figure out a basic price that hits a balance between covering your costs, reflecting market realities, meeting your likely ticket-buyers' ability to pay, and—if you're paying the performers a cut of the proceeds—satisfying the performers that they're likely to net a reasonable amount. After all that, you may just have to go with standard market price. For example, for the Suitcase Clinic Benefit Concert described above, Simon Wang explains, "Based on the price of other concerts on campus, we felt it right to charge $8 for presale tickets, and $10 at the door. We sold over 200 tickets at our 2010 concert—but our biggest source of profit from the event was actually proceeds from the silent auction." (This isn't atypical—many groups report that their main source of income from a benefit concert or lecture is not from ticket sales, but from other sources, such as food and beverage sales.)

If some seats are better than others, you can sell tickets at varying prices, just like in theaters. Also consider offering VIP tickets, perhaps in the $100-plus dollar range. The benefits should include a good view, being wined and dined (hopefully with donated goods), and ideally a "meet-and-greet" with the artists or other exciting personality. You don't want to give your VIPs an unlimited backstage pass, however, which tends to put too much pressure on the artists. Robyn Lydick adds, "Some artists don't even like people, and you must cater to their needs. If they agree to do a meet-and-greet, be sure to put this in their contract, specifying exactly what time it will be held at and how long it will last. It's worth the effort of arranging this— in the end, you sometimes make your real money on the VIP tickets."

It's also fine to put out a donation jar at your entrance or ticket booth. If it's a Lucite or see-through box, seed it with some bills—ideally some one dollar bills and a twenty. If people see coins, they'll donate coins.

Also post signs or literature reminding people that your group is sponsoring the event, and providing information on what you do and how they can get further involved. C.J. Hirschfield adds, "Don't be afraid to be creative with the displays. At Children's Fairyland, we have our different departments put on displays showing what their work involves: The horticulture department might fill a wheelbarrow with potted plants and a rake; the animal department might bring out the miniature donkey to meet people; and the art and restoration department might do a before-and-after paint job on a storybook set. This makes our work real for people, and we give them a chance to donate on the spot."

TIP

Performers often want to sell their CDs, DVDs, and other merchandise. Do your best to accommodate them—even if the venue's rules don't allow commercial sales. For example, Robyn Lydick explains, "Let's say you're in a condo association and you're using the community room. The association may have a 'no commercial use' policy. You might be able to get around this by having your nonprofit do the selling and taking a percentage, usually no more than 7%. You may have to raise the sales price to accommodate this. In any case, for the sake of your volunteers, tell the customers a flat amount that they owe, such as $15 or $18, with the sales tax (if any) already figured in."

Select a Location

Choosing and securing a location is one of the earliest details to take care of. You'll have to make sure the space will be available, and get any permits taken care of. You may also want to start announcing the event to your membership, on your website, and to any community calendars.

Renting a place that's already a performance venue is an obvious choice. Though it may cost more than the local church, it's also likely to have appropriate sound and technical equipment in place (which is of paramount importance if you want happy performers and audience members), have other staff you can hire to help, and possibly even promote your event within its regular channels.

On the other hand, you'll need to have up-front cash to invest in such a rental—probably several thousand dollars. So if that's out of the question, go back to the lower-cost venues, and work on finding affordable—but high-quality—sound equipment. C.J. Hirschfield says, "Finding the venue is often the biggest cost you'll face. Ask around—you may be able to find an unusual and low-cost location. Here in Oakland, for example, there's a high-end auto-body shop—a beautiful one, in a historic brick building, with an architecturally designed interior where they play classical music, serve espresso, and hang art exhibits. Best of all, they'll let people use the space free for fundraisers."

Arrange Airfare, Accommodations, and Meals

If you're going for a big-name band from out of town, you may—unless you can catch them in mid tour—be expected to pay for their airfare and accommodations. (We're assuming you wouldn't take this on unless the band was going to be a big draw and earn you lots of profits!) You'll obviously want to place tight controls on the amounts to be spent. For meals, you can either give the performers a set amount (such as $25) per meal, or cater the meals yourself.

Robyn Lydick adds, "Even if you're giving the performers a set amount, you've got to have someone who knows where the best restaurants are for vegan, kosher, allergy-free, macrobiotic, and other such foods. If you're not giving them cash, then assign a volunteer with cooking skills, and a willingness to accommodate various needs, to handle feeding them."

Plan What to Sell for Added Income

Figure out ways in which to raise additional money for your group—such as with refreshment sales or a raffle. Of course, you'll want to make sure these don't conflict with or overshadow any merchandising by the performers.

C.J. Hirschfield says, "I saw a great example of raising added income when an Oakland middle school did a production of *Charlotte's Web* in our theater. They created, in an adjacent area, a darling county fair environment, tying in the *Charlotte's Web* theme. They sold cookies in the shape of pigs, jars of jam, and more. It was a big success."

Promote and Attract Media Attention

As with any event, having your volunteers and board members sell tickets to their friends, and promoting it on your own website, Facebook page, and so forth, is an important first step. However, if your benefit might attract people outside its membership, promoting it more widely will be key—and a big part of where you should assign your volunteers. Chapter 7 contains tips for event promotion. Also note that this might be your nonprofit's first opportunity to place a story with the entertainment page of your local paper.

Talk to your performers about how you can help them reach out to their fan base. Supply a description of your group and its mission, details about the event itself (date, time, location, and where to buy tickets), Web links, and photos that they can tweet about, email to their mailing list, post on their Facebook page and fan forums, and so forth.

TIP

What if tickets are selling too slowly to fill the house? Aside from asking your volunteers to ramp up their efforts, C.J. Hirschfield suggests, "You can sell tickets via a discounting service or website such as Goldstar or Groupon. Don't use this strategy until you have to, because the discounts are deep ones. But you can, at least, place a limit on the number of tickets to be sold this way, and you may reach people outside your usual audience or immediate geographic area."

Solicit Cash Sponsorships From Businesses

According to Robyn Lydick, "Benefit concerts are not a guaranteed moneymaker. You absolutely have to go after sponsorships to tip the balance toward profitability." How to approach businesses for cash sponsorships is described in Chapter 4.

C.J. Hirschfield also notes, "When it comes to music, there are some natural partnerships that you can create. For example, we're talking with a local radio station about copresenting one of our concerts. I've got a popular children's band in mind, but we can't afford them on our own—the station might make the difference for us."

Solicit Donations of Food or Supplies

You'll want donated food and drink for two purposes. The first is to nourish your performers, particularly if they've come from out of town. Robyn Lydick emphasizes, "Always, always, always, feed your artists and give them beer!" (Of course, use discretion if they're sitting in front of an audience of children.)

The second purpose of bringing in food donations is to resell at the event, in order to raise extra funds. Chapter 4 describes how to solicit in-kind donations from businesses.

Prepare Programs

Your guests will expect a printed program describing who is performing and at exactly what times (don't forget to mention how long the intermission will be), background information on the performers themselves, and some interesting, related articles to read while waiting for the show to begin. You might add an article about some of the great work your group has been doing, which the concert will help support. Enlist someone with journalistic skills to make this interesting—no one wants to read the sort of prose you'd put in a grant proposal when they thought they'd come for a fun night out.

Don't forget basic safety and other relevant information. The program is also an important place to thank your sponsors.

Arrange for Safety and Security

The degree to which you'll need to take extra security measures depends on the type and scale of event. For the concerts at Children's Fairyland, for example, which C.J. Hirschfield expects to attract up to 1,000 children and parents, she says, "We'll hire at least one security guard, and have several other staff members on hand (who are pros at dealing with issues like lost kids). We don't expect problems, but for a group this size, hiring security is simply what you do."

Big-name performers may bring their own security people, but you'll need to foot the bill for them. Even for a smaller-name act, designating volunteers to keep people off the stage and away from the sound equipment is an excellent idea. For a smaller event, such as at a school, you may be able to borrow its existing security personnel, or designate parent volunteers to keep an eye on the action.

First-aid is also an issue. A large event outdoor concert may require an ambulance standing by, while for a smaller one, a first-aid booth or kit may be sufficient. And, as discussed in Chapter 7, don't forget the portapotties!

Purchase Insurance

Chapter 7 discusses the wisdom of buying insurance to cover your event, or at least checking with your carrier to make sure that your existing policy adequately covers your planned benefit concert or lecture. As insurance expert Mike Mansel explains, "The risks might be small at something like a chamber orchestra recital, where the typical audience isn't known for throwing beer bottles. But even then, someone could catch a heel on the carpet and break an ankle."

If you'll be renting a venue, don't be surprised to find that it requires proof of a certain level of insurance to protect it from lawsuits by injured guests and perhaps for damage to the rented property (which is probably also included in your liability policy).

The performers should, if they're professionals, carry their own insurance for injury to others (including workers' compensation for their employees) and for damages to their equipment. To protect your group from the possibility of lawsuits by the performers, ask for proof of liability and workers' comp insurance ahead of time. Of course, if it's the local working-dads-with-midlife-crises rock band, they probably won't carry business liability insurance. Your best bet is to ask them to sign a document saying that they'll hold your group harmless for any injuries, damages, or other potential legal claims.

Plan "Day of Event" Assignments

Figure out every possible task that people might need to handle on event day, and then either assign volunteers or hire professionals to carry them out. The job assignments might include, for example:

- Coordinator with the venue (someone to pick up the keys or otherwise interact with whoever's in charge of the space and with any staff you've hired for the event)
- Setup crew
- Drivers to pick up and deliver the performers (from the airport or from the hotel, for example for the sound check) and for gathering any donations of food, drink, decorations, or other items from off-site
- Food preparers and bartenders (if you're creating your own food)
- Ticket sellers and takers, as well as ushers
- Volunteers to guard the stage and sound equipment
- Performer hospitality crew (to make sure the performer has snacks and is otherwise attended to)
- Photographers, to take pictures for future publicity and for your website or newsletter
- A few miscellaneous volunteers, to call upon for backup or special assignments

- Cleanup crew
- Two financially responsible people to count up and deposit any earnings, and possibly pay the performers, either from ticket purchases or other on-site sales (see the suggested financial controls described in Chapter 1).

Call or email your volunteers a day or two before the event, asking them to confirm their attendance, and reminding them of any requirements (such as that ushers wear black).

Create a Day-of-Event Timeline

Like any event, whoever is in charge needs to know exactly what must happen when—from what time the performers' plane arrives to when the beer must be picked up—and who is in charge of seeing that it all happens. The best way to do this is with a timeline, as shown in Chapter 7.

Holding the Event

It's show time! Hang on to your timeline, and don't enjoy the performance too much—you'll need to watch for any glitches before they turn serious. Be sure to take some time during intermission to remind people that this is a benefit, and to solicit further donations. C.J. Hirschfield adds, "If it's not too cheesy, think about bringing out the people who benefit. I'll have kids from our theater program come out in costume. They love to do it. It makes the need very real, especially for people who don't have kids that age. When they see inner-city kids doing great stuff and creating community, the reaction is, 'Wow.'"

Follow-Up to the Event

If you haven't already paid the performers and any other vendors their contracted-for fee, this is one of your first tasks. Then follow the advice in Chapters 2 and 7 regarding sending thank-you letters and making records of what you did, for the sake of your group's future planners. ●

Home and Garden Tours

Meet Your Adviser

Philip Skabeikis, Founder and annual chairperson of the Richmond Hill House and Garden Tour, which has, since 1996, been the main fundraising event put on by the Richmond Hill Chapter of the Friends of the Queens Library in New York City. Their efforts help provide community-based support for local branches of the Queens Public Library system, one of the largest systems in the country.

What he does: "I'm an enthusiastic volunteer with the Friends, with a firm belief in the goal of providing community man- and woman-power to supplement existing library services, particularly in times of budget shortages and service curtailments. I've not only served as chairperson of the House and Garden Tour since 1996, but am the primary house recruiter and 'biographer.' (And by the way, this is on top of my day job at the Social Security Administration.)"

Earliest memory of taking part in a charitable activity: "That would be as a Cub Scout, before I was ten years old, collecting clothing for the needy. I was raised with the philosophy to always try to give something back, in whatever way your time, talents, and interest permit."

Likes best about his work: "I really enjoy getting to know about each house and writing up its story for visitors to read in our guidebook. My interest stems partly from the fact that I was raised in Richmond Hill and, after marriage, raised my family here. We bought an 1897 Victorian home, and started to delve into local history. Also, I love how working with the Friends lets us see tangible results—we can say that our funds bought this bookcase, or those CDs, or put art on the walls of the children's section."

Top tip for people new to nonprofit fundraising: "When choosing a particular fundraiser, try to make sure it has a ripple effect on different levels, for example by not only raising money, but by helping bring people together. Also determine your own knowledge, skills, abilities, and interests, and those of other volunteers, to create good matches with the jobs that need to be done. As an example, I've never been comfortable asking people for monetary donations face-to-face, but we're lucky to have volunteers who are both personable and aggressive, and very successful at this."

Organizing a successful home and garden tour usually involves convincing a group of private home or garden owners to open their space to members of the public—who then buy tickets for the privilege of wandering through these gorgeous—or at least interesting—inner sanctums. They're a wonderful way to make money from something you get for free, and to bring positive attention to your organization.

One of the greatest appeals of home and garden tours, according to adviser Philip Skabeikis is, "people's curiosity to see what's inside the various homes or gardens. Before we started the Richmond Hill House and Garden Tour, there were local walking tours offering a 'from-the-curb view,' but I wanted to appeal to people's desire for a unique experience—to be let in on a secret."

Is a Home or Garden Tour Fundraiser Right for Your Organization?

The ideal nonprofit organization to hold a garden tour is one that not only has a number of volunteers willing to commit to organizing and running the event, but also a mission with some thematic tie-in, perhaps to local history, nature, or art, and existing contacts with people with lovely homes or gardens.

Yet not all of these elements need to be in place. For example, when Philip Skabeikis started the Richmond Hill House and Garden Tour, "Our first year," he says, "we didn't know any likely homeowners, and our board of directors was seriously doubtful that I could convince people to open their doors to strangers. I literally started by walking my dog around the neighborhood of the library's service area and identifying houses that I'd like to see myself. I mailed a letter of invitation to each homeowner, then tried face-to-face invitations. At last, we came up with six suitable houses, all within walking distance of each other."

If the tour stops are attractive enough, people will even be willing to drive a bit. Philip Skabeikis remembers, "One year, the home of an antique dealer/collector became available for the tour—including a three-story collection of antiques and a remarkable secret garden. But it was situated a mile away from the neighborhood. We took a chance, and it stole the show that year."

Christy Fell, who coordinates Tulsa's Living With Art in the Garden Tour, suggests another strategy for motivating people to visit out-of-the-way gardens: "Have a drawing signup at that particular location. That worked for us one year, when one garden was about five miles away from the rest. We gave away garden art, donated by the artists."

Another plus is that a well-run home and garden tour will attract people outside your immediate membership. That makes these tours a good bet for schools, religious organizations, and other groups that might not be able to convince neighbors and other community members to, for example, attend their dinner or auction. A tour that's intriguing enough will attract tourists and out-of-towners.

TIP

Your tour might reignite community spirit. "As a direct result of the Richmond Hill House and Garden Tour," says Philip Skabeikis, "the local historical society was revived by folks who met each other on the tour. It went on to do a great deal of research and education on local history, while networking with other historical groups in New York City. In the years immediately following the first tour, the neighborhood experienced a mini-restoration movement, including the formation of trade exchanges for siding, painting, plastering, landscaping, and sharing of expertise on antiques and historical accuracy."

But will your tour make money? Typical garden tour tickets cost between $10 and $60 when bought in advance, with a $5 to $10 markup for people buying on tour day. The costs to your group are relatively low, especially if you can borrow basic supplies like tables, and get donations of supplies or refreshments. So assuming you can line up some nice places to tour, your chances of at least breaking even look pretty good. Then it's just a matter of promoting like crazy, in order to maximize attendance.

How Much Planning and Work Will Be Required?

The challenging part of putting on a home and garden tour is the amount of organizing required. You've got to start well in advance to find appropriate homes or gardens, and negotiate with the owners to make them available on the appropriate day. Philip Skabeikis says, "There are a number of moving parts. It takes us at least nine months of planning and organizing each year, with about six to ten people involved in the lead-up stages, and 25 to 30 people on tour day. It would take more people if we weren't lucky to have critical knowledge, skills, and abilities amongst that core group of volunteers."

Michael Crowe, a board member with the Oakland Heritage Alliance in California, offers this tip for lining up volunteers: "Our Fall House Tours highlight particular neighborhoods in the Bay Area, so we've found that, by contacting local community groups and getting them involved, we can often gain more people to help on the day of the tour."

After identifying a set of homes or gardens, you'll need to gather information about them and write up descriptions for a guide book that visitors can carry with them. Unless you're lucky enough to identify homes and gardens within walking distance of each other, one of your volunteers will have to personally drive to every destination in order to write up clear directions. Also, you'll need to organize those volunteers for the day of the tour, to handle tasks like checking tickets at each stop and standing at key points to answer questions and make sure visitors don't step on the tulips or pocket the silverware.

Key Preparatory Steps

Here are the key things to arrange, or assign to committees to prepare for your home or garden tour.

Give Your Tour a Theme and Name

With any luck, your home or garden tour will be so popular that you'll want to repeat it year after year. In that case, it needs a theme and name that people will remember.

Going with a basic "Home and Garden Tour" theme might be a bit generic, unless you're the first one in town. Some interesting home and garden tour concepts we've come across include the "Candlelight Tour of Historic Homes and Landmarks" in New Orleans' French Quarter; the "Secret Garden Tour" of Newport, Rhode Island; the "Heritage Home Tour" of historic homes in Portland, Oregon; the "Living With Art in the Garden" tour in Tulsa, Oklahoma; the "Heart of the Home Kitchen Tour," in Wilmington, Delaware; and the "Bainbridge in Bloom" tour, held in July on an island near Seattle, Washington.

Poster from the Living With Art in the Garden tour

Set an Attendance Goal—And Limit

As you begin planning, figure out how many ticket buyers you'll need in order to make your efforts worthwhile, and whether selling that amount is likely given your mailing list and interest levels in your community. Also think about the maximum number of people that your event—and the property owners—can handle, whether it's 50 or 500.

"We feel like 400 people is the limit for our Living With Art in the Garden Tour," says Christy Fell, who has helped coordinate this event (benefiting Living Arts of Tulsa, a contemporary arts center) for the past nine years. "Any more people than that and the wear and tear on the six or seven gardens we include gets to be too much. We've had owners who had to put in new sod after the tour. Fortunately they were savvy enough to know this might happen, and didn't ask us for compensation."

Pick a Date

Choosing an appropriate date and time for your event can be critical to its success. Check your calendar and any community calendars carefully for competing holidays or other tours or major community events, and preferably avoid times when many people will be out of town. Watch out for any weeks that bump up against three-day weekends, especially in summer.

Set a Schedule

The classic tour is held on a Saturday or Sunday, from approximately 10 a.m. to 4 p.m. (unless it's a "candlelit" or other evening tour). Variations are possible, of course. The Living With Art in the Garden Tour in Tulsa, for example, is held over a two-day period, with tickets good for both days (10 a.m. to 5 p.m. Saturday and 1 to 5 p.m. Sunday). Chairperson Christy Fell explains, "We have a lot going on in the gardens, and want people to enjoy it without feeling rushed. In addition to the art that the owners have placed there, we'll also arrange for performance art shows, such as sound artists or contemporary dancers, and for installation artists to create site-specific works. Visitors often spend an hour or more in each garden."

TIP

Would some of your audience pay for a more exclusive tour? If so, that might be a different reason to divide your event into two days—one for a small number who buy limited-edition tickets, and the next day for the general admission and last-minute ticket buyers. You might also arrange a special shuttle bus for the limited tour (sometimes called a "preview day").

Set Rules for Attendees

Most house and garden tours are self-guided, as opposed to organized walking tours. In other words, participants can visit the tour stops in whatever order they like, and spend as much time in one house or garden as they like. Decide in advance what restrictions to set for the visits. For example, the Richmond Hill tour prohibits children under 12, spiked heels, cameras, smoking, pets, and food. According to Philip Skabeikis, "The single incident where we had to enforce the no-kid rule was when one of our board members brought her five-year-old grandchild. We were terribly sorry to have to turn the child away, but once you've got a rule in place, you've got to enforce it."

Michael Crowe, a board member and Fall House Tour planner with the Oakland Heritage Alliance, says, "Last year I stopped a guy taking photos, and it turned out he didn't even have a ticket—he was a gate crasher. I told him to leave immediately. Other than that incident, however, everyone on our tours tends to be very respectful."

Of course, you'll need to allow seeing-eye dogs and other working animals.

Choose Homes or Gardens to Feature

A crucial part of planning a tour that people will return to, year after year, is finding homes or gardens with something special about them. Between six and 15 homes or gardens is enough for the typical tour. They don't all have to be palaces of the rich and famous—but according to Michael Crowe of the Oakland Heritage Alliance, "Tourgoers do like to see big, grand houses. No matter how much you talk up the virtues of more modest homes on your tour, they may stay away entirely if you don't present at least some grand ones."

Not everything special about the house has to be immediately visible, however. An interesting history (or rumored haunting!), or a homeowner's stories of dealing with challenges—such as undoing some badly done remodeling, or finding native plants that can survive the shade of an oak or redwood tree—can all add to a home's interest, making it a fine stop on the tour.

Why are some people willing to open their homes up to the public? Philip Skabeikis says, "I think they're proud to show what they have, not in a bragging sort of way, but as a mark of pride in their community and what they've been able to accomplish. Perhaps they've restored a neglected house or tastefully modernized it. Also, people really do want to connect. We don't require that homeowners stay in their house during the tour, but many choose to, and eagerly take visitors through, telling them stories, like, 'We did that ourselves,' or, 'We found that at a salvage yard.'"

Of course, some people won't be willing to open up their home to strangers. Don't be offended. Even Philip Skabeikis waited until the second year of the tour to put his own restored Victorian on show. (See the drawing from that year's tour pamphlet, below.) You may also encounter a few people who eagerly push to have their homes or gardens put on your tour, despite being unworthy of a stop—you'll have to politely say no to them.

Once you've selected the homes or gardens for your tour, work carefully with each owner to learn the place's history, stories, and relevant information, such as the names of plants, architects, designers, and so forth. Decide whether some of this information might be presented not only in your guidebook, but by displaying photos or storyboards on site. Also find out which information the homeowner would prefer not be published, and which areas they'd prefer not be made open to the public. Plan to rope off areas that will remain private, and post signs if appropriate.

Drawing of Skabeikis Home, for House and Garden Tour Pamphlet

> ⚠ **CAUTION**
>
> **What if you can't find enough homes or gardens?** Of course, you'll do your best to avoid that happening, but as Philip Skabeikis explains, "Between 1996 and the present there have been a couple of years where we didn't hold the tour, primarily because we just weren't able to enlist enough new homeowners' participation. We felt it better to hold off a year than to disappoint people with a tour that had numerous repeats."

Decide Whether to Present Lectures

To add to the appeal, many home and garden tours schedule lectures, for example by experts in interior design, gardening, landscaping, architecture, or history. The home or garden owners themselves can be invited to give lectures. These can be held at your reception area and/or at various stops throughout the tour. Such lectures are usually free to ticket-holders—and lucky for you, the lecturers will often provide their services for free, especially if they're professionals looking for a way to market their business or services.

Choose a Registration Method

While you can simply send people a map and instructions and say, "Have at it," you might prefer to ask participants to start at a particular registration point on the day of the tour. And some organizations let people pay, register, and pick up their materials at any stop along the tour.

Whichever method you prefer, we recommend creating a reception area for visitors. Philip Skabeikis says, "We give people the guidebook to the homes and all the information they need when they register, but we also hold an all-day reception, usually at the library. This helps get people familiar with the library and learn about its history (it was among those funded by Andrew Carnegie)."

Having a registration area and reception also allows people to feel welcomed, meet up with friends, pick up any last-minute information (such as a cancelled stop on the tour), and perhaps shop at booths that you've arranged. You can also set this area up for picnicking, thus attracting even more people back to your vending booths at the lunch hour.

Set an Entry Fee Amount

Choose an entry fee amount that fits your likely audience and the exclusivity of the homes or gardens they'll be visiting. If it's your first year, for example, you might make your advance tickets a modest $20 and your day-of tickets $25. (Tickets should be made nonrefundable.)

TIP

How about a "single-home" ticket option? If you've got a highlight home on your tour that the whole neighborhood has been dying to get a look at, or you want to make room for curious passersby or people who don't want to go on a whole tour, you can offer the chance to buy tickets to one house only, at the door, for, say, $5 to $10.

Plan a Budget

Chapter 7 contains a detailed discussion of how to create an event budget. Don't forget to include amounts for advertising and other printed materials (such as flyers, posters, guide booklets); refreshments; supplies for the day of the tour (such as banners, balloons, and ticket tables outside the various stopping points); legal fees to review your participant waiver; thank-you gifts for homeowners and volunteers; and anything else specific to the event. Of course, you'll want to get as many of these loaned or donated as possible.

Asking your visitors to supply their own transportation is fine, but some tours also arrange for a shuttle bus or similar transportation, or create a luxury tour for a limited audience who all travel together. The bus rental will, of course, be a major item on your budget, unless you can get it donated.

Solicit Business Sponsors

A home or garden tour is a fine opportunity for soliciting business sponsors, who give either cash or goods (as described in detail in Chapter 4). Many businesses like to be associated with something that highlights their community's best features.

Beyond cash sponsorship, you can probably think of many in-kind items that you'd like to ask for, from refreshments to graphic and printing services to balloons to thank-you gifts for the home and garden owners (as described below). Michael Crowe, with the Oakland Heritage Alliance, says: "We've had florists donate floral arrangements—which are displayed during the tour, and which the homeowners get to keep afterwards."

Philip Skabeikis says, "We've had successful sponsorships by local dining establishments that agree to donate up to 15% of the tabs of tourgoers who show their guidebooks or tickets when having lunch or dinner on the tour day."

> **TIP**
>
> **Get sponsorship decisions wrapped up early.** For the sake of your graphic designer, printer, and others, you'll need to have all the logos figured out well in advance—at least several weeks, if not months.

Plan to Earn Extra Through Sales, Ads, or Raffles

Ticket sales will be an important part of your proceeds from this type of event—but as always, are just a starting point. For example, Philip Skabeikis explains, "We've starting selling ad space in our guidebook to community businesses as well as individuals, which has proved an even bigger fundraiser."

If your group has T-shirts, greeting cards, or other paraphernalia to sell, your reception area provides a perfect place for a booth. Refreshments are a guaranteed seller, too. You might also hold a raffle or sell grab bags (if games of chance are legal in your state). See Chapter 5 for tips on raffles.

Beyond booths with your own products, you might invite sponsors or individual craftspeople and restaurant owners to set up sales booths at your reception area (preferably thematic ones, with sales of home décor items or landscaping materials). It's fine to charge a fee to the vendors, anywhere from $30 to $250, depending in part on booth size. This little fair can become a drawing point in itself. The 2010 Bainbridge in Bloom Garden Tour, for example, had four different nurseries selling plants at their main festival site, and individual artist booths (a total of 12, whose work included garden sculptures, mosaics, pottery, photography, and painting) in two of the gardens. You can make the fair open to anyone in the community, not just ticket-holders.

In a variation on this theme, the Living With Art in the Garden tour brings artists into the individual gardens to sell their work. Tulsa Living Arts board member Christy Fell explains, "In keeping with the theme, we choose only artists who sell outdoor art, such as ceramics, or metal and glass sculptures. The artists pay us 20% of what they sell, on the honor system."

Plan for Health, Safety, and Security Issues

You're probably not looking at a lot of safety risks, but there's always the possibility that someone will fall while navigating a rocky garden or steep staircase. Fortunately, you can presume that the homeowners' insurance liability and medical payments insurance will respond to invitee accidents and injuries.

Another possible issue is theft by the visitors. Although these, too, would be covered by the typical homeowners' policy, the practical truth of the matter is that most homeowner deductibles are upwards of $250, many in the $1,000 range, so the theft would have to be a major one for the coverage to kick in. Another possible issue is that the homeowners might not notice what's missing until weeks later, and therefore have to report a "mysterious disappearance" instead of a theft, which probably wouldn't be covered by their policy.

The bottom line is that prevention is always your best bet. Take a careful look around each property, and find ways to deal with risks, put up warning signs about unsafe areas, hide anything valuable or easily stolen, and plan to have volunteers watching the property at strategic points.

As a matter of basic health, your participants will need access to restrooms. Some home tours ask homeowners to provide these; but it's best to do so in downstairs bathrooms where people don't keep personal items or prescription medications (which are vulnerable to theft). Another option is to either direct people to local public restrooms or rent portapotties for some (but not necessarily all) of the stops.

Prepare Instructions for Property Owners

To prevent miscommunications, prepare a written document explaining what the property owners can expect from your group, and vice versa. Some of the most important information will be logistical, like, "Our friendly volunteers will arrive at your home one-half hour before the tour opens at 10 a.m. Please make arrangements for any pets and secure any valuables. Do let us know whether you plan to stay at the property or elsewhere that day. The tour will end at 4 p.m., and our volunteers will depart after helping with any cleanup." You'll also want to thank the owners again, and remind them about the great cause they'll be supporting. And we recommend advising them to double-check their homeowners' insurance to satisfy themselves that any property damage or injuries to guests that occur in the course of the tour will be covered.

TIP

It's okay to verbally assure property owners that lawsuits and security problems are rare. As Philip Skabeikis says, "The home-and garden-tour crowd tends to be friendly and respectful of the properties. Despite our and homeowners' fears that some ticket buyers would, say, case the joints for future robberies, we haven't had any problems in the many years we've been running the tour." Of course, that's not the kind of information you want to put in writing, lest people view it as a promise they can rely on—and sue over.

Be sure to stay in touch with homeowners in the months and weeks before your tour. Some have been known to change their mind or forget. By checking in periodically, even with updates like, "How do you like the photo of your place we've chosen for the guide book?" you'll demonstrate how seriously you take their participation and help discourage last-minute defections.

Create a Registration System

You'll need to create a way for participants to sign up for the event, whether in person, by phone, or online. For the Richmond Hill tour, for example, participants can buy tickets at the library or at certain local churches, and must pay by cash or check.

Apart from gathering basic information and payment, we recommend that your sign-up materials ask participants to waive their right to sue your group or any of the home or garden owners if they're injured on the tour and feel that it's owing to your carelessness. (Recklessness or intentional injuries are another matter—if one of your volunteers slugs a visitor, get ready for a justified lawsuit.) The waiver should also give you the rights to use participants' "likenesses" (photos or videos) for promotional purposes.

Sample Participant Registration and Waiver

Buffalo Neighborhood Improvement Foundation

I am purchasing _2_ tickets to attend the Buffalo Remodeled Basements Tour, scheduled to take place on May 4, 20xx from 10 a.m. to 4 p.m.

Name(s): Ted and Karen Black
Address: 4567 Warrenwood Drive
  West Amherst, New York
Phone(s): 321-456-7888
Email: tedandkaren@sendmail.com

Waiver, Assumption of Risk, and Release of Liability

I recognize that, by participating in the Buffalo Remodeled Basements Tour (the "Event"), I may face hazards or risk personal injury from various causes, such as the weather, uneven paths, rocky landscapes, fellow participants, steep or uneven staircases, and other local conditions. I promise to follow the rules and any instructions given to me by Event officials and their agents, and to remain on designated pathways. I voluntarily assume the risks reasonably associated with participation in the Event. **I further waive any and all rights that I or my heirs and assigns might have to bring a lawsuit or present claims based on my participation against the Buffalo Neighborhood Improvement Foundation or its directors, officers, members, staff, hired event staff, volunteers, property owners, sponsors, vendors, the City of Buffalo, State of New York, or other agents, even in cases where the aforementioned persons, entities, or organizations acted negligently or carelessly and caused my harm, injuries, or losses.**

Photo and Media Release

I understand that during the Event, various photographs, video recordings, and other media will be taken by the Foundation and others. I grant full permission for the Buffalo Neighborhood Improvement Foundation to use any photographs, video recordings, or other media of the Event that contain my likeness, for promotional or other legitimate purposes, without compensating me.

Signature(s): *Ted Black*
  Karen Black

Date: *February 22, 20xx*

Our sample Participant Registration and Waiver form will give you an idea of how to word this. However, we don't suggest that you simply copy it, and we haven't made it a fillable form for this book. Instead, a visit to an attorney may be worth the expense, in order to be sure that your waiver will "work." Each state's waiver guidelines are unique, sometimes mandating such fine points as font size. By the way, we're fully aware that many garden tour registrations trim this clause down, often to one sentence. It sure looks friendlier, but it's less likely to protect you. The person can too easily tell a judge that his or her attention wasn't fully drawn to the risks being assumed or the waiver being made.

Prepare Written Materials for Participants

Once people have signed up, they'll need detailed information on the where, what, and how of your event, plus attractive descriptions and information about each stop. You can either send an initial confirmation letter and instruct guests to pick up their guidebook at your registration area, or combine it all into one booklet, which people receive upon registering or soon thereafter. Include all of the following information:

- name of the event
- name of your group and, if applicable, its status as a federally recognized 501(c)(3) nonprofit organization
- a brief statement of the wonderful things your group is striving to achieve, which will be supported by ticket fees
- contact information (your group's address, and the telephone, fax, and email addresses, and website where people can most quickly reach the organizers or gain more information)
- a reminder that tickets are nonrefundable
- date of the event, including opening and closing times, and the statement "rain or shine," assuming you won't plan a rain date (most tours don't)
- starting location, with directions on how to get there

- directions to all stops on the tour (don't rely on MapQuest alone—it may not provide all the information your participants will need, such as landmarks to look for along the way, temporary detours, and suggested parking areas)

- detailed, intriguing, and informative descriptions of each spot on the tour, with photos or drawings, historical and plant or product information, interesting stories, the homeowners' names, and the names of any landscapers and interior designers who were involved in creating the current look of the place (they'll appreciate the marketing, and tour visitors will appreciate knowing whom to call)

> **TIP**
>
> **Home or garden images make fine gifts for the owners.** For the Richmond Hill House and Garden Tour, Philip Skabeikis says, "Our first year, a local art student donated a sketch of each house on the tour for our guidebook. In later years, a young architect in the neighborhood, who himself was restoring his home, did the sketches. After the tour, we give each homeowner the original sketch, framed, as a 'thank you.' (And we give thank-you gifts to the artists too, such as art books or supplies.)"

- information on which homes or gardens are wheelchair and stroller accessible, and which have or are close to open restrooms

- instructions on what happens if it's an outdoor event and bad weather threatens. Many tours are "rain or shine," but for those that aren't, information on how to get cancellation notices (ideally, posted on your website)

- if you won't be setting up lunch booths, information on local places to dine

- other tourist information, for people who might come from out of town to attend, and

- a thank-you to your sponsors.

💡 **TIP**

You may want to independently research the homes and neighborhood. That's what the Oakland Heritage Alliance does for its Fall House Tour—appropriately enough, given its mission to help preserve and protect Oakland's architectural, historic, and other resources. Michael Crowe, who writes the entries for their tour book, says, "I'll include a history of the neighborhood, plus a house history, the names of its original owners, and information on the architect. People enjoy getting some education along with the chance to look inside beautiful houses."

Prepare Job Descriptions for Volunteers

On the day of the event, you'll need numerous volunteers to host and direct people at each stop on your tour. These aren't your core group, who already understand the basic goals and parameters of your effort. Some of them may show up only once a year, because they enjoy the event itself, and want free tickets to attend (a common perk for volunteers).

Write up a detailed job description explaining what they're expected—and not expected—to do, what to tell people about your organization, and how to handle difficult situations. Mention any perks, such as whether they will indeed get free tour tickets. (Of course, if you offer this, you'll need to schedule shifts—not a bad idea anyway.)

Publicize the Event

See the general tips in Chapter 7 on generating event publicity. You've got a good chance of getting the mainstream media interested. Even if they don't present an entire article on your tour, they might include it in a roundup of local home and garden tours.

Also think of targeted ways to create publicity within niche outlets, for example by sending announcements to the blogs or newsletters of local home or garden clubs, historical associations, or neighborhood groups. In Richmond Hill, for example, the Queens Cable TV network sent out a cameraman and reporter a week before the tour to do a feature that then ran during multiple time slots during the days leading up to the tour.

Create a Check-In System for the Tour Itself

On tour day, you need a way for participants to prove they have tickets for entry to each home or garden. One common way to do this is with a separate page in your guidebook, either containing a limited number of tear-out tickets or a page with squares, where check-in hosts can place stamps indicating that the person stopped there. Other possibilities include a bracelet that's taped onto each attendee's arm or a sticker for their lapel. (For obvious reasons, you want something that's not easily reused by another person.)

Plan "Day of Event" Assignments

Figure out every possible task that people might need to handle on event day, at every stage of the event. Then either assign volunteers or hire professionals to carry them out. The job assignments might include, for example:

- Setup crew, for the reception/registration area and to help deliver and set up tables at individual tour stops
- Parking attendants, if you'll have a lot of people arriving at the reception area at the same time
- Reception area crew. If everyone will check in at once, have at least four people ready to process their admission and hand them any additional materials.
- House captains, to supervise and be the point person for the crew described in the next bullet point
- Host/security crews, to stand at designated points within each home or garden, perhaps in shifts, beginning one half hour before the tour opens, and ending when all the attendees have gone. Their role is a mixed one: to keep an eye on the property, direct traffic, and answer questions. Philip Skabeikis says, "Each house needs multiple hosts, who are willing to be on their feet for a while, stand at key places for security, and appear welcoming. We assign at least one per floor of each home. We also assure them that their role as security guards is limited—they should call the police if anything goes wrong, not endanger themselves by intervening."

- Lecturers or information specialists, for example master gardeners, who are named in your brochure and are available at certain stops for inquiries and guidance
- Booth staffers at your reception area, if you'll have a separate information table or sell goods
- A few miscellaneous crew members, to call upon for backup or special assignments
- Photographers. Be sure to gain advance permission from the property owners, however, and observe any limitations they place on areas to be photographed.
- Breakdown, cleanup, and trash-disposal crew
- Party hosts, servers, and associated crew if you plan an after-party.

Prepare Participant Thank-You Gifts and Prizes

Try to have a little thank-you gift for each homeowner participant, such as the framed home sketches that the Richmond Hill House and Garden Tour provides. The Oakland Heritage Alliance often gives out homemade jam or jelly made by Michael Crowe as well as free tickets to go on the tour, plus additional copies of the tour booklet.

Plan an After-Celebration

Some tours plan an after-party, at which homeowners and participants can relax, network, and continue their conversations. At the Oakland Heritage Alliance's Fall House Tour, for example, they hold registration at one location, and an afternoon reception—during the late hours of the tour—at another, usually in someone's home or backyard. Board member Michael Crowe explains, "This is a favorite tradition of the tour, and a great chance for everyone involved to talk and meet—the tour attendees, the board members, and the homeowners, who by now have seen one anothers' houses (we give them all free tickets to the tour), and love the chance to meet and compare notes and homeowner tips."

Holding the Event

After all your careful planning, the event should simply roll out as intended. Your volunteers know their assignments, your participants have been advised of the rules, and you should have enough group leaders on hand to deal with surprises.

Surprises are, of course, inevitable. Michael Crowe relates, "We vet the houses on our tour pretty carefully. But one year, on tour day, there was a mattress in one of the hallways of an otherwise lovely house! You just never know." (That's another good reason to have your volunteers arrive at the house a half hour early.)

You'll find that some attendees may skip a few houses, and aim for the top draws. (In fact, they'll pump your registration table people for advice on which are the not-to-be-missed tour stops.) That can lead to large numbers of people arriving at certain tour stops all at once. If your hosts see that a house is getting overcrowded, they should be advised to restrict the number of people coming in at one time. Simply asking people to wait a few minutes, and then watching when others leave, will do the trick.

Event Follow-Up

Your key steps, such as evaluating the event and assembling a written file for future event organizers, are described in Chapter 7. Send thank-yous to all involved—to home and garden owners, volunteers, and business sponsors. Keep careful records of which homes made especially good stops, both in terms of appeal and ease in working with the homeowners. You might want to repeat a select few of them—not next year, but in future years.

Walkathons, Contests, Games, and Sporting Events

Meet Your Adviser

Gary Stewart, Director in the Office of Government and Community Relations at Cornell University, in Ithaca, New York; and a longtime supporter and past board of directors' member for Hospicare & Palliative Care Services, also in Ithaca.

What he does: "My 'day job' is to represent Cornell within the local community, which includes things like media outreach and creating a gateway by which local nonprofits can connect with Cornell's resources. On the Hospicare board, I not only helped with operational matters, but volunteered with the annual Women Swimmin' fundraiser, in which 300 women (ages 18 and up) join in a mile-and-a-quarter community swim across Cayuga Lake. It's not a race, but a personal challenge to finish, and to raise sponsorship pledges. I've done everything for the event from publicity to dealing with traffic to crowd control when the swimmers reach the shore."

Earliest memory of taking part in a charitable activity: "Selling holiday candles for Cub Scouts. It's been so long, I don't even remember how I liked it, or whether we sold any candles. But I haven't seen any other candle sales lately!"

Likes best about his work: "I believe we each have a moral and ethical responsibility to make our communities better, especially for those without a voice. People who are fortunate enough to have time, passion, resources, health, and sense of place, need to step up and lead, not sit and watch QVC. Undoubtedly, there's a selfish component to volunteerism—it makes me feel good about myself and where I live. But at the end of the day, we have one (albeit expanded) shot to leave the earth better than we found it, at least in our own little corner of it."

Top tip for people new to nonprofit fundraising: "Keep it simple. Don't over-engineer it. And have fun! If it's not fun for you, it won't be fun for the people who want to come. And choose people who will work on their own fundraising ideas. A lot of people have good ideas, but really, the idea is only a small percentage of the mix. On your team, you want the person who says, 'Here's my idea, I'm willing to work to get it done and will follow through until it's a success.'"

One of the best ways to get people involved in a fundraising activity is to make it fun. And for some people, there's no greater source of enjoyment than participating in games or sports, healthy outdoor activities, or various types of competition. Examples include races, fun runs, marathons, walkathons or other "athons" (swim, dance, jump-rope, bike, hula hoop, and so forth), relay races or walks, scavenger hunts, chess, Scrabble, crossword, tennis, or ping-pong tournaments … the list goes on. As adviser Gary Stewart says, "This is one of the best ways to tap into people's spirit of wanting to be active and do something. Plus, a well-promoted event will get people thinking, 'Everyone else is going to be there, I want to be there too.'"

Athletic events can also tie in well with people's personal motivations. You've probably heard at least one friend say, "For my upcoming birthday, I've decided to run a marathon for charity." And for young people, such challenges can provide one of their first experiences of setting a high goal and then reaching it.

These events work as fundraisers in various ways, depending on the nature of the participants' involvement. Participants typically (either as individuals or as teams):

- pay an entry fee or promise to solicit pledges from others (either flat sums or amounts conditioned on how many miles they cover or some other achievement), or both

- sometimes receive preparatory training or guidance (perhaps months in advance, for major events like a marathon)

- enjoy a rousing time participating in some sort of competitive activity or personal challenge, with cheers from the sidelines, assistance (water, please!) from your organization and other sponsors, and perhaps the opportunity to meet participating celebrities

- receive prizes based on either fundraising success or winning the actual competition or race (or both)

- join in a postevent celebration or meal, and

- after the event, collect on and submit to your group any pledges that weren't collected in advance.

This chapter will cover how to choose, plan, and carry out such an event.

> **TIP**
>
> **It doesn't have to be athletic.** The Friends of the Packard Library of Yuba County, California, made about $1,000—slightly under their usual earnings from an annual four-day book sale—by having volunteers do guerrilla readings of poems by Emily Dickinson at various locations around Marysville, after collecting sponsorships. Part of the concept was bringing poetry to unusual locations, such as a bar, a diner, a gas station on Highway 70, a shoe repair shop, a bank, a laundromat, and a commuter bus.

Some People Create Their Own Pledge Activity

Not all pledge-driven events need to be organized by your group. The press is full of examples of people who've undertaken their own personal challenge for a good cause, often enlisting their friends through social networks such as Facebook.

In 2010, for example, at least a dozen people reportedly planned walks or runs across the United States to raise money and awareness for everything from Crohn's disease to war veterans. Others have gone to greater extremes, whether by ski-sailing across the Greenland icecap or participating in the "Mongol Rally," a 1,000-mile race from Europe to Ulan Bator, in which participants raise money for various charities.

What will you do if someone contacts your group about plans to undertake such a challenge? Be ready with offers of publicity, materials, and other support. Also ask to sit down and talk out the details, to make sure this really will be mutually beneficial. ("Oh, a naked run across the state? Would you consider modifying that so that we'd feel more comfortable supporting you on publicity efforts?")

Is a Competitive or Pledge-Based Event Right for Your Organization?

For schools and other nonprofit groups with lots of kids and families, tournaments or pledge-based events can be an excellent way to tap into a broad membership base. A simple event such as a fun-run or walkathon can be a good fit if you're based in a low-income area, where small amounts can be solicited from a large number of people and the low setup costs won't require charging high entry fees.

At the other end of the spectrum, events like celebrity golf tournaments work best in areas where people can afford, and are interested in, rubbing shoulders with celebrities and other luminaries at the local country club. The setup costs are greater, but with the right preparation, the rewards can be worth it.

Basing the Event on Your Existing Assets

Take a closer look at the group assets and resources you identified in Chapter 3, and make sure that a good number of them match the attributes listed below. This will help not only to assure you that this type of event makes sense for your group, but will give you ideas for particular sports or competitive fundraisers:

- A broad membership base, from which to draw both attendees and volunteers
- A mission or shared interest among your members in health and fitness, or in a particular activity, game, or sport—for example, if you're trying to raise money for the school band, a march-a-thon might be a good choice
- A volunteer who is an expert on a game or sport; for example, someone who knows where to go for high-quality crossword puzzles, or how a typical chess tournament is run

> 💡 **TIP**
>
> **Don't let your expert over-professionalize the event.** You'll most likely turn away participants if they need to have significant experience or be members of a certain club or federation. Ask your expert to help set the bar for maximum participation, perhaps by creating different tracks for different skill levels within the competition.

- Numerous other volunteers who will not only help with planning and preparation, but can be mobilized on the day of the event to set up and staff registration tables, support booths, the after-celebration, cleanup, and more

- Access to sponsors who might donate anything from use of a track, pool, or other venue to supplies such as refreshments, musical entertainment, giveaways such as sunscreen, caps, and balls, and trophies or other prizes.

> 💡 **TIP**
>
> **Keep tying the event back to your mission, if possible.** As Saoirse McClory, Director of Community Support at Hospicare, explains of their Women Swimmin' event, "This is more than just an athletic event. People often swim in memory of someone, or as an activity to motivate and inspire during their own recovery from illness. Honoring that has helped the event. For example, we ask people participating to share stories of why they're doing so, online and by being available to the media. This keeps the bigger picture in mind, and reminds the public why it might want to sponsor a swimmer. Some fundraisers lose this mission piece."

Beyond the Walkathon: Making Your Event Unique

Because so many groups rely on raising money through various races and "a-thons," the public can get tired of being asked to participate. To overcome this resistance, try to make your event different, while remaining true to your mission and reaching out to your most likely audience.

For example, school and libraries have found that readathons are effective fundraising tools that also fit their mission. Students get pledges based on how many books or pages of books they read. Alternatively, some base the pledges on the amount of minutes spent reading (which avoids penalizing the slow readers or making kids feel rushed to skim without understanding). It's best, for obvious reasons, to do this in a supervised setting, or to have the children read out loud to one another.

The organization Camp Happy Days, a tiny nonprofit of three and one half staffpersons, provides support and special programs to children with cancer. In 2010 it decided to hold its first annual "Charleston Bed Race." With this offbeat theme, it hoped to attract support from the 18-to-35-year-old crowd. Dubbed "the second most fun you can have in bed," the group invited participants to design and decorate a bed on wheels, with prizes for the fastest, slowest, best decorated, most outrageously decorated, "What were you thinking?" and People's Choice Award. Instead of asking participants to raise pledges, it charged an entry fee and relied on sponsorships from local businesses. Although the Camp Happy Days' custom T-shirts didn't sell well, the event still turned a profit (and did so with an organizing committee of only ten people, meeting weekly for four months). Next year, says

2010 Winner of Charleston Bed Race's "What Were You Thinking Award"—The "Redneck Bed"

Development Director Alix Robinson Tew, "We're going to try working in pledges, and bringing in money in other ways, perhaps by charging $1 to place each vote in the People's Choice awards."

How Much Planning and Work Will Be Required?

We've heard stories of successful events produced flawlessly with very little planning—a charity ping-pong tournament, for example, that was planned in as little as three weeks. That's all very well, but the organizers of said tournament described their effort as "ridiculously hard." Better to allow a minimum of two months or more—up to six to ten months, depending on the scale of the event—for assembling committees and volunteers and actually preparing and holding the event. Exactly how far in advance you need to start your planning may depend on forces outside your control, such as a city permitting department that requires six months' notice of an event that will use city streets or other public places.

In terms of your level of effort, a competition that doesn't include much equipment and can be done on-site won't stretch your volunteer corps too much. Examples include chess, Scrabble, Sudoku, and other game tournaments, scavenger hunts, and swim and other sports tournaments.

The various "a-thons" (walkathons, bikeathons, swimathons, bowlathons, 10Ks, and so forth) are appealingly simple in certain ways, because your primary needs will include a route or pool, some paper for participants to use as sponsor sign-up sheets, refreshments to hand out along the way, and prizes for those who finish first and/or collect the most in sponsorship money. You'll still need plenty of volunteers for the day of, however—an event like this can use up to 100 helpers. And the bigger the event gets, the more you'll need to handle other issues like city permits, traffic, and other logistics.

Moving up the scale, larger events will require more equipment as well as more people. For example, a marathon or other timed race will require medical assistance (in some cases, an on-site EMT is a condition to obtaining event insurance), bike mechanics, police support, professional referees or officiants, and more.

One way to make the administrative parts of the job easier is to use an online service that coordinates such events. Instead of having to deal with registration forms, enter handwritten pledge information into your database, and oversee participants' efforts to collect sponsors' cash and checks; such services create a central point for gathering information and processing credit card payments. You'll typically need to send your participants and donors to the host company's website, but you'll be able to customize your page with your own logo, messages, and more.

Using one of these outside sites can also add value to your fundraising efforts by letting you communicate in compelling ways with your participants and supporters (such as by using videos describing your cause and the importance of supporting event participants), providing pages for participants to customize with messages to their friends or photos, posting regularly updated information about your fundraising progress (such as a graphic thermometer), and so on.

Talk to friends at fellow organizations about which online services have worked best for them. Some of the better-known ones include DoJiggy's "Pledge" product (www.dojiggy.com; flat fee), Convio, with "TeamRaiser," (www.convio.com), and FirstGiving, (www.firstgiving.com).

Key Preparatory Steps

Here are the basics to setting up a sports, game, or walkathon type of event, after you've mobilized a group of volunteers using the tips in Chapter 2. Many of the categories below might be appropriate for a small committee to work on.

Give Your Event a Name

Start with the assumption that this event will be so popular that you'll want to repeat it year after year. In that case, it needs a recognizable name. Adviser Gary Stewart says that the name "Women Swimmin'" has worked very well for Hospicare, by "instantly conveying what the event is about, while adding a touch of whimsy. You just can't put a price on a good name for an event."

Women Swimmin' Flyer

You might even want to buy the Internet domain name for your event, as the Charleston Bed Race did. (You can also, of course, create a link from your own website, but that might be impractical if your site is still in its infancy or there isn't room to give the event much visibility on your home page.) Waiting until you're successful to register a domain name will only assure that someone else gets to it first—with the idea of reselling it to you later at a markup. Initial registration should cost you less than $50, and annual renewals even less. To check that the name you want hasn't already been snapped up, search for it at www. networksolutions.com. Websites that offer domain registration are listed at www.internic.net/alpha.html. For more information on website development for nonprofits, see *Starting & Building a Nonprofit; A Practical Guide*, by Peri Pakroo, J.D. (Nolo).

Set a Participation Goal

As you begin your planning activities, start by figuring out what level of participation you'll need in order to make your efforts worthwhile. And, although over-participation may at this point seem like an unlikely problem, you'll also need to know the maximum number of people that your event can handle, whether it's 20 or 2,000.

Don't automatically discount a small event. Even a 20-person event can raise a significant amount of money, if the participants are enthusiastic and given solid guidance on raising pledge money.

Decide Rules, and How Winners Will Be Chosen

Every event needs basic parameters, like a start and end time, minimum age or experience of participants, what it takes (in a competitive event) to win or get a prize, and any other standards of behavior that will make the experience pleasant and fair for everyone.

For example, for a simple kids' fun run, you'll need to decide what ages or grades will race against each other, and at what times the various races begin. For an adult race or walkathon, you might want to specify not only basic race rules, but that wearing iPods or other headsets or bringing dogs will not be allowed. For a chess tournament, you might specify not only whether contestants will be playing against a clock and that boards and pieces will be provided, but that participants may not bring their own pieces (which, if they're oddly shaped enough, can throw off competing players). For other board games, such as crossword puzzles, it's wise to prohibit use of electronic devices or headphones during the tournament rounds (this prevents people from contacting their friends or the Internet for help).

Certain competitive activities will, of course, need to comply with the basic, preset rules of the game or sport. Be sure to research these carefully, communicate them to participants, and arrange for on-site judges or referees. Depending on the ability level of expected participants, you may want to coordinate with a local sports or game federation to bring in authorized judges or refs.

> **TIP**
>
> **Kids love prizes!** If you're trying for an event with lots of community participation, make it easy to win something (even if there's serious competition for the top prizes). After years of experience cochairing Silicon Valley Puzzle Fest (which raises funds for the Morgan Hill Library Foundation), Emily Shem-Tov has found that, "The grownups aren't really doing it for the prizes, but kids like to walk away with something. So we've created prizes for things like 'Best handwriting on a crossword puzzle' (that one, which also applies to adults, helps the judges out, too) and 'Person who traveled farthest for the tournament.' Plus, we give out certificates to everyone who turns in perfect puzzles in all rounds, even though they weren't the fastest and therefore didn't qualify for the final rounds. One of our sponsors, a bookstore, has donated giant pencils—literally two feet long—Sudoku Rubik's cubes; and puzzle books. (We try to stay on the theme.) We gave out savings bonds the first year, but the kids thought those were lame."

Plan Your Scoring System

Tracking results is a key part of the process. Emily Shem-Tov explains, "The serious crossword and Sudoku people among our participants are detail-oriented. So we need to have a really good, quick system for scoring, judging, and reporting of the scores. If there are any discrepancies they'll be right on it!" The first year of Puzzle Fest, Emily says, "We put the scores on dry erase boards, or posterboard sheet, which we hung on the walls, while I did the math. But that was ridiculously worky, and didn't allow for printouts. By year two, we had projectors and computers, with me typing the scores in as they came in, all on display. Everyone wants to know not only how they did, but how they compared to everyone else."

You may also be able to buy scoring software for your event (search online for "software" and the name of your sport or game).

Set an Entry Fee Amount

Charging an entry fee is almost always a good idea, to bring in a baseline level of profits. Having people register and pay in advance also assures you of a certain level of participation.

The entry fee should be high enough to communicate that this is a serious endeavor—but not so high as to discourage participation. In cases where most of the participants will be young people, entry fees of around $10 to $25 are common (and you can do a sliding scale, or create a family fee). For the Charleston Bed Race, for example, entering one bed cost $125—but with five team members allowed per bed, this worked out to $25 per person. You can also ask participants to commit to raising a certain amount on top of their entry fee.

When more adults than children will be involved, or the event will be comparable to one that people normally pay to attend, some organizations set the entry fee quite high. For example, they may charge $3,000 to enter a marathon, perhaps with the proviso that participants can reduce this by the amount of pledge money they successfully raise. The purpose is to ensure that participants don't treat the event as a mere personal exercise and neglect the fundraising side of it.

Design a Pledge-Collection System

As with any form of nonprofit fundraising, the mantra "make it easy to give" is important here. Your job is to figure out how to best apply it when it comes to helping your participants collect sponsor money.

Assuming each volunteer will approach multiple sponsors, provide them with a form they can use to inform prospective sponsors of their obligation, and to use later when gathering pledges (see the sample below). The form also instructs volunteers on how to complete the form (gather the pledges).

Think twice before committing to a "pay when the goal is met" method of securing support, however. "Tracking sponsors down after an event is over can be difficult," warns adviser Gary Stewart. The excitement has died down, and your organization may start to feel like it's nagging the participants to nag their sponsors.

Flat-fee pledges are much easier to collect in advance. You can suggest donation levels, such as $15, $25, $50, $100, and Other. If you've got the tech resources, an even better approach is to convert this form into an online sponsorship method. At Women Swimmin', people go straight to the website to sponsor a swimmer, paying immediately by credit card.

TIP

Offer incentives to getting early pledges. According to Saoirse McClory, "Some people are slower to get their fundraising going, so at a minimum, we require that everyone raise at least $100 (in addition to their $25 registration fee) by the Friday before the event. But we offer a prize if people raise $1,000 by approximately one month before the event. This inspires people to start fundraising early. Swimmers will send emails or visit asking, 'How am I doing? Are checks arriving for me?' They're excited about the prize! We also give prizes to the swimmers who have raised the most money by the evening before the event."

Give your participants plenty of guidance on gathering sponsors. Recommend that they ask friends, both in person and via email and other online methods. Hospicare, for example, gives participants a button to wear that says, "Ask me about Women Swimmin'."

Below is an example of how to use the Donor Pledge Log. The italicized portions are examples of the information that you will enter when you create the Log for your event, and the faux-handwriting portions show what the donors will fill out. (You'll find a blank copy on the CD-ROM.)

Sample Donor Pledge Log

Friends of Maintown Public Library Read-a-Thon

Donor Pledge Log

Friends of Maintown Public Library is a nonprofit, 501(c)(3) organization committed to working toward **widespread community access to information and promoting the joys of reading**. Thank you for participating in this year's **Read-a-Thon**, which will raise money for the important goal of *creating a new young-adult section of the library*

Sponsors

Please fill in the first three columns below. You may indicate a maximum pledge. Your pledges are tax deductible to the extent allowed by law. If you are writing a check, please enter **Friends of Maintown Public Library Read-a-Thon** on the memo line, so that your check will serve as a receipt.

Participants

Please fill in the last three columns. Calculate the amount you earned, and state the date the pledge amount was collected and what form of payment you received (cash or check). Return this pledge sheet and collected pledges to **Maribeth Reeder.**

Donor's name	Donor's phone number/ address	Pledge amount	Amt. due	Date collected	Form of payment
Joseph Reeder, Sr.	1234 Center St., Maintown, WI, 12345	$5 ☒ per book ❑ flat amt.	$25	12/4/2011	☒ cash ❑ check
Aileen Zhang	4321 Wide St., Maintown, WI, 54321	$10 ☒ per book ❑ flat amt.	$10	10/31/2011	☒ cash ❑ check
		$ ❑ per book ❑ flat amt.			❑ cash ❑ check
		$ ❑ per book ❑ flat amt.			❑ cash ❑ check

Schedule Wisely

Check your calendar and any community calendars carefully for competing holidays or other community events, and preferably avoid times when many people will be out of town (watch out for any weeks that bump up against three-day weekends, especially in summer). If the event is going to be outdoors, that will obviously limit your scheduling options.

Think carefully about time of day, as well. Adviser Gary Stewart counsels, "You've got to be considerate of peoples' time. Not everyone is willing to give up a big chunk of their precious weekend. The Women Swimmin' event starts early in the morning. It's still so dark when people arrive that all our volunteers wear orange vests and lights. But everyone is done by 10 a.m., so they can get on with their day. There's a little ceremony at the end, which no one is obliged to attend, though many do, because it's a party atmosphere and a proud achievement for the swimmers."

Choose a Location, Route, or Course

Perhaps you already have a location in mind, such as your school's pool, your library's meeting room, or the track in your neighborhood park. If so, double-check the scheduling, and look into whether any permissions or permits will be required. For example, you'll need city permits and police support to close any roads.

If you haven't chosen a location or course, your volunteers have a little research task ahead of them. Events like walkathons, marathons, and bike races need both a starting and ending point that are easily reached by your participants, where large crowds can gather, change into athletic clothes, and ideally use the restroom, all of which may require getting permission for use of public land, negotiating use of private space, and hiring a fleet of Porta Potties. Don't forget to check into wheelchair accessibility. For some events, you may need wireless Internet access.

The Women Swimmin' event, for example, starts out at the Ithaca Yacht Club (which donates its facility). A boat takes everyone across the lake to the starting line, where the women jump out and swim back to the yacht club. Swimmers are in organized "pods," accompanied by numerous kayakers and boaters. (If you map out a loop or out-and-back course, that's one less venue to arrange.)

In some instances, you may want to map out more than just one route. Creating alternate courses for participants of different levels can maximize participation, allowing people of varying abilities and stamina to choose appropriate distances. Particularly if you have children taking part, you don't want some of them lost or in tears at the 10K point of a 20K walk. Participants choose the course they want when they register.

For outdoor activities, each route will need to be measured and plotted out. Your volunteers should look for any dangerous or difficult-to-navigate spots—for example, a place where the sidewalk disappears. Prepare directional and warning signs ahead of time. Also create markers to post at each mile or kilometer, to motivate participants.

The longer the route and the greater the number of participants, the more restroom options or portable bathrooms you'll need to arrange for. At least two potties for every one and a half to two miles is standard, and someone will need to keep an eye on toilet paper supplies. (This is serious—the Internet is full of posts by angry and disappointed charity runners or walkers who faced inadequate or badly maintained pit stops.)

TIP

Don't forget to choose a scenic route! I remember participating in a walkathon as a teenager, and thinking at approximately kilometer 16 that they couldn't have chosen a less interesting stretch of paved-over Seattle suburb for us to drag our feet through. I never signed up for another walkathon. By contrast, Gary Stewart notes of the Women Swimmin' route, "It's truly visually inspirational. There you are on the calm lake early in the morning, with the sun's first light illuminating the colorful swim caps."

Plan a Budget

Chapter 7 contains a detailed discussion of how to create an event budget. For a competitive event, don't forget to include amounts for, as appropriate: permit fees and the cost of police presence and an ambulance; advertising and other printed materials (such as flyers, posters, and race results booklets); insurance (as discussed in Chapter 7); legal fees to review contracts you'll be signing; security personnel (discussed under "Plan for Health and Safety Issues," below); scoring software; purchase or rentals of tables, chairs, and sports or game supplies; refreshments for rest or break areas, aid stations, and the finish line; banners for start and finish lines; a microphone or megaphone; a large digital clock or timer; bib numbers for participants; safety pins; paint for marking the course; trash cans and bags; awards for participants; thank-you gifts for volunteers; and anything else specific to the event. (Get as many of these loaned or donated as possible.)

Solicit Business Sponsors

A competitive event is perfect for soliciting business sponsors, who give either cash or goods (as described in detail in Chapter 4). Many businesses like to be associated with something active and exciting, and you'll have lots of opportunities to publicly post their logos.

Don't forget to approach businesses that you're paying for services associated with the event itself. For example, if you'll be renting bowling lanes, and the bowling alley owners weren't willing to donate the actual rental costs, see whether they'll throw in some free passes that you can use as raffle or participant prizes. Alix Robinson Tew of Camp Happy Days says, "The guy we ordered our event T-shirts surprised us by saying, 'Oh, I've got a racing bed in my garage,' and he entered the race!"

For large-scale events, your more generous sponsors might be invited to set up booths of their own, selling goods, offering freebies like ice cream samples or blood pressure checks, or otherwise promoting their services.

Plan to Earn Extra Through Sales or Raffle Booths

The core of your proceeds from this type of event will be entry fees and pledges brought in by the participants. These aren't the only ways to make money, however. Your event is likely to attract not only participants, but their family members and friends, who will deliver them or cheer them on. That gives you a great opportunity to raise a little extra money for your cause.

If you've got T-shirts, greeting cards, or other paraphernalia that your group has been trying to sell, your meeting area provides a perfect place for a booth. If the up-front costs are minimal or you can get goods donated, this is also a good time to sell other thematic items, such as sports or game gear.

Refreshments are a guaranteed seller, even if they're as simple as cans of soda on ice and store-bought cookies, sandwiches, or energy bars. You might also hold a raffle or sell grab bags (if games of chance are legal in your state). See Chapter 5 for tips on raffles.

Plan for Health and Safety Issues

For sit-down events like a chess or Scrabble tournament, you're probably not looking at a lot of health or safety risks—unless a fight breaks out, or someone's blood pressure goes through the roof. For more strenuous events, however, especially those that involve a lot of people, involve personal challenges for nonathletes, or are outdoors, health and safety are important concerns.

Try to imagine various scenarios—everything from a player having an asthma attack to a beach cleanup crew member sticking a finger with a syringe to a swimmer getting cramps or hypothermia—and what would be the most efficient response method.

Making sure to have a first-aid kit handy is a good start for the less physical events, such as board games. Soliciting a doctor or nurse from among your volunteer corps would also be good for these smaller events—or at least a volunteer, with cell phone turned on, ready with a van for minor emergency trips home or to a doctor. For larger events, you might want—and in fact be required by your insurance carrier—to have an ambulance in waiting. (The Women Swimmin' event has been fortunate to get the services of one ambulance, two EMTs, and a physician donated every year.)

Being able to nip trouble in the bud is also important, and will save you needing that ambulance. At the Women Swimmin' event, for example, they arrange to have 150 people out in kayaks and other boats, assigned to accompany the pods of swimmers, and ready to pull people out of the water if they're in any sort of distress. Saoirse McClory adds, "Every year of the event we learn something new, and that has allowed us to refine our safety plan. The year 2009 was a tough one, with cool weather and choppy water. Eight swimmers got out of the water early, feeling cold. We were ready with Red-Cross-donated blankets. But we realized then that we also needed to tighten up coordination and make sure the boaters know exactly where to bring someone, and to contact a central command center so that we can let the family know right away. We've also started writing up an internal incident report of the person's experience and following up by phone to see how they're doing. To our surprise, among the swimmers with whom we followed up, their primary worry was usually that we might not allow them to swim next year! They kept assuring us that they'd be fine."

And then there's the matter of protecting your group's income or expensive equipment. Hiring security personnel can be well worth the cost in cases where large amounts of money will be in one place (such as your registration booth) or you'll be leaving equipment outdoors or in a public space overnight.

Prepare Registration Materials for Participants

Once people have signed up or shown interest, they'll need detailed information on the where, what, and how of your event. Nothing turns off participation faster than feeling like the organizers can't give clear instructions.

For starters, all of the following information should be included in your flyer or other written instructions (preferably posted online as well, if that isn't already your main place for giving out information):

- name of the event
- name of your group and, if applicable, its status as a federally recognized 501(c)(3) nonprofit organization
- a brief statement of the wonderful things your group is striving to achieve, which will be supported by participants' pledges
- date of the event, including registration and starting times
- type of activity and what level of participant expertise is required or encouraged, or how many people are required per team

- location (including start and finish points for races or walkathons and course distance)
- directions on how to get there
- detailed description of the course (an elevation map is ideal for challenging walks or runs)
- instructions on what happens if it's an outdoor event and bad weather threatens
- entry fee or pledge expectations
- instructions on soliciting pledges, including safety advice if children will be involved (some organizations, for example, advise kids not to go door-to-door without an adult), a request to make sure that sponsors supply complete information as requested on the form, and a recommended pledge goal (usually at least $100 per person)
- registration deadline
- awards
- contact information (your group's address, and the telephone, fax, email addresses, and website where people can most quickly reach the organizers or gain more information), and
- a list of sponsors.

Create a Registration and Waiver Form

You'll need to create a registration and waiver form so that participants can formally sign up and, most importantly, waive their right to sue you (or make claims on your insurance policy) if they feel that your carelessness has harmed them. The waiver should also give you the rights to use their "likenesses" (photos or videos of participants) for promotional purposes. If kids will be participating, you'll need the signatures of their parents or guardians. (This is also a good time to alert parents to volunteer opportunities.)

Our sample Participant Registration and Waiver form will give you an idea of how such a waiver might look. However, we do not suggest that you simply copy it, and we haven't made it a fillable form for this book.

Sample Participant Registration and Waiver

Participant Registration and Waiver

Yes, I'd like to participate in the _Petaluma Prance_, scheduled to take place on _May 4, 20xx_.

Name: _Jennifer Blake_

Address: _457 Gardenia Way_

Petaluma, California

Phone(s) _123-456-7891_

Email: _jenniferblake@coldmail.com_

Date of birth: _June 13, 1988_

Emergency contact:

Name: _Marvin Blake_

Relationship: _father_

Phone(s) _123-456-8899_

Waiver, Assumption of Risk, and Release of Liability

I recognize that, by participating in the Petaluma Prance (the "Event"), I may face hazards or risk personal injury from various causes, such as the weather, nearby traffic or other local conditions, fellow participants, and my own exertions. I attest that I am in adequate physical shape, have discussed any relevant medical concerns with my doctor, and have trained sufficiently for the Event. During the Event, I promise to follow the rules and any instructions given to me by Event officials and their agents, and to make every effort to act sensibly and within my physical limits. I voluntarily assume the risks reasonably associated with participation in the Event. **I further waive any and all rights that I or my heirs and assigns might have to bring a lawsuit or present claims based on my participation against the Daisy School Foundation or its directors, officers, members, staff, hired event staff, volunteers, sponsors, the City of Petaluma, County of Sonoma, State of California, or other agents, even in cases where the aforementioned persons, entities, or organizations acted negligently or carelessly and caused my harm, injuries, or losses.**

Photo and Media Release

Daisy School Foundation may give my name to members of the media in connection with the Event, for potential interviews or personal coverage. I understand that during the Event, various photographs, video recordings, and other media will be taken by Daisy School Foundation and others. I grant full permission for Daisy School Foundation to use any photographs, video recordings, or other media of the Event that contain my likeness, for promotional or other legitimate purposes, without compensating me.

Signed: _Jennifer Blake_

Date: _January 5, 20xx_

Parental or Legal Guardian's Consent (Must be completed if participant is under age 18):

_____ (child's name) has my permission to participate in the Petaluma Prance and to collect pledges afterwards.

Signed: _____

Date: _____

Instead, this is one time that a visit to an attorney is well worth your time and expense. Here's why: Each state's waiver guidelines are unique, and you want to be absolutely sure that your waiver will "work" if, heaven forbid, a participant is hurt at your event and decides to sue you by challenging your waiver in court. With any luck, you'll find a local attorney willing to donate services to your cause. Also take another look at the suggestions for providing insurance in Chapter 7.

> **CAUTION**
>
> **Waivers protect you only from lawsuits by participants.** As Camp Happy Days Development Director Alix Robinson Tew notes, "You can't make every spectator sign a waiver. No one got hurt at this year's bed race, but we realized—especially after a certain photographer insisted on getting very close to the action, refusing to take care of himself—that we need to block off spectators next year."

Supply Training Information for Participants

If this is the first such event your group has organized, providing actual training for entrants is probably more than you should take on. But there are ways to start small—for example by providing written materials with training tips and lists of places to practice, or, as Women Swimmin' does, scheduling short, optional trainings to be given by a local fitness center (the participants pay). At the Silicon Valley Puzzle Fest, they actually devote all of Saturday to instructional workshops and lectures, and then hold the tournament on Sunday.

Publicize and Recruit for the Event

You're looking for several types of publicity for an event like this—advance publicity to encourage people to participate or to support participants by pledging, viral publicity as friends tell friends about the event and their participation in it, and "day-of-event" publicity that will get the public excited about your cause and encourage them to support you in other ways or join up next year. For the Charleston Bed Race, Alix Robinson Tew says, "We put up a banner across a busy street downtown—the permit cost only $200! In fact, while we were arranging it, the city staff got so enthusiastic, they ended up putting two beds in the race."

See the general tips in Chapter 7 on generating event publicity. Face-to-face recruiting among your members will have the best results. With the right hook or interesting visuals, you might also get the mainstream media interested. Contests of any sort tend to make good media fodder. There's always a winner and, particularly if you've got cute kids involved, some good photo opportunities.

Also think of targeted ways to create publicity within niche outlets, for example by sending announcements to be placed in the newsletters or mentioned in blogs of others likely to participate. Making personal contact or sending announcements to local sports clubs, games shops, recreation centers, or religious organizations might also be good bets. The Charleston Bed Race actually rolled a bed out to various public places to advertise their event—"an ugly old cot," says Alix Robinson Tew. "But it worked great. People would walk by and stop to talk or have their picture taken."

This type of event is tailor-made for individual social networking. Prepare sample Facebook, Twitter, or blog entries that you give to every registered participant. (You shouldn't put words in their mouths, but show them how to work important facts into their posting, such as the name of your organization and the name and date of the event.) Gary Stewart reminds us that, "There's an emotional component to people's participation in an event like this, and letting them tell their own story to friends about why they're taking part is often the most powerful way to get the word out." Providing a JPG photo from a previous year's event can help their efforts, too.

The day of the event is one of your best opportunities for publicity. Make sure that everyone who's participating, volunteering, or just plain hanging around is made aware not only of what's happening, but of the cause it's helping to support. Banners and signs can help with this, as can a separate booth where volunteers pass out flyers and answer questions.

Plan "Day of Event" Assignments

Figure out every possible task that people might need to handle on event day, at every stage of the event. Then either assign volunteers or hire professionals to carry them out. The job assignments might include, for example:

- Setup crew. (Look for people willing to get up really early, because everything will need to be ready when the participants arrive.)

- Parking attendants to direct people arriving at the venue or starting area. (This will be the attendee's first impression of how well-run your event is.) In some cities and locations, you'll be required to arrange for a police officer to direct traffic.

- Referees, officiants, judges, or assistants. (At Silicon Valley Puzzle Fest, for example, high school students volunteer to serve as "runners," who pick up participants' completed crossword puzzles when they see a raised hand, note the time they finished, and run them back to the judges.)

- Registration table crew. For large events, create separate check-in areas for separate alphabetic groups of names. One volunteer for every hundred attendees is usually enough.

- Information booth and sales booth staffers

- Aid station and other support crew (remember the toilet paper)

- A few miscellaneous crew members, to call upon for backup or special assignments

- Finish line crew. (In some cases, as with Women Swimmin', you'll want all the finishers to check in, just to make sure they've all made it out of the water or safely finished the course.)

- Trained first-aid personnel, including on-site ambulance for large athletic event

- Police, for large-scale events in public spaces

- Photographers. Photos are great for future publicity and for your website or newsletter.

- Emcee or award presenter

- Breakdown, cleanup, and trash-disposal or equipment-return crew.

Prepare Participant Thank-You Gifts and Prizes

Most people love to have their achievements recognized. Try to have a little thank-you gift for each participant, such as a commemorative cap, T-shirt or wristband, or even chocolate (it's considered healthy these days). Think creatively about thematic thank you gifts—the Red Cross, for example, has given out mini first-aid kits to walkathon participants.

Of the Women Swimmin' event, Gary Stewart notes, "No one's in it just for the prizes, but we've always got some good ones. This year, swimmers who raised at least $500 in pledges received a fleece scarf, and those who raised at least $1,000 received a canvas fold-out chair. For the top fundraisers, we've had such prizes as theater tickets, stays at B&Bs, or a hand-built canoe."

For races or competitions that have winners, you'll also want to plan prizes for the top three. However, don't feel you have to pass out traditional trophies, which turn into dust gatherers. An official certificate, suitable for framing, is a good and inexpensive substitute. Here are some other interesting gifts you can use to make the winners feel special—at no cost, if they're donated:

- gift certificates to local businesses
- a framed photo of the person taking part in the event
- sports apparel, or
- something thematic to the sport or game, such as a high-quality ping-pong paddle or chess clock.

Plan Awards Ceremony or Other Celebration

Your event participants as well as volunteers may have challenged themselves in any number of ways to take part. Mustering up the courage to ask for pledges, making the effort to train or learn new skills, or simply getting up early in the morning for hard work or a physical challenge aren't necessarily easy. But they not only made it, they helped out a good cause. Here's your chance to recognize these efforts.

Your awards ceremony needn't be long—some participants will be eager to leave and celebrate with friends and family—but it should provide an efficient, sincerely felt way to say "Thank you."

Holding the Event

This is the shortest section in this chapter, because, after all your careful planning, the event should simply happen on its own momentum. Your volunteers know their assignments, your participants have been advised of the rules, and you should have enough group leaders on hand to give things a nudge or make a quick decision when needed.

Help assure your readiness by thinking through the whole event beforehand, perhaps even doing a walk-through where possible. Start at the parking lot, go to the registration area, begin the route (if it's a walk or something similar), visualize how it will all work for people with strollers and wheelchairs, check whether people will be able to see the signs and banners you've planned on posting, imagine where participants are most likely to look for a garbage can, and so forth.

Don't forget to have fun, take lots of pictures, and keep your cell phone on!

Event Follow-Up

Apart from the follow-up tasks described in Chapter 7, your most important job now is to monitor and encourage completed pledge collection. This can be a bit of a chore—but a necessary one. Communicate with all participants immediately after the event, congratulate and thank them, and then give them crystal-clear instructions on how to proceed with collecting and turning in their pledges.

Don't be surprised if you have to repeat your reminders two or three times over the next few weeks. To avoid sounding like a nag, remind participants of how much they've achieved already, and how every added amount that they raise will make an important difference to your cause. ●

How to Use the CD-ROM

The CD-ROM included with this book can be used with Windows computers. It installs files that use software programs that need to be on your computer already. It is not a stand-alone software program.

In accordance with U.S. copyright laws, the CD-ROM and its files are for your personal use only.

Please read this appendix and the Readme.htm file included on the CD-ROM for instructions on using the CD-ROM. For a list of files and their file names, see the end of this appendix.

Note to Macintosh users: This CD-ROM and its files should also work on Macintosh computers. Please note, however, that Nolo cannot provide technical support for non-Windows users.

How to View the ReadMe File

To view the "Readme.htm" file, insert the CD-ROM into your computer's CD-ROM drive and follow these instructions:

Windows *XP, Vista,* and *7*

1. On your PC's desktop, double-click the **My Computer** icon.
2. Double-click the icon for the CD-ROM drive into which the CD-ROM was inserted.
3. Double-click the file "Readme.htm."

Macintosh

1. On your Mac desktop, double-click the icon for the CD-ROM that you inserted.
2. Double-click the file "Readme.htm."

Installing the Files Onto Your Computer

To work with the files on the CD-ROM, you first need to install them onto your hard disk. Here's how:

Windows *XP, Vista,* and 7

Follow the CD-ROM's instructions that appear on the screen.

If nothing happens when you insert the CD-ROM, then:

1. Double-click the **My Computer** icon.
2. Double-click the icon for the CD-ROM drive into which the CD-ROM was inserted.
3. Double-click the file "Welcome.exe."

Macintosh

If the **Fundraising Resources CD** window is not open, double-click the Fundraising Resources CD icon. Then:

1. Select the **Fundraising Resources** folder icon.
2. Drag and drop the folder icon onto your computer.

Where Are the Files Installed?

Windows

By default, the files are installed to the **Fundraising Resources** folder in the **Program Files** folder of your computer. A folder called **Fundraising Resources** is added to the **Programs** folder of the **Start** menu.

Macintosh

The files are located in the **Fundraising Resources** folder.

Using the Word Processing Files to Create Documents

The CD-ROM includes word processing files that you can open, complete, print, and save with your word processing program. All word processing files come in rich text format and have the extension ".rtf." For example, the Donor Thank-You letter discussed in Chapter 1 is the file "DonorThankYou. rtf." RTF files can be read by most recent word processing programs including *MS Word, Windows WordPad,* and recent versions of *WordPerfect.*

The following are general instructions. Because each word processor uses different commands to open, format, save, and print documents, refer to your word processor's help file for specific instructions.

Do not call Nolo's technical support if you have questions on how to use your word processor or your computer.

Opening a File

You can open word processing files in any of the three following ways:

Windows users can open a file by selecting its "shortcut."

- Click the Windows **Start** button.
- Open the **Programs** folder.
- Open the **Fundraising Resources** folder.
- Open the **Forms** subfolder.
- Click the shortcut to the file you want to work with.

Both Windows and Macintosh users can open a file by double-clicking it.

- Use **My Computer** or **Windows Explorer** (Windows *XP, Vista, 7*) or the **Finder** (Macintosh) to go to the **Fundraising Resources** folder.
- Double-click the file you want to open.

Windows and Macintosh users can open a file from within their word processor.

- Open your word processor.
- Go to the **File** menu and choose the **Open** command. This opens a dialog box.
- Select the location and name of the file. (You will navigate to the version of the **Fundraising Resources** folder that you've installed on your computer.)

Editing Your Document

Here are tips for working on your document.

- Refer to the book's instructions and sample agreements for help.
- Shaded underlines (known as fields) indicate where to enter information,

frequently including bracketed instructions. Put your cursor in the field to select it, then begin typing. Your entered text won't be shaded or underlined.

- Signature lines should appear on a page with at least some text from the document itself.

Editing Files That Have Optional or Alternative Text

Some files have optional or alternate text:

- With optional text, you choose whether to include or exclude the given text.
- With alternative text, you select one alternative to include and exclude the other alternatives.

When editing these files, we suggest you do the following:

Optional text

Delete optional text you do not want to include and keep that which you do. In either case, delete the italicized instructions. If you choose to delete an optional numbered clause, renumber the subsequent clauses after deleting it.

Alternative text

First, delete all the alternatives that you do not want to include. Then delete the italicized instructions.

Printing the Document

Use your word processor's or text editor's **Print** command to print your document.

Saving Your Document

Use the "Save As" command to save and rename your document. You will be unable to use the "Save" command because the files are "read-only." If you save the file without renaming it, the fields in which you entered your information will be lost, and you will be unable to create a new document with this file without recopying the original file from the CD-ROM.

Using the Spreadsheet

The CD-ROM includes spreadsheets that you can open, complete, print, and save with Microsoft Excel and other spreadsheet programs that read XLS files.

The following are general instructions. Because each spreadsheet program uses different commands to open, format, save, and print documents, refer to your spreadsheet program's help file for specific instructions.

Do not call Nolo's technical support if you have questions on how to use your spreadsheet or your computer.

Opening a File

You can open spreadsheets in any of the three following ways:

Windows users can open a file by selecting its "shortcut."

- Click the Windows **Start** button.
- Open the **Programs** folder.
- Open the **Fundraising Resources** folder.
- Open the **Forms** subfolder.
- Click the shortcut to the XLS file you want to work with.

Both Windows and Macintosh users can open a file by double-clicking it.

- Use **My Computer** or **Windows Explorer** (Windows *XP, Vista, 7*) or the **Finder** (Macintosh) to go to the **Fundraising Resources** folder.
- Double-click XLS file you want to work with.

Windows and Macintosh users can open a file from within their spreadsheet program.

- Open your spreadsheet program.
- Go to the **File** menu and choose the **Open** command. This opens a dialog box.
- Select the location and name of the file. (You will navigate to the version of the **Fundraising Resources** folder that you've installed on your computer.)

Printing Your Document

Use your spreadsheet program's **Print** command to print your document.

Saving Your Document

Use the "Save As" command to save and rename your document. You will be unable to use the "Save" command because the files are "read-only." If you save the file without renaming it, the fields in which you entered your information will be lost, and you will be unable to create a new document with this file without recopying the original file from the CD-ROM.

Using Print-Only Files

The CD-ROM includes useful files in Adobe PDF format. To use them, you need Adobe Reader installed on your computer. If you don't already have this software, you can download it for free at www.adobe.com.

Opening PDF Files

PDF files, like the word processing files, can be opened one of three ways.

Windows users can open a file by selecting its "shortcut."
- Click the Windows **Start** button.
- Open the **Programs** folder.
- Open the **Fundraising Resources** folder.
- Open the **Forms** subfolder.
- Click the shortcut to the file you want to work with.

Both Windows and Macintosh users can open a file by double-clicking it.
- Use **My Computer** or **Windows Explorer** (Windows *XP, Vista, 7*) or the **Finder** (Macintosh) to go to the **Fundraising Resources** folder.
- Double-click the file you want to open.

Windows and Macintosh users can open a file from within their word processor.
- Open your word processor.
- Go to the **File** menu and choose the **Open** command. This opens a dialog box.
- Select the location and name of the file. (You will navigate to the version of the **Fundraising Resources** folder that you've installed on your computer.)

Filling In PDF files

The PDF files cannot be filled in using your computer. To create your document using one of these files, print it and then complete it by hand or typewriter.

Reading the Bonus Chapter

The CD-ROM contains a bonus chapter, "Applying for Grants From Foundations, Corporations, or Government" (BonusChapter.pdf). To open and read the chapter, follow the instructions above, "Opening PDF Files," in "Using Print-Only Files." If you like, you can print the chapter too.

Listening to the Audio Files

This section explains how to play the audio files using your computer. All audio files are in MP3 format. For example, Interview With Author Ilona Bray is on the file "InterviewWithAuthor.mp3." At the end of this appendix, you'll find a list of the audio files and their file names.

Most computers come with a media player that plays MP3 files. You can listen to files that you have installed on your computer or directly from the CD-ROM. See below for further information on both.

The following are general instructions. Because every media player is different, refer to your media player's help files for more specific instructions. Please do not contact Nolo's technical support if you are having difficulty using your media player.

Playing the Audio Files Without Installing

If you don't want to copy 50.4 MB of audio files to your computer, you can play the CD-ROM on your computer. Here's how:

Windows

1. Insert the CD-ROM to view the **Welcome to Fundraising Resources CD** window.
2. Click "Listen to Audio."

If nothing happens when you insert the CD-ROM:

4. Double-click the **My Computer** icon.
5. Double-click the icon for the CD-ROM drive you inserted the CD-ROM into.
6. Double-click the file "Welcome.exe."

Macintosh

1. Insert the CD-ROM. (If the **Fundraising Resources CD** window does not open, double-click the **Fundraising Resources CD** icon.)
2. Double-click the **Audio** icon.
3. Double-click the audio file you want to hear.

Listening to Audio Files You've Installed on Your Computer

There are two ways to listen to the audio files that you have installed on your computer.

Windows users can open a file by selecting its shortcut.

- Click the Windows **Start** button.
- Open the **Programs** folder.
- Open the **Fundraising Resources** folder.
- Open the **Audio** subfolder.
- Click the shortcut to the file you want to work with.

Both Windows and Macintosh users can open a file by double-clicking it.

- Use **My Computer** or **Windows Explorer** (Windows *XP, Vista, 7*) or the **Finder** (Macintosh) to go to the **Fundraising Resources** folder.
- Double-click the file you want to open.

Files on the CD-ROM

The following are RTF files:	
File Name	**Form Name**
Donor Thank-You Letter	DonorThankYou.rtf
Volunteer Application	VolunteerApplication.rtf
Letter to Business	LetterToBusiness.rtf
Business Pledge	BusinessPledge.rtf
Phonathon Call Sheet	PhonathonCalls.rtf
Pledge Confirmation	PledgeConfirmation.rtf
Silent Auction Bid Sheet	SilentAuctionBids.rtf
Silent Auction Recorder Sheet	SilentAuctionRecorder.rtf
Auction Pickup Receipt	AuctionReceipt.rtf
Application for Exhibit Booth Space	ApplicationForSpace.rtf
Participant Registration and Waiver	ParticipantRegWaiver.rtf
Pledge Log	PledgeLog.rtf
Press Release	PressRelease.rtf

The following spreadsheets are in Microsoft Excel format (XLS):	
File Name	**Form Name**
Phonathon Summary Sheet	PhonathonSummary.xls
Fundraising Goals	FundraisingGoals.xls

The following are PDF files:

File Name	Form Name
Bonus Chapter: "Applying for Grants From Foundations, Corporations, or Government"	BonusChapter.pdf
Fundraising Goals Worksheet	FundraisingGoals.pdf
Projected Special Event Expenses	ProjectedEventExpenses.pdf
Projected Special Event Income	ProjectedEventIncome.pdf
Grant Priorities Summary Chart	GrantSummaryChart.pdf
Grant Prospects Research Overview	GrantResearchOverview.pdf
Applying for Grants From Foundations, Corporations, or Government	ApplyForGrants.pdf

The following are audio (MP3) files:

File Name	Form Name
Interview With Author Ilona Bray	InterviewWithAuthor.mp3
Bringing Creativity to Your Fundraising Efforts	BringCreativityToEfforts.mp3
The Down Economy's Impact on Grassroots Fundraising	DownEconomyImpact.mp3

Index

The letters "CD" preceding a page number indicate the bonus chapter on grant writing located on the CD-ROM.

The letters "CD" preceding a page number indicate the bonus chapter on grant writing located on the CD-ROM.

The letters "CD" preceding a page number indicate the bonus chapter on grant writing located on the CD-ROM.

G

The letters "CD" preceding a page number indicate the bonus chapter on grant writing located on the CD-ROM.

The letters "CD" preceding a page number indicate the bonus chapter on grant writing located on the CD-ROM.

The letters "CD" preceding a page number indicate the bonus chapter on grant writing located on the CD-ROM.

The letters "CD" preceding a page number indicate the bonus chapter on grant writing located on the CD-ROM.

The letters "CD" preceding a page number indicate the bonus chapter on grant writing located on the CD-ROM.

The letters "CD" preceding a page number indicate the bonus chapter on grant writing located on the CD-ROM.

The letters "CD" preceding a page number indicate the bonus chapter on grant writing located on the CD-ROM.

The letters "CD" preceding a page number indicate the bonus chapter on grant writing located on the CD-ROM.

The letters "CD" preceding a page number indicate the bonus chapter on grant writing located on the CD-ROM.

The letters "CD" preceding a page number indicate the bonus chapter on grant writing located on the CD-ROM.

The letters "CD" preceding a page number indicate the bonus chapter on grant writing located on the CD-ROM.

The letters "CD" preceding a page number indicate the bonus chapter on grant writing located on the CD-ROM.

1 Go to Nolo.com/newsletters to sign up for free newsletters and discounts on Nolo products.

- **Nolo Briefs.** Our monthly email newsletter with great deals and free information.

- **Nolo's Special Offer.** A monthly newsletter with the biggest Nolo discounts around.

- **BizBriefs.** Tips and discounts on Nolo products for business owners and managers.

- **Landlord's Quarterly.** Deals and free tips just for landlords and property managers, too.

2 Don't forget to check for updates. Find this book at **Nolo.com** and click "Legal Updates."

Let Us Hear From You

3 Register your Nolo product and give us your feedback at Nolo.com/book-registration.

- Once you've registered, you qualify for technical support if you have any trouble with a download or CD (though most folks don't).

- We'll also drop you an email when a new edition of your book is released—and we'll send you a coupon for 15% off your next Nolo.com order!

⚖ NOLO *Lawyer Directory*

Find a Nonprofit Attorney

- *Qualified lawyers*
- *In-depth profiles*
- *A pledge of respectful service*

When you want professional help with crucial issues involving a nonprofit corporation, you don't want just any lawyer—you want an expert in the field, who can give you and your family up-to-the-minute advice. You need a lawyer who has the experience and knowledge to answer your questions about key issues such as deciding to incorporate, gaining 501(c)(3) tax-exempt status, dealing with board of directors disputes, and helping with legal issues raised by foundation, government and individual funders.

Nolo's Lawyer Directory is unique because it provides an extensive profile of every lawyer. You'll learn about not only each lawyer's education, professional history, legal specialties, credentials and fees, but also about their philosophy of practicing law and how they like to work with clients.

All lawyers listed in Nolo's directory are in good standing with their state bar association. Many will review Nolo documents, such as a will or living trust, for a fixed fee. They all pledge to work diligently and respectfully with clients—communicating regularly, providing a written agreement about how legal matters will be handled, sending clear and detailed bills, and more.